Liberia

The Ethnography of Political Violence

Cynthia Keppley Mahmood, Series Editor

A complete list of books in the series is available from the publisher.

Liberia

The Violence of Democracy

Mary H. Moran

PENN

University of Pennsylvania Press

Philadelphia

Copyright © 2006 University of Pennsylvania Press
All rights reserved
Printed in the United States of America on acid-free paper

10 9 8 7 6 5 4 3 2 1

Published by
University of Pennsylvania Press
Philadelphia, Pennsylvania 19104-4112

Library of Congress Cataloging-in-Publication Data

Moran, Mary H., 1957–
    Liberia : the violence of democracy / Mary H. Moran.
        p.   cm. — (The ethnography of political violence)
ISBN-13: 978-0-8122-3907-2
ISBN-10: 0-8122-3907-5 (cloth : alk. paper)
    Includes bibliographical references and index.
    1. Political violence—Liberia. 2. Democracy—Liberia. 3. Liberia—History—Civil War,
1989–. 4. Liberia—Politics and government—1980–. I Title. II. Series
DT636.5 .M69   2006
966.6203'3—dc22   2005042347

In memory of my parents, John F. and Helen I. Robinson Moran

and

For my Glebo foster family, the late William Sodo Newton, Viola Klade Wesley Newton, and all the Newton family, in the hope of more peaceful days to come for all Liberians.

Contents

Introduction:
Liberia, Violence, and Democracy

Violence and democracy are words that do not sit easily together in the same sentence. Indeed, our tendency as Westerners is to see them as opposite ends of an evolutionary scale; the successor to widespread violence, we often imagine, *is* democracy, a system in which rulers are freely chosen by their people and in which everyone is allowed to voice their opinions and concerns. If such conditions exist, what need is there to resort to violence?

In the 1990s and into the current century, war and genocide in the Balkans, the Middle East, and numerous African countries have been attributed to the absence of democratic institutions. Processes of "democratization," including "capacity-building" workshops and efforts to promote "civil society," are prescribed as post-conflict solutions to support the "free and fair" elections which are the ultimate goal. Indeed, the ability to hold a "transparent" election is held to be the real test of whether or not democracy has "taken root" in a formerly troubled society and is seen as a bulwark against further outbreaks of war. Democratic societies, we are told, do not make war on their neighbors, but must be poised to intervene when nondemocratic regimes threaten to overstep their boundaries. But are democracy and violence really separate (or separable) ontological states, or is there violence in democracy and democracy in violence? Can both be viewed as means of communication between higher and lower levels of political organization; for example, between the local community and the state? In what instances does the discourse of democracy, grounded in the expectation of "a fair discussion among equals" (Guinier 1995, cited in Wonkeryor et al. 2000: 52), fail? When does the state resort to imposing its will by force, and the local population resort to resistance or aggression? Conversely, what conflicts between local and national elites can be accommodated by the ritual forms of elections and designated representatives? How do leaders on both the small and the large scale manage to allow disparate voices to be heard without compromising their own legitimacy? Can a people really be said to "choose" democracy over war, and vice versa?

Liberia, resting on the great bulge of West Africa, is the setting in which I investigate these questions (see Figure 1). It is in many ways a paradoxical place, often cited as the exception to most sweeping generalizations about sub-Saharan Africa. Unlike the rest of the continent, Liberia was never formally colonized by a European power; its pseudocolonial "mother country" is the United States. It was born out of the contradictions inherent in the founding of the United States itself; a nation predicated on individual liberty which at the same time condoned and profited by chattel slavery. Although frequently characterized in the Western media as "founded by freed slaves," Liberia was initially imagined as a haven for "free people of color," descendants of Africans who by luck, birth, or their own efforts were no longer legally enslaved. The country was literally the philanthropic project of a private, white, benevolent organization founded in 1816, the American Colonization Society. Its establishment in 1822 of an American outpost on the West African coast served multiple interests. Slaveowners saw repatriation as a means of removing unwelcome examples of independent, self-supporting free blacks from the view of their slaves. Some white abolitionists who felt slavery as an institution was immoral were nevertheless uncomfortable with the prospect of actually living in a multiracial society. Evangelical Christians, inspired by the Second Great Awakening, envisioned a divine plan to "redeem" African heathens through the example of black missionaries and Christian communities. American merchants, competing with their European counterparts, welcomed a secure landing place on the African coast and an advantage in the emerging "legitimate trade" in palm oil, coffee, and other tropical products (see Adeleke 1998; Beyan 1991; for older accounts, see Staudenraus 1961; Shick 1980, among others).

Although most American abolitionists, white and black, rejected the colonization movement, between twelve and thirteen thousand colonists were settled in Liberia between 1822 and 1867 (Liebenow 1987: 19). Of these, roughly 4,500 had been born free, while the others were emancipated from slavery on the condition that they emigrate to Africa. These numbers were augmented by about 6,000 "recaptive" Africans taken from impounded slave ships before they ever crossed the Atlantic. Along with a few hundred immigrants from Barbados arriving after the abolition of slavery there, this group over time became the national elite known as Americo-Liberians, "Congoes," or simply "Settlers."

The remainder of Liberia's population of between two and three million have affiliation with one or more of over sixteen indigenous ethnolinguistic groups, often glossed as "tribes." As is commonly the case in Africa, these groups are not bounded, internally organized, or historically continuous political units, but rough approximations of regional and

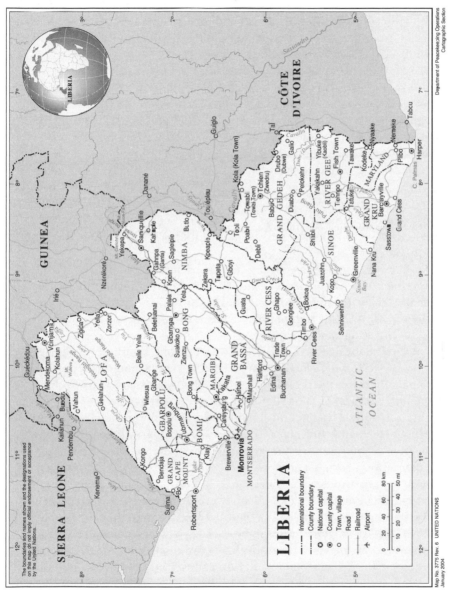

Figure 1. Map of Liberia. Courtesy United Nations Cartographic Section (map number 3775, revised January 2004).

sometimes religious identity. Intermarriage and internal migration have made it possible for many Liberians to invoke more than one "tribal" affiliation, despite the fact that all the indigenous groups subscribe to an ideology of patrilineal descent (see d'Azevedo 1969–70: 111–12). Although "tribalism" has been invoked as an explanation for the violence in Liberia in recent years, local histories point to more evidence of conflict *within* than *between* ethnic categories.

It is hard for me to believe that I first went to Liberia more than twenty years ago, in 1982. This book has evolved over those years of my involvement with the country, taking a different shape from the way it was first imagined as a "followup" to my work on gender and prestige among the Glebo people of the southeast (Moran 1990). At various times, it was to be a study of local and national interpretations of political events, then it became a book on civil war and state collapse, and, finally, it has taken its current shape as a study of themes of democracy and violence in Liberia, past and present. It has taken me a long time to parse the relationship between these two terms, so often represented as polar opposites, and to understand them as persistent and mutually constitutive themes in Liberian history.

In the early nineteenth century, the American missionary John Payne characterized the Glebo of southeastern Liberia as practicing "the purest of democracies" (cited in Martin 1968: 15). In 1847 the African American settlers declared their independence from the American Colonization Society, affirming their commitment to an American-style constitution and its attendant democratic institutions. For one hundred and thirty-three years following, elections were held at regular intervals for both national offices like the presidency and local positions such as town chief. Although members of the settler group maintained a monopoly on state institutions and the indigenous people were not fully enfranchised until the 1960s (Liebenow 1987: 63–65), there is substantial evidence that some principles of transparency and accountability were employed even during the period of single-party rule (1877–1980) by the True Whig Party. "There was, first of all, the observance of constitutional norms, which apparently had high value to the legally minded Americo-Liberians. Secondly, it did provide for at least a biennial discussion of the party's goals and permitted new generations to be socialized . . . the personnel of government did change as a result of this active discussion" (1987: 94; see also Sawyer 1992; Liberty 2002). Before centralized power was fully consolidated in the executive branch by William. V. S. Tubman (1943–71), recognized corruption in political office was severely punished; several Liberian presidents were impeached or forced to resign, and transitions were relatively peaceful.

Why then did Liberia, with a longer experience of political independence than any other nation in Africa, fall victim to the syndrome of violent civil war and state collapse which swept the continent in the 1990s? Following a military coup in 1980, the situation deteriorated into outright war from 1989 to 1996, leading to complete national disruption, foreign occupation, and the deaths of up to 200,000 people, most of them civilians. Even after a brokered peace agreement and internationally supervised elections in 1997, Liberia could not enjoy an end to violence. Charles Taylor, who had begun the war in 1989, received 75 percent of the vote in what were widely described as free and transparent elections, yet within two years he was challenged by another armed faction and spent his five-year term as president trying in vain to hold off "rebels" who occupied more and more of the country. Taylor was forced into exile in Nigeria in 2003, and a transitional government is preparing for new elections in 2005. Along with its neighbor Sierra Leone, Liberia in the 1990s gave the world ghastly images of child soldiers, "warlord" politics fueled by "blood diamonds," and utter, regionwide devastation.

Explanations have been offered from a variety of perspectives for this puzzling phenomenon. Some analysts have seen the combination of rising populations, ecological degradation, deep-seated "tribal" animosities, and marginalization from the global economy as enough to throw any society into irrational chaos and anarchy (see Kaplan 1994, 2000). Other scholars reject this "New Barbarism" argument and locate the source of the conflict in the very rational competition for resources amid rising but unfulfilled expectations that underlies civil wars in Angola, Sierra Leone, and Congo as well as Liberia (Reno 1995b, 1998; Richards 1996a). Still others point to the postcolonial "politics of the belly" that has, in the absence of an industrial sector, made state institutions the primary means of accumulation and distribution of wealth (Bayart 1993; Chabal and Daloz 1999). There is an extensive literature on Liberia which argues that elections and other "democratic" trappings were never more than show pieces to begin with; that since its inception the nation has been dominated by the small settler elite through the mechanisms of a one-party state, an "imperial" presidency, and a set of exclusive institutions ranging from churches and schools to Masonic lodges (Dolo 1996; Dunn and Tarr 1988, Gershoni 1985; Sawyer 1987, 1992; Leibenow 1987; Holphe 1979; Osaghae 1996, among others). Finally, it has been suggested that the peculiar "religious" orientation of Liberians, related to a regional "politics of secrecy," may have influenced both the shape and the extent of the violence (Ellis 1999; for Sierra Leone, see Ferme 2001).

This book is a response, from an anthropological perspective, to the literature on state collapse, reintegration, and democratization in Africa, through the lens of the particular case of Liberia. Specifically, I hope to make three related contributions to the current scholarship. First, this project contributes to the goal of "denaturalizing" violence and warfare, directed particularly at essentialist commentators like Kaplan (1994, 2000) and Huntington (1993, 1996).This project has dominated the "anthropology of violence" during the 1990s and into the present century (Warren 1993; Nordstrom 1997; Daniel 1996; Besteman 1999; Richards 1996a; Taylor 1999, Besteman and Gusterson 2005, among others). Second, I contest the characterization of Liberia and other Guinea Coast societies as dominated by secrecy, distrust, and hierarchy; as religious and cultural systems that explicitly impede democratization (Ellis 1999; Bellman 1975, 1984; Ferme 2001). These authors, of course, acknowledge that a range of political orientations exists within the region, but see alternatives to hierarchy and secrecy as suppressed or underdeveloped. I argue that there are strong indigenous traditions of participation, voice, and empowerment, otherwise known as "democratic values," embedded in the governmental structures of local communities and in the operative conceptions of personhood used by these populations. Although these structures and values have undeniably changed over time, there is also a remarkable continuity in the language people use to talk about what they expect from political leaders, both local and national. Following Piot (1999), I argue that these democratic traditions are fully "modern," in the sense of being part of the repertoire of daily life, and are the result of global historical processes involving the indigenous people of Liberia, while at the same time insisting that they represent an *alternative* model of political process to that which has its origins in Western Europe. Third, I suggest that violence and democracy are not conceptually opposed in Liberian political discourse but are aspects of the same understanding of legitimacy. Liberian history can be understood as an ongoing interplay between themes of democracy and violence enacted on both local and national levels. This point is particularly crucial in the context of American foreign policy of the early twenty-first century, in which the establishment of democracy (by force if necessary) is seen as a solution to regional instability and the ensuing threat to strategic resources.

This analysis requires an interrogation of both terms, "democracy" and "violence," as discourses that are deployed, contested, and altered by participants in small communities, in the national capital, and within the state apparatus. At all these levels, actors must also refer to *international* definitions of democracy and "human rights" as these are tied to multilateral aid packages and relations with foreign powers. A key feature of the scholarly and policymaking literature on political transition in Africa is the tendency to view representational democracy as unproblematic, an obvious "good" that will only benefit all sectors of society. Furthermore, democracy is often represented as alien to Africa, a recent import from the West; much of the debate within the discipline of political science has centered on whether or not Africans are "ready" for democracy, generally defined as the ability to hold transparent elections (for one example, see Diamond, Linz, and Lipset 1988). Strongly evolutionary assumptions underlie this line of argument, since preexisting political institutions, kin, and ethnic ties are described as "patrimonial" and are believed to be antithetical to more modern forms of rational bureaucracy and efficiency (Clapham 1985, but for a rethinking of these models, see Joseph 1999). Several African scholars have contested these assumptions (Ake 2000; Monga 1996), but they continue to underlie a great deal of the foreign policy of the Western powers regarding Africa. I will argue that this approach not only obscures the democratic possibilities in indigenous political arrangements, but blinds Western scholars from interrogating the meaning and operation of democracy in general.

As an anthropologist, I want to consider seriously what led John Payne to recognize "democracy" in the political organization of nineteenth-century Glebo towns. What characteristics of governmental structure and conceptions of the person and of individual rights led him to this evaluation? Are these features still salient today, after over one hundred years of violent confrontation with an expanding colonial state? Following Geschiere (1982, 1997), I focus on the differences and similarities between local and national understandings of legitimate political process and the legitimate use of force. I examine how these differences are mediated by both local and national elites, the so-called "civilized people" of both indigenous and settler background. Acknowledging that greater power, in the raw sense of the ability to enforce compliance, may rest with the national government, I look at local forms of resistance and expectations of how and when violence should be deployed.

Stephen Ellis has suggested (1999) that the particular shape and character of the Liberian civil war was a result of religious ideas about power, life, death, and blood. He follows a long scholarly tradition of emphasizing the occult, cosmological aspects of Liberian politics (Harley 1941, 1950; Bellman 1975, 1984). Clearly, Liberians hold a variety of religious beliefs, some of which are widely shared. I will argue that an explicitly *political* discourse is also at work, one which is recognized as such by those who participate in it. I will argue that an ongoing contest over the nature of democracy and political legitimacy has characterized the Liberian experience for over a century, not just in the last few decades. Moreover, the "political" is not just a hegemony imposed from the center over the local community, but a product of the interaction between them. In the following chapters, I trace the struggle over the meaning and value of democracy and violence through five selected aspects of Liberian society.

Methodologically, the core of my research draws on fifteen months of fieldwork in southeastern Liberia in 1982–83, as well as on interviews, news reports, Internet sources, and ongoing conversations with Liberians over the past twenty years. My initial fieldwork was during the period between the military coup led by Samuel Doe in 1980 and the beginning of the civil war in 1989. When I arrived in Liberia, the country was under military rule, the constitution of 1847 was suspended, and a commission was drafting and debating a new constitution for the second republic. It was an historical moment in which the country seemed poised to make some kind of transition. The seventies had been characterized by considerable political openness as the ruling one-party state responded to increasing demands for greater participation in government by intellectuals, rural people, and those of indigenous background. The young military men who took power violently in 1980 represented themselves as acting in the interests of the disenfranchised: the rural and urban poor, the "tribal" people who had been excluded from real power for the previous 130 years. Promising to hold elections and return the country to civilian rule in five years, the military temporarily allied themselves with the activists and university-based intellectuals who had been agitating for change. People seemed cautiously optimistic.

From my field site in the extreme southeastern part of Liberia, I observed the reaction of local Glebo people to what was going on in the capital, Monrovia. In the course of carrying out a "classic" ethnographic study for my dissertation, I lived with a Glebo family, struggled with the language, and attended a wide range of public and private events and ceremonies. I conducted a house-to-house census of six communities containing a total of about 3,000 people on the outskirts of Harper, the regional capital. My dissertation and subsequent book centered on understanding women's lives and status aspirations in a period of economic decline that offered few options for educated or "civilized" people (Moran 1990). At the same time, I was intrigued by what was going on in the country at large, and recorded many conversations with local people about national events as we listened to the radio (both the government station and the BBC, VOA, and Radio Moscow) or passed around my subscription to one of the independent Monrovia dailies (which arrived in large batches every few weeks, invariably several months out of date). I amassed a large clipping file on various topics from these papers and others purchased on my infrequent trips to Monrovia. The local celebrations of national holidays like Independence Day, Flag Day, the birthday of former president William V. S. Tubman, and "Redemption Day" (the anniversary of the 1980 military coup) were all carefully described in my fieldnotes. I hoped to return in a few years for a new project focused on the relationship between the community and the state.

Shortly after I left Liberia, in December 1983, Head of State Samuel

K. Doe moved to convert himself from a military leader to a civilian candidate. The election of 1985 was widely acknowledged to have been stolen by Doe and his party, although it was certified as "free and fair" by the Reagan State Department. Various attempts were made to unseat Doe, resulting in armed incursions against the home regions of his rivals. For his own protection, the soldier-turned-president surrounded himself with members of his own small ethnolinguistic group, the Krahn, and embarked on a deliberate policy of creating and manipulating ethnic antagonisms. In late 1989, one rival, Charles Taylor, entered the country with a small group of Libyan mercenaries and succeeded in coordinating local resistance into full-scale civil war. By the summer of 1990, his forces and those of breakaway factions were closing in on Monrovia.

I had planned to return for new fieldwork during a leave in 1988–89, but was convinced by well-meaning advisors to prepare my tenure dossier instead. Unfortunately, that year was probably the last moment that I could have done ethnographic fieldwork in Liberia. When the war started, it was very difficult to get any reliable news about what was happening in the country. American journalists were preoccupied with the situation which would soon become the first Gulf War, and the few international news sources were difficult to access. I employed work-study students whose job consisted of photocopying everything they could find on Liberia in the news magazine *West Africa* and the *International Herald Tribune*, information that was "only" one or two weeks old by the time I got it. Late in the summer of 1990, as Monrovia was cut off from water, power, and food by the surrounding rebel factions, a telephone tree was set up with one of the few remaining Americans in Monrovia, an anthropologist. A group of us here in the States had a system whereby someone would call her every few hours to get news on the situation, her safety, and the safety of others who were staying with her. Then, the caller would call two other people and pass the word along. It was cumbersome and expensive, but it worked. Finally, all phone communication was cut off and the anthropologist was evacuated by the U.S. Marines.

For the next few years, it was almost impossible to get any news at all. My Glebo foster family was in a refugee camp in the Ivory Coast and managed to get a letter out once in a while, but did not seem to be receiving mine. The war dragged on. Occasionally there was something on NPR or CNN, or in the *New York Times*, generally on the theme of how "ancient tribal hatreds" were sending Africa back to the "Heart of Darkness." A multinational West African force controlled the capital city, up to seven warring factions had carved up the countryside, and unless you could get access to non-American news sources, it was very hard to hear anything at all. I tried to remain in contact with friends at the UN and the African American Institute, and began a new project, interviewing

Liberian expatriates in the United States, including former student leaders, labor activists, and government officials, about their experiences during the 1970s and '80s. I was hoping to combine their views with my understanding of how local populations reacted to national events.

Then, about 1995, everything changed. I refer, of course, to the rise of the Internet, which has significantly altered the prospects for anthropologists who work on countries in conflict. In this case, a dedicated group of volunteers known as Friends of Liberia started an e-mail news service. Composed mostly of former Peace Corps volunteers with experience in Liberia, FOL had acted as an advocate for the country throughout the war, lobbying Congress to cut funding to the Doe regime, working to regularize the immigration status of Liberians in the United States, and raising funds for refugee relief. The e-mail news was a free service that brought together anything in the international media that mentioned Liberia. All at once, sometimes several times a day, I was getting the latest reports on peace negotiations, refugee issues, and Liberians abroad. Coverage included the AP and Reuters, the BBC and other European news outlets, PANA (the Pan-African News Association), and even the Chinese news service. There were also links to the web sites being created by Liberian communities in the United States and other countries. At the time, I had been considering giving up on Liberia and beginning research in another African country, as many colleagues were doing. All at once, it seemed possible to stay connected, to remain current enough to consider going back in the future, even to use the information I was getting to write critically, as an anthropologist, about events in Liberia. I began to think of it as "virtual fieldwork."

At roughly the same time, my foster family reestablished contact. My foster brothers, who had been in college and high school when the war began, traveled to Monrovia in 1996 to see if they could pick up their disrupted educations. Telephone trees became important once again; I would be awakened at four or five in the morning by a call from a Liberian expatriate in New Jersey or Pennsylvania. "I just spoke with your family in Monrovia," they would begin, "take down this number, they are waiting by a phone right now for you to call." When I would get through, the first part of the conversation was always, "When we finish, please call this number and tell them their family members are here, it's their turn next." The few working private telephones in Monrovia were being used to maintain complex transnational networks, into which I had suddenly become incorporated. When Monrovia was threatened by armed insurgents again in June 2003, such telephone trees were once again called into service. Ironically, technological change had a less positive effect in this instance, as cell phone service was far more unreliable than the old land lines.

Unfortunately, in April 1996 the peace agreement on which my broth ers had pinned their hopes fell apart. The armed factions, which had been allowed to bring their troops into a ring around the city, began fighting among themselves, looting and destroying Monrovia in the process. The international peacekeeping forces from the Economic Community of West African States (ECOWAS) stood aside or joined in the looting. As battles raged all over the city, my brothers somehow found themselves trapped in an apartment with a phone that could make international collect calls. They did not have a working radio, so they had no idea what was happening except for the sounds of shooting and shelling going on all around them. Over the next few days, we had some very bizarre conversations.

"We're close to the port," they said, "maybe we could get to a boat and get out of here." "No!" I screamed into the phone, having just read about "ghost ships" of Liberian refugees on my e-mail news. "None of the other West African countries are accepting more Liberian refugees. There are overloaded boats floating along the coast that are not being allowed to land; the people have no food or water and there is cholera breaking out! Don't get on a boat!"

"But we have no food here. We have to try and get out and find some, but we don't know which way to go."

"Well, I've seen on the news that most of the soldiers are concentrating on looting the NGO offices around the UN compound, so don't go over there. Try to go toward the Waterside Market."

The Internet was providing me with information not just for my personal or scholarly use, but with a life-or-death importance to the people I was in contact with. Ironically, I sometimes knew more about what was going on in any given section of Monrovia than people who were physically there. It was a moment that brought home forcefully the eroding distinction between being "in" and "out" of the field for anthropologists in the digital age. This situation replayed itself during the summer of 2003, when I became the point of contact for my three foster brothers, located in three different cities along the coast. All were able to reach me by phone, but they could not communicate with each other from within the country. For each of them, I was the source of information that the others were still alive.

As the crisis of 1996 resolved itself in still another peace agreement and the country moved toward elections in 1997, new players entered the Internet news scene. The Hirondelle Foundation, a Swiss NGO committed to funding independent news media in countries struggling with democratic transitions, initiated STAR radio, an independent station staffed by Liberian journalists telling their own stories. Liberia has a long tradition of crusading, critical journalism in spite or because of its autocratic history. STAR radio's daily broadcasts, added to the international news services, were soon joined by articles from the many independent Monrovia newspapers which were being published as soon as they could get access to the city's one remaining printing press. The character of what came over my e-mail each day began to change as recognizably Liberian voices and concerns took over the bulk of the transcripts. From being dominated by the reporting and analysis of foreigners, the news now began to sound like "being there." I could use my expensive telephone time actually to discuss the news with my foster family, who were astonished by how much I seemed to know. The "fieldwork" was beginning to feel more real than virtual. Only in the last few years have my foster brothers gained access to e-mail accounts of their own; once again, a new means of communication has opened between us.

Having this access has kept me committed to doing research on Liberia, with Liberians, there, over the Internet, and in the United States. I no longer feel compelled to find another field site. Even though Charles Taylor shut down STAR radio in 1998 and continued to harass and close independent newspapers, the wonderful Liberian genius for subversion came through the writing that still made it onto the Friends of Liberia news. Within weeks of Taylor's departure during the summer of 2003, STAR Radio was back on the airwaves and the independent press was more vibrant than ever.

All these sources of information have contributed to this book. Although I did not personally witness the violence of the war and its aftermath, my experience of living the daily life of a Glebo community before the war contextualizes my analysis of what I read on the Internet. I look for ways in which local people interpret, resist, and accommodate national events and institutions and look back in my notes to the stories they told me of how they interacted with the national government in the past. Like them, I hope to resist the tendency to overvalorize events taking place in the capital city. This is not to understate the terrible devastation and disruption that have taken place in Liberia during the long years of civil conflict, but rather to suggest that people's responses to the tragedy may hold the key to a reconceptualization of the national state.

Here in the United States, I have struggled to analyze the interviews conducted with Liberians in the diaspora. Many of these were with scholars, activists, and important national figures who honestly saw themselves as acting on behalf of "the people" and were dealing with a profound sense of failure. Some were searching desperately for answers and solutions to the ongoing conflict and were willing to entertain whole new perspectives on the history of the national state. Others continued to locate the seeds of the present war in the mistakes of the past, citing the inherent racism of the American Colonization Society's project and the deliberate concentration of power in the presidency afforded by the 1847 constitution. A significant body of work published by Liberian politicians and intellectuals lays out their analysis of past failures and visions for the future (among them Wonkeryor et al. 2000; Liberty 2002; Sawyer 1992). In early 2003, I participated in a small conference of Liberian intellectuals and former government officials as they struggled to rethink completely their assumptions about citizenship, constitutionalism, and "traditional political institutions." After years of reading stinging critiques of "Africanist" discourse and the colonialist construction of indigenous otherness by anthropologists from scholars like Mudimbe (1988, 1994) and Mamdani (1996), it was something of a shock to be asked, by a roomful of prominent Liberians, if I could please provide them with an account of rural political institutions of their country, in the hopes that these might serve as an alternative to the American-derived structures which had failed so spectacularly. This process, which is still ongoing, will be addressed in Chapter 7. The overall goal of this work is to elucidate the tension between these two levels of experience, the national and the local, without reducing one to the other.

Tragically, what happened in Liberia during the nineties and first decade of the twenty-first century was not unique. Although the years between the Gulf War and the events following September 11, 2001, are generally regarded as a period of "peace and prosperity" in the United States, many other parts of the world experienced terrible instability and violence. In the rest of this chapter, I will review some of the recent literature on violence and war produced by anthropologists during the last decade. I seek to locate my work within this body of literature, because I see it as countering a dangerously simplistic model of conflict which has been called the "New Barbarism Hypothesis" (Richards 1996) This set of ideas, which predominates in foreign policy studies, political science, and much political journalism, seems to provide an explanation for the fundamental difference between the "rational" deployment of American military might and the "senseless" terrorism of others. Certainly, most Western audiences have gained their understanding of "African wars" and the relationship between democracy and violence within this paradigm. In subsequent chapters, I consider how indigenous Liberians construct and enact the expression of individual voice and autonomy and what they consider justifies the use of violence (Chapter 1). I then trace the interaction of these ideas with those emanating from the national center in five specific contexts: representations of the past (history, Chapter 2), struggles over prestige, identity, and lifestyle (modernity or "civilization," Chapter 3), the conferral of political legitimacy (elections, Chapter 4), discourses of local and national economic transformation (development, Chapter 5), and the tensions between elders and youth (generation, Chapter 6). I argue that contests in each of these areas make use of a range of conceptions of political legitimacy and the legitimate use of force. The national state, rather than simply dictating and enforcing its policies at the local level, has had to adapt to these local interpretations and demands, just as local populations have often been forced to adapt to the demands of the state.

According to Richards (1996: xiv-xvii), the central tenets of the New Barbarism thesis are best articulated in the work of journalist Robert Kaplan in his influential article, "The Coming Anarchy" (later expanded into a book by the same name), in *Atlantic Monthly* in 1994. The *Atlantic Monthly* piece was considered so important by policymakers that it was faxed by the U.S. State Department to every American embassy around the world and sparked a confidential meeting by top officials at the United Nations (Richards 1996: xiv; Ellis 1999: 19–20). The three basic ideas, of what Kaplan himself has called his "paradigm for the Post-Cold War era" (2000: xiii), are relatively familiar: one might say that Kaplan has only articulated "common sense" notions about Africa held by many Americans (see also Keim 1999).

First, cultural identity, either "ethnic" or "tribal," is presumed to be stable, enduring, and almost unchangeable. Cultural differences between human populations are seen as leading inevitably to conflict (Richards 1996: xiv). This idea has been extended by the political theorist Samuel Huntington in his famous 1993 article (and later book by the same name, 1996) "The Clash of Civilizations," in *Foreign Affairs* and has enjoyed wide acceptance in political science and policy studies. Anna Simons notes that the military analyst Ralph Peters, writing for a Defense and State Department audience in the journal *Parameters*, has taken up these ideas and reworked for them for policymakers. Peters believes that certain societies, which seem to be coterminous with national states, are "rooted in culture." Such countries are those which restrict the free flow of information, subjugate women, do not assign responsibility for individual and collective failure, have the clan or family as the basic unit of social organization, are dominated by a restrictive religion, and place a low value on education and low prestige on work (Peters 1998, cited in Simons 1999). These societies are in a constant state of struggle against the more "rational" polities of the West, but are doomed to failure by their inefficiency; they are simply culturally inferior to the West (Simons 1999: 93; see also Huntington 1996). One can easily recognize in this "laundry list" the features attributed to Iraq under Saddaam Hussain or Afghanistan under the Taliban. The enemies of freedom and democracy at the turn of the millennium are trapped in their outmoded and irrational cultures, just as the communist demons earlier in the century were trapped by their unworkable socialist ideology. Simons notes that these "grand theories" all use "catchall terms—anarchy, civilization, culture—to explain phenomena that have local roots" (1999: 92). The whole construction, therefore, divides the world neatly into two sides, or in Huntington's terms, "civilizations." One represents the rational modernity of the West, while the other consists of less evolved cultures still dominated by religion, kinship, and "tradition." The argument rests on the evolutionist assumption that the West has somehow progressed "beyond culture" as a cause of violence and conflict; if and when *we* go to war, it is to defend "democratic principles," to "make the world safe from terrorism," or to secure the strategic resources (like oil) which make this benevolent intervention possible. The democratic government of the United States conducts rational "policy debates," holds hearings, and considers opinion polls before making the reasoned judgment to go to war. In contrast, other regions of the world seem to be prone to "spontaneous" outbreaks of warfare which erupt from time to time, rather like a volcano.

The second tenet of the New Barbarism thesis is that the post-Cold War context of globalization has thrown the monopoly of the nation-state over the means of violence into question. Weapons are cheaply made and easily transported; they are small and light, and can be operated even by children. Sovereign states can no longer contain the ambitions of warlords, criminals, and just disaffected teenagers (Richards 1996: xiv). Since postcolonial states in the Third World and central Europe are no longer needed as buffers and proxies by two competing super powers, there is no one to step in and clean up the mess when such states "fail" or "implode."

Driving all the above, the third tenet holds that overpopulation in the poorer parts of the world leads to inevitable environmental degradation, which causes competition for resources, resulting in local conflict. With no "big brother" to intervene, these conflicts become national and regional rather than local. Since, as described in the first tenet, some "civilizations" or cultures are simply more "barbaric" than others *and* since these nations are multiethnic and different ethnic groups will naturally want to fight each other, such conflicts consist of assaults on civilians, bizarre masquerades, acts of unspeakable cruelty, and outright genocide, as in Bosnia and Rwanda.

Kaplan's argument, which appears to wrap up a range of variables into one satisfying explanation, has been systematically and effectively dismantled by a number of scholars (Richards 1996; Besteman 1996; Besteman and Gusterson 2005, and others) but continues to influence both popular understandings and policy responses to "foreign wars." One reason for its popularity is that it resonates with Western evolutionist assumptions that cultural difference can be understood as a function of time. In many years of teaching undergraduate anthropology, I have frequently noticed that my undergraduate students are surprised to discover that customs such as polygyny, belief in sorcery, or veneration of ancestors "still" exist in the contemporary period (see also Fabian 1983, 1991, for a discussion of the use of time in categorizing human societies). My students share with Kaplan and Huntington the idea that some unfortunate people have made it into the twenty-first century with social and political institutions more suited to an earlier era. When reading media accounts of "tribal" conflicts in Liberia or Rwanda (or Afghanistan or Iraq), most Westerners imagine a premodern, "traditional" form of violence grounded in "ancient tribal hatreds." Yet there is striking evidence that these supposedly primordial identities can be manufactured and mobilized with great speed. In Liberia, where group identity had historically been fluid, localized, and situational, politicized "tribalism" emerged only after 1980, when the young leader of the military coup, Samuel Doe, moved to surround himself with friends and kin from his home region in Tuzon, Grand Gedeh County, purportedly the home of the Krahn "tribe." Doe and his originally multiethnic group of young soldiers had articulated a vague justification for the coup by defining themselves as indigenous "redeemers" and liberators who had overthrown the alien Americo-Liberian minority. The great sin of the previous administration, described as selfish and insular, was its unwillingness really to share both the national wealth and the promise of democratic participation with all Liberians, regardless of ethnicity. By the mid-1980s, the increasing presence of coethnics in Doe's inner circle invited grumbling about the "Krahn people's government." After Doe declared himself the winner of obviously rigged elections in 1985, a coup attempt by a former military associate almost succeeded in overthrowing him. For the first time, Doe retaliated not only against his rival but against the rival's rural homeland. The army, now composed mostly of recruits from Grand Gedeh, was sent to this region, identified with the "Gio" and "Mano" people, and went on a rampage of killing, looting, and raping. At the same time, Doe purged the army and civil service of Gio speakers, and well-known Gio citizens in Monrovia began to "disappear."

Four years later, another aspirant to unseat Doe, Charles Taylor, brought a small force of Libyan-trained mercenaries into the country through this same area. Doe, predictably, sent the army back to the towns and villages they had so recently ravaged. The people there responded to Taylor's invitation to join his uprising, swelling his forces from two hundred to over twenty thousand in a few months. Since Taylor's troops were now mostly Gio and Mano and Doe's army had been made solidly Krahn, the conflict was represented in the American and European press as an ethnic war grounded in, as the *New York Times* reported, "ancient tribal hatreds." As is clear from the above account, the antiquity of those hatreds amounted to less than a decade.

The story of how the Liberian conflict became a "tribal war" was not unique in the 1990s, especially as events in Africa have been reported. Catherine Besteman has documented the same process at work in the reporting on Somalia, in which rival "clans" took the place of "tribes" in that conflict (1996: 121). "The crisis in Somalia has been caused by intense clan rivalries, a problem common in Africa, but here carried out with such violence, there is nothing left of civil society, only anarchy and the rule of the gun" (CNN 1992, quoted in Besteman 1996: 121–22). Besteman points out that, far from being a homogeneous, egalitarian, kinship-based society, Somalia was in fact deeply divided by class and race (defined as the difference between northern Somalis and those of southern "Bantu" or slave origins). Economic stratification and a growing gap between rural and urban populations led, ironically, to increasing identification with "clans," which had formerly been just one among many status positions that Somalis could assert. During the 1980s, as external "development" aid poured into Somalia and "the state became a primary source of wealth and resources, competition among the new urban elite who gained prominence . . . often played out along bloodlines. This urban-based elite struggle for personal enrichment through acquiring state resources is what came to be known as tribalism or clannism, although it bore little, if any resemblance to traditional lineage mediated interactions" (Besteman 1996: 126–27). Just as in Liberia, the cleavages of contemporary warfare are not relics of the past; rather, they are new constructions, employed for specific purposes in contexts that are the result of changes often initiated from abroad.

Likewise, the horrific genocide in Rwanda, represented as the outcome of "age-old" struggles between Tutsi and Hutu, has been analyzed differently by Christopher Taylor, who demonstrates how European colonial powers built upon existing status differences to produce rigid ethnic categories, beginning in the late 1880s. According to the so-called "Hamitic hypothesis" favored by Europeans to explain the status hierarchies they observed, the tall, "Caucasian-featured" Tutsi were the biblical lost sons of Ham and so were the natural rulers of the shorter, more "African" Hutu (Taylor 1999: 55–97). The fact that these supposedly separate groups speak the same language and have intermarried for generations made little difference in the colonial policies of the region. A variant of this hypothesis was later used by competing political factions as justification for the wave of massacres that began in April of 1994. The willingness of international bodies like the United Nations to believe that the killings were "tribal" and therefore somehow unavoidable led to the withdrawal of peacekeeping troops and the escalation of the violence.

All three of these examples from Africa demonstrate the fallacy on which the first tenet of the New Barbarism hypothesis is based: that archaic cultural identities are essentially stable, historically unchangeable, and the source of conflict in the present day. Why do we find it so satisfying to believe that other people are rooted in culture while we ourselves have somehow evolved beyond tribalism to rational politics? One answer is that this makes complex events easier to understand. "Tribal violence" functions as both a description and an explanation; once something has been designated as tribal, we no longer feel we need additional information. Besteman suggests another way in which this view responds to anxieties closer to home: "Viewing Somalis as caught in a destructive spiral of 'tradition' allows us to imagine them as very different kinds of human beings, to pity them, and feel safe" (1996: 130). We feel safe, she argues, because as long as we are so different from those "others," the horrors they experience could never happen to us. More significantly, displacing the source of conflict away from issues of race and class and onto tribes and clans "allows us to ignore the legitimacy of these categories and our growing inability to manage their 'dangerous' mix within our own societies, borders, and world" (Besteman 1996: 130). In other words, as national borders become more permeable and "others" take to living as our neighbors, it becomes harder to ignore the inequalities and injustices of our own society. Understanding violent conflict as an outcome of primordial hatreds rather than as a product of the complex interaction of numerous factors and local histories is comforting under these circumstances.

Recently, the "othering" of supposedly traditional cultures has become even more pronounced as the United States settles into an extended "war on terrorism." In seeking to understand the motivation behind the suicide bombings of September 11th, the notion that the perpetrators were products of "cultures of terror" was given wide currency. During the brief military intervention in Afghanistan, anti-Taliban Afghans were represented as unreliable allies due to their "tribalism" and the fact that "Pashtuns have always hated Uzbeks." Even long-term alliances have come under recent scrutiny as fears of "Islamic culture" grow. In an editorial on August 9, 2002, entitled "Saudis pose a threat to U.S.," the syndicated columnist Cal Thomas describes a briefing commissioned by the Pentagon from the Rand Corporation. The report characterizes Saudi Arabia as "a regime that oppresses women, denies human rights and favors a privileged few at the top over the mostly poor and illiterate at the vast bottom." While this may in fact be an accurate portrayal of the Saudi state, the same conditions held ten years before, when the Saudis were American allies in the Gulf War against Iraq. What was tolerated then as merely a "different" form of government has taken on sinister connotations in the new "cultural war." The columnist concludes, "The United States is being invaded by the immigration of such people." The implication, of course, is that "such people," already dangerous by virtue of their ancient cultural commitments, are violating both spatial and temporal boundaries through immigration ("invasion"). As transnationalism becomes a way of life and economic globalization demands the constant shifting of labor and capital, the barriers separating "us" and "them" dissolve in both time and space.

To anthropologists, the idea that some people have "culture" while others have moved on to a superior rationality is absurd. Anthropologists understand "culture" to be our species' means of adapting to the physical world and creating systems of meaning through which experience can be interpreted; *all human beings*, by definition, are rooted in culture. As Clifford Geertz noted, cultureless humans (if such were possible) would not be "talented apes," but "unworkable monstrosities with very few useful instincts, fewer recognizable sentiments, and no intellect: mental basket cases. As our central nervous system . . . grew up in great part in interaction with culture, it is incapable of directing our behavior or organizing our experience without the guidance provided by systems of significant symbols" (1973a: 48).

Yet New Barbarism theorists suggest that we in the West have somehow transcended or evolved beyond this most human of capacities, leaving others to stagnate. Until those others are also able to leave behind their warlike, mystical, and irrational cultures, they will be unable to participate fully in the modern world of the West, forced to occupy a kind of half-life as unreliable allies if not outright threats.

The appropriation and misrepresentation of the anthropological concept of culture by policy analysts who use it in this static, reductionist way must be challenged. The examples from Liberia, Somalia, and Rwanda make clear that culture is a dynamic process of making meaning from ongoing events, not a fixed position on an evolutionary scale. After all, what is the New Barbarism thesis itself if not a cultural product of our own assumptions about the world and our place in it, one that conveniently disguises the role of major powers like the United States in violent conflicts elsewhere in the world?

I now turn to the second tenet of the hypothesis: the argument that Cold War policies in the post-World War II period served the purpose of keeping local conflicts "under control." All classic social science definitions of the state include the observation that under this form of political organization, the central government (rather than the kin group or the local community) reserves to itself the legitimate use of violence. In other words, if I kill someone for my own purposes, the act constitutes murder and is defined as a crime, but if I do so while in a police or army uniform pursuing my official duties, the same act may be defined as heroism. From the point of view of the victim, of course, there is no difference, but from the perspective of the state one killing is legitimate and the other is not. One of the defining features of the "failed" states of the 1990s—from Bosnia to Somalia to Liberia—was the state's loss of control over the means of violence and their usurpation by "non-state actors," defined as militias, warlords, or terrorists.

It has been asserted that the Cold-War era superpower competition kept such tendencies in check during the post-World War II period (Kaplan 2000). Using the world as a giant chessboard, the United States and the Soviet Union distributed financial aid and military equipment to a carefully balanced assortment of client states, clearly identified as "ours" or "theirs." While admittedly some of the leaders of "our" clients were rather unsavory characters (Mobutu of Zaire comes to mind), at least they provided stability if not democracy and kept tribal and other factional tendencies in check. In this sense, the Cold War was seen as having brought benefits to countries in Africa and Eastern Europe, giving them a much needed break from their own "natural" cycles of internal tribal conflict. The emergence of wars in these regions after the demise of the Soviet Union, on the other hand, was viewed as an unfortunate side effect of the triumph of the United States as the sole remaining superpower and of capitalism as the uncontested, dominant form of economic organization on the planet. The fact that the former Soviet Union is no longer capable of supporting client states and the United States no longer needs them is the regrettable cause of the "descent into anarchy" experienced by these now expendable nations.

Such a formulation, like the assertion of cultural difference in the first tenet of the hypothesis, sounds reasonable, but it ignores several alternative understandings of the Cold War period and the question of who bears responsibility for the wars of the 1990s. In the first place, the model ignores the fact that both Cold War antagonists had active programs to destabilize each other's clients. Superpower competition *generated* rather than prevented warfare in Angola, Mozambique, and Ethiopia, among other countries. Development aid, often granted with no mechanisms for accountability, rewarded cooperative clients but exacerbated the kind of class stratification that Besteman noted was key to the outbreak of conflict in Somalia (1996: 126). Moreover, the tremendous influx of weapons, all manufactured in the developed world, saturated African countries with the means of violence while profits accrued to those at a safe distance. During the height of Cold War tensions in the first Reagan administration (1980–84), tiny Liberia, with a population of two and a half million people and an area the size of the state of Ohio, was the "beneficiary" of the second largest package of United States military aid in the world (after Israel). This was presumably to keep Liberia safe from the "communist threat," but these were the same weapons that

Samuel Doe turned against his own civilian population in 1986. With the breakup of the Soviet Union, arms manufacturers in Ukraine and other newly independent republics, as well as in the United States, have depended on demand from the African market to maintain domestic employment in their aging industrial plants (Ellis 1999: 90, 180; Reno 1993: 181). The militarization of Africa was a deliberate Cold War strategy and continues to benefit its principal architects, long after the Cold War itself was declared over.

A second problem with the "Cold War peace" formulation is that the tendency to view warfare in the non-Western world as simple "anarchy" obscures the very "rational" economic incentives that fuel long-term conflicts. Charles Taylor quickly learned that he did not need the legitimacy of the Liberian state in order to profit from the country's natural resources. With control over roughly three-fourths of the country, including significant timber and diamond reserves, Taylor was able to build his personal wealth over the many years of the Liberian civil war, even though an international peacekeeping force occupied Monrovia and a series of helpless interim governments struggled to bring him to the negotiating table. The logic of global capitalism dictated that international firms were more than willing to buy the products Taylor had to offer, whether or not he had the "legitimate" right to sell them (for an extended analysis, see Reno 1993, 1998). In fact, the rationality of pricing made Taylor an even more attractive trading partner to countries like France and China, since as a "warlord" he was not bound by any cumbersome environmental or labor restrictions. A similar economic rationality supported the flow of "blood diamonds" from Sierra Leone and petroleum from Angola, while both countries were trapped in seemingly endless wars. Rather than mindless anarchy, the post-Cold War conflicts of Africa are the logical outgrowth of the triumph of capitalism and economic globalization, achievements celebrated by the same authors who decry the barbarism of their victims.

The final element of the New Barbarism hypothesis would appear to be the most "natural": that overpopulation and natural resource depletion are driving the world's poor into a desperate struggle for existence. Richards has dubbed this aspect of the model "Malthus-with-guns" (1996a: xiv). Kaplan dwells at length on a frightening metaphor of the developed world as a luxury limousine, with its few occupants temporarily insulated from the teeming hordes just beyond the tinted windows (1994: 62). Kaplan attributes this population explosion in Africa to "loose family structures" and polygyny, which he sees as "largely responsible for the world's highest birth rates and the explosion of the HIV virus on the continent" (1994: 46). The pressure of this burgeoning population on a fragile and already depleted environment, Kaplan argues, will ultimately overwhelm the continent and the comfortable lives of those in the developed world, as the violent, the diseased, and the dispossessed overflow out of Africa to engulf the planet.

I am not a demographer, and so will leave it to others to dissect Kaplan's Malthusian argument in detail. I will note, however, just a few fallacies in its logic. One is that in using Sierra Leone and Liberia as examples of the corrosive relationship between overpopulation and anarchic violence, Kaplan chose two countries that have among the *lowest* population densities in sub-Saharan Africa (this point has been made by Richards 1996a: xvi). Rather than driving up population, polygyny is generally considered by demographers to have, if anything, the effect of *decreasing* average fertility per woman. While multiple wives may increase the number of children claimed by an individual man, other men will have no wives at all and women in polygynous unions are likely to have fewer children than their monogamous counterparts. At its root, Kaplan's analysis seems to rest on the old racist trope of the oversexed African, unable to control his "natural" impulses.

With regard to the supposition that population pressure and resource depletion, especially deforestation, drive young people to violent behavior, it is once again unfortunate for Kaplan's thesis that he chose to base it on Liberia and Sierra Leone. New research by Fairhead and Leach on this region of West Africa has suggested that "the extent of forest loss in the twentieth century has been vastly exaggerated . . . calling into question the commonplace view of population growth and deforestation as linked one-way processes" (1998: xiv). While there may be environmental crises elsewhere in Africa, they are not coterminous with the wars that Kaplan attributes to them.

On all his major points, therefore, Kaplan is rehashing old, disqualified ideas and assuming that the events he witnessed during his brief visits were the outcome of ageold structures and processes. His observations have much in common with the travel writing of the Victorian era, in that he generalizes widely from single examples and assumes in advance that he is witnessing a "clash of civilizations." His "master stroke" and the secret of his ability to "touch a chord with Western policy makers," according to Ellis, was his suggestion that barbaric wars driven by overpopulation and environmental mismanagement "would soon be breaking out in other parts of the world too, and that West Africa was ahead of the trend" (1999: 19). Yet, as we have seen in the case of Liberia, neither environmental factors nor the end of the Cold War nor "ancient tribal hatreds" can fully explain why 200,000 people lost their lives and over the half the population was displaced during a fourteen-year period. Sadly, none of these explanations reassure us that "it could never happen here."

Faced with an integrated, seemingly logical construction like the New Barbarism thesis, what critical tools can anthropology provide to serve as an alternative? The United States is currently the only global superpower, capable of destroying entire nations and regions as well as enforcing peace agreements in those contexts where we choose to intervene. Such immense power confers responsibility not only on our political leaders but on all citizens. The ability to cut through the mythology of the "cultural other" is crucial to understanding and evaluating what we are told about the deployment (or decision not to deploy) American military power abroad. I believe that anthropological analyses can serve to bring to light naturalizing assumptions about violence and war.

Richards notes that the "New Barbarism pays scant regard to the insurgents' own claims concerning the purposes of their movement (that they took up arms to fight for multiparty democracy and against state corruption)" (1996a: xvi). Rather, Kaplan talked almost exclusively to elites in the African countries he visited, elites who have their own reasons for defining young fighters as out-of-control criminals. In contrast, anthropologists attempting to understand the violence and disruption bearing down on the people they work with and care about use ethnographic methods of long-term participant observation in specific local situations, often returning to the same place to build a deeper understanding of communities through time. In recent years, many anthropological studies have explored the impact of warfare and violence on local communities, both historical and contemporary. Michael Taussig (1987), building on Foucault (1979, 1983), documented the deliberate construction of "cultures of terror" and the ways that local populations respond by drawing on existing traditions and creative innovations. Kay Warren examined the revitalization of older religious practices among Mayan populations in Guatemala—including the idea of multiple "selves" capable of operating independently and taking on supernatural qualities—as a way of answering the question: "Whom can I trust in a world in which I may be betrayed by my neighbors?" (1993: 12). Likewise, Carolyn Nordstrom emphasized the resilience and creativity of Mozambicans in constructing alternatives to the terror and violence of a seemingly endless war (1997).

Although the "ethnic" character of the Guatemalan violence is commonly highlighted (indigenous Maya against Hispanicized *ladino*), Warren showed that local people recognized that the troops of the government's counterinsurgency force were also Mayan and in actuality, their own neighbors (1993: 26–27). Similarly, Valentine Daniel, in decoding Tamil/Sinhala (also often framed as Buddhist/Hindu) conflict in Sri Lanka, wrote that "many Sri Lankans have either forgotten or do not know that there was a time in Sri Lanka when where one lived mattered more than what language one spoke or what one's religion was" (1996: 16). Historicizing and denaturalizing ethnicity have been central to anthropologists' alternatives to the New Barbarism accounts.

Other ethnographers have refuted the notion that Third-World wars are anarchic and inscrutable forms of violence, as opposed to the technologically "clean" or "surgical" havoc wreaked by Western militaries. The effort to make conflicts understandable by placing them within a local cultural context is a key theme of this literature. For example, Christopher Taylor explained some of the peculiar mutilations and tortures employed in Rwanda in terms of broadly shared understandings of movement, impediment, fluidity, and blockage employed in folk medicine and ideas of how the health of land, cattle, and people is maintained (1999: 99–149). I felt compelled to respond to demeaning and frankly racist stories in supposedly serious magazines like *Atlantic Monthly* and *Esquire* that ridiculed Liberian fighters who dressed in women's wigs and dresses. The authors of these pieces could not resist referencing Conrad's *Heart of Darkness*, and they assumed that the bizarre attire of the fighters either was due to ignorance of Western clothing (and hence was evidence that the fighters were unsophisticated tribesmen) or was motivated by "juju" or other magical beliefs. I argued, rather, that far from displaying primitive ignorance, these fighters were asserting the gender ambiguity of the traditional warrior through intentional transvestism, in ways that I had observed numerous times in funeral dances before the war (Moran 1995).

The work of these and other anthropologists undermines the New Barbarism hypothesis by exposing the fallacies on which it rests. First, it underlines the incorrectness of any evolutionary assumption that "progress" is linear and unidirectional, with all human societies moving inexorably toward something resembling contemporary Western life. No society or people can evolve "beyond culture" to a universal rationality, because all human products (including the belief that one is rational) are cultural by definition. The combatants in African and Middle Eastern wars are behaving rationally according to their own understandings of the world. They may also have very real grievances against the West that our own cultural frameworks do not recognize or acknowledge. By positing archaic "culture" as the cause of violence in the developing world, this framework blinds us to the tensions and antagonisms of race, class, and inequality existing in our own communities—a far more dangerous situation than that presented by "invading" immigrants (Besteman 1996: 130). The New Barbarism thesis also imposes historical blinders, as when ethnic or tribal identities are projected into the primordial past rather than understood as products of colonial and postcolonial power struggles.

Finally, the New Barbarism framework falls back on a reductionism that attributes violence, in the final analysis, to "natural" causes, both those seen as endemic in humans and those, like population growth and resource competition, that have to do with human interactions with the environment. This view leads to the inescapable conclusion that nothing can be done; "those people" will continue to kill each other and we had best not get involved beyond erecting barriers that will prevent their conflicts from spilling into our territory. Anthropologists insist on returning local histories of conflict, and their relationship with global political and economic forces, back to the center of the analysis.

The events of September 11, 2001, may have reinforced the sense that many Americans have of themselves as the endpoint of a progressive evolutionary process, waiting as the rest of the world—jealous and resentful—tries to catch up. The New Barbarism hypothesis fits neatly into this understanding of self and other, but it is based on a systematic misunderstanding of both culture and history. A critically aware citizenry, able to see through the essentialism and reductionism of such notions, is our best hope that we will be able to find a peaceful future. The archeologist Philip Walker has argued that the message of the deep historical record is one of equality and universality; no people, in any time or place, have been immune from war and, conversely, none have held a monopoly on it (2001: 590).

There is also the danger, pointed out by Nordstrom and others, of making *too* much sense of violence: "A concern with the reasons of war comes dangerously close to a concern with making war reasonable" (Nordstrom 1995: 138). Likewise, our emphasis on the resilience, resistance, and creativity of populations under fire may result in the feeling, as voiced by one of my students after reading Nordstrom's book on Mozambique, that "They're doing all right, we don't have to worry about them." The overcelebration of local resistance or "the allure of agency," as Rosalind Shaw refers to it, can result in the misreading of every action on the part of subjugated people as deliberate and strategic (2002: 18–20; see also Abu-Lughod 1990). Although convinced that local actors and their responses have more impact on national events than has been recognized, I strive to avoid the romanticizing impulse inherent in "orientalizing" discourses of otherness (see Piot 1999: 20–21), while still insisting that we have much to learn about democracy and violence from rural Liberians.

I locate this study within this evolving literature. The Liberian war, like that in neighboring Sierra Leone, has been taken as emblematic of the "barbaric" nature of wars conducted by non-Western combatants using low-technology weapons. Contesting this characterization, of Africa and the rest of the non-Western world, is indeed one of the most important contributions that anthropologists can make. We must no longer allow whole peoples and cultures to be described as "naturally warlike" or barbaric. The chapters which follow seek to extend this project while also encouraging a critical reevaluation of how violence and political legitimacy are interrelated.

Chapter 1
The Case for Indigenous Democracy

The scholarly literature on democracy is, like that on war and violence, voluminous and at times contradictory. That portion of it dedicated to Africa has come primarily from political scientists, who have devoted much time and care to constructing typologies and definitions (although anthropologists have contributed important insights to the study of democracy worldwide; see Owusu 1992, 1997; Comaroff and Comaroff 1997; Karlstrom 1996; Schaffer 1997, 1998; Snyder 2001; West and Kloeck-Jenson 1999; Gutman 2002; Paley 2001, 2002; Greenhouse and Kheshti 1998, among others). In what follows, I address only a fraction of that literature, and only in terms of how it can enhance or limit our understanding of both local processes and postcolonial states in some parts of Africa. But I also want to emphasize the aspect of this literature that has been given most attention by the popular press and by policymakers, contributing to an evolutionist discourse in which the continent and its people are configured as "not ready" for democracy.

Africa in general has long been constructed in the Western imagination as the opposite of the West on a number of points of contrast. One of these contrasts is between the supposedly open and "transparent" nature of Western political institutions and those seen as "indigenous" to Africa, said to be characterized by secrecy, mystical religious beliefs, and outright autocracy. Specifically, the claim has been made that African political institutions were "patrimonial" in the precolonial past and, rather than evolving properly as "modern" rational-legal bureaucracies, they are "neopatrimonial" in the present (Hyden 2000; Jackson 1977; Jackson and Rosberg 1982; Clapham 1985; Bratton and van de Walle 1997; Reno 1995a, b, 1998). The term was first employed by Max Weber, who was attempting to create a typology of different forms of political structures worldwide. Weber defined patrimonialism as a form of prebureaucratic organization emerging from the "natural" patriarchal authority of men over women and children (1978: 1006–7) Patrimonialism is "at first . . . only a decentralization of the household when the lord settles dependents (including young men regarded as family members) on plots within his extended land-holdings" (1010). Unlike the patriarchal father, the patrimonial lord does not have direct physical control over his dependents, since they are not residing in his household. In the absence of bureaucratic institutions like codified laws and contracts, the relationship is grounded in personal loyalty and mutual self-interest. As we shall see, some contemporary scholars believe that these personalistic or clientalistic relationships are the antithesis of good governance, especially when office holders are supposed to attain their positions through credentials, merit, and achievement. Neopatrimonialsim in African governments has been invoked to explain the failure of development initiatives, free market and privatization reforms, and the lack of "civil society" all over the continent.

I will argue in this chapter that the characterization of African political institutions as patrimonial or neopatrimonial rests on a fundamental misreading of Weber. Such a characterization misrepresents the actual dynamics of political authority in rural West African communities and shifts the blame for the abusive behavior of some African rulers onto the passivity and tolerance for corruption of the suffering masses. This imaginary African politics obscures the role of international commodities traffickers, development "experts," and post-Cold War strategists in the abysmal record of many contemporary African states. By characterizing Charles Taylor as a neopatrimonial ruler, these analysts imply that he is behaving like a "traditional chief," only on a larger scale. What is obscured is the role of United States policy in supporting and funding men like Taylor and his predecessor, Samuel Doe, as described in the previous chapter. Also missing is the global economic context that rewards the "entrepreneurial" efforts of men like Taylor to lease, sell, and pocket the profits from national resources. As we shall see below, the fact that African rulers like Taylor may *claim* the prerogatives of "traditional" chiefs does not mean that local populations accept these claims as legitimate. The neopatrimonialism school has too often taken these claims at face value, arguing that the majority of the African population accepts blatant corruption and autocracy as simply a part of life. People may indeed turn to religious or magical understandings of the world to explain political events and place their trust in prophets, priests, and spirit mediums rather than in political organizing and grassroots demands for reform (see Ellis 1999: 266–80). Yet such an analysis cannot account for the proliferation of organized groups that have flourished in Liberia before and during the war nor for the long history of dissent, resistance, and opposition that preceded it (see Moran and Pitcher 2004; Sawyer 1992). Such activities are inexplicable if we assume that the people have little sense of social justice, no understanding of their own rights as citizens, and little faith in coordinated human action to change their social and political environment.

At first glance, this particular part of West Africa seems an unlikely setting in which to encounter principles of egalitarianism and shared decisionmaking. The Upper Guinea Coast is a region of humid tropical forests, stretching from the Gambia to Cape Mount in northern Liberia (Rodney 1970: 1–2) and from there usually extended to at least the St. Paul River in central Liberia (d'Azevedo 1962b). Long viewed as a kind of backwater to the savannah empires of Ghana, Mali, and Songhai to the north, the region became strategically significant in the fifteenth century when European traders, moving along the coast in ships, began to compete for trade goods with the overland trans-Saharan caravan routes. The rise of the Atlantic slave trade after the colonization of the New World further altered the relationship between the inhabitants of the forests, their powerful savannah neighbors to the north, and Europeans along the coast.

In the literature of both anthropology and political science, this part of West Africa is understood as one of "stateless societies" or shifting alliances of uncentralized chiefdoms built around individual strongmen or warlords (d'Azevedo 1962b; 1969–1970; 1989: 103–4; Holsoe 1974) These political units competed with each other for access to land and trade routes and were characterized by a hierarchy of founding and "latecomer" lineages, close control over secret information (especially genealogical and historical knowledge), and "clientalism" or autocratic rule by individuals who managed to gather enough resources to offer protection to a collection of followers (see Murphy and Bledsoe 1987). These local-level arrangements, which some scholars have identified with traditional rulers elsewhere in Africa, are said to have infiltrated the structure of postcolonial nation states, where they become the "neopatrimonialism" associated with corrupt, abusive governments in many parts of contemporary Africa. This literature asserts that "the institutional hallmark of African politics since independence has been neopatrimonialism. . . . Neopatrimonialism is the opposite of democracy in that it is characterized by the absence of public accountability. It lies in the very nature of this system that it is kept private and secret" (Hyden 2000: 18, 21; see also Jackson 1977, Jackson and Rosberg 1982, Clapham 1985, Bratton and van de Walle 1997, among others). Therefore, the Guinea Coast, where indigenous precolonial societies are said to be characterized by secrecy and autocracy, becomes the perfect venue for the development of the neopatrimonial postcolonial state.

The ethnographic literature on the Guinea Coast is further characterized by an emphasis on the influence of Mande-speaking peoples, who are said to have brought state-influenced political institutions into the region sometime between the thirteenth and fifteenth centuries. As mentioned above, this area of humid forests has conventionally been treated as a regional system in attempts to recreate its precolonial history, distribution of populations and languages, and environmental features (e.g., Rodney 1970, d'Azevedo 1962b, Fairhead and Leach 1998). The standard historical narrative emphasizes the arrival of Mande-speaking "invaders" from the savannahs of the north and west who brought with them agriculture, iron-smelting technologies, concepts of social stratification, and politico-ritual complexes, including universal initiatory organizations or "secret societies" of Poro for men and Sande or Bundu for women. The prior inhabitants of the forests, designated as "Primitives" by Rodney (1970: 6–7), were subsumed in processes of displacement or assimilation by the Mande speakers (11). The limits of Mande expansion, as measured by linguistic distribution, have been used as the boundaries of somewhat arbitrary "culture areas," such as Rodney's "Upper Guinea Coast" or d'Azevedo's "Central West Atlantic Region" (1962b), both of which cut off northern Liberia from the south and east. By contrast, the Kruan-speaking (or Kwa) peoples of the south are usually characterized as less hierarchical, more recently adapted to agriculture (from their presumably primordial state as foragers), and are defined by the *absence* of secret societies. The northwest-to-southeast direction of this diffusion, bringing at least a limited "complexity" to the "simpler" people of the south, was conceptualized as essentially unidirectional and has only rarely been challenged (see McEvoy 1977; Fairhead and Leach 1998). The overwhelming bulk of ethnographic research in the region has focused on the Mande speakers and those, like the Gola, who have adopted the secret initiation societies and who participated in building complex trading confederacies linking coastal, forest, and savannah zones (d'Azevedo 1969–70).

New research, however, points to evidence of extensive, established rice production "often independent of any obvious 'Sudanic influence'" in the southeastern Kwa-speaking regions (Fairhead and Leach 1998:49). A picture is emerging of the entire region as one of dynamic interaction and cultural interchange among peoples of different linguistic and cultural traditions. It therefore seems both arbitrary and illogical to view the southeasterners as merely the isolated, passive recipients of northern "civilization." Cultural contact and exchange is always a two-way process, and ideas, products, and people move in multiple directions. Yet the ethnographic literature on the Bassa, Kru, Grebo, and Krahn-speaking peoples of southern Liberia pales in comparison with that which has been compiled about their northern neighbors: the Kpelle, Mende, Vai, Gola, Dan, and others. As a result, most writing on "traditional Liberia" contains a distinct "Mande-centric" bias.

The aspect of social and cultural life most emphasized by ethnographers of the Mande-speaking peoples is the high value placed on regimes of secrecy (Bellman 1975, 1984; Murphy 1980, 1981, 1988; Ferme 2001). Political power is understood as controlled through ritual hierarchies which reinforce the ability of highranking persons and lineages to command the labor and resources of others (Bledsoe 1980, 1984). Given that the most spectacular and defining features of this region are the so-called "secret societies" of Poro and Sande, universal initiatory and educational associations that hold the power of transforming children into adults, the emphasis on secrecy is clearly not misplaced. Yet there are also counter discourses of political legitimacy that the attention on secrecy has helped to obscure. The very fluidity and lack of centralized historical states have served to maintain multiple systems of organization and constructions of group membership. For example, Warren d'Azevedo recorded the following statement from an informant during his fieldwork among the Gola in the early 1960s: "No one can say that I am not a real Gola, but also no one can say that I am not a Mandingo, De, or even Vai . . . I learned to be a leader for many kinds of people, and I was able to show them that I could turn my face to each of them and be one of them" (1969–70: 11). Such a basis for political legitimacy would seem to depend on the wide sharing of information ("no one can say") and the deliberate overlapping of multiple identities.

Even if strict hierarchical principles were brought from the Sudanic states into the forests, it is likely that they would become attenuated in the emerging economic system created by the demands of European traders on the coast as well as the multiethnic, multilingual context of intermarriage. And is it not at least possible that competing notions of political process may have diffused *to* the north from the less hierarchical, more egalitarian Kwa-speaking people of the southeast? Rather than simply excluding them from the definition of "the region," would it not make sense to consider how their influence may have modified the overwhelming power of high-ranking elders, secret-society officers, warlords, and wealthy traders over other members of the community?

I have not had the opportunity to investigate this question empirically among Mande speakers, but there is evidence in the ethnography of multiple discourses of power and influence and of extensive strategizing by individuals to avoid relationships of dependency and obligations to superiors (Bledsoe 1980; Ferme 2001). I do not contest the centrality of principles of hierarchy and secrecy in the formal arrangements of political participation and decisionmaking in the Upper Guinea Coast. Also, it is clear that both domestic slavery and participation in the Atlantic slave trade had a great impact on the societies of the north (Ferme 2001;

d'Azevedo 1969–70; Shaw 2002), contributing to the greater concern with hierarchy and with controlling knowledge of genealogy and personal identity. D'Azevedo and Holsoe have both documented the multiple forms of political authority, some based on lineage and others on achievement, which operated in tandem (d'Azevedo 1989; Holsoe 1974). The work of these sensitive ethnographers also documents the reciprocal nature of dependency and dominance, as well as the historical fluidity of rank and identity in this region.

The subtlety of the anthropologists' accounts is sometimes missed by political scientists seeking to construct explanations for contemporary state failure, especially in Sierra Leone and Liberia. As mentioned above, an extensive literature views African states as "neopatrimonial," a concept derived from Max Weber's ideal typology of forms of political authority (Hyden 2000: 18–19; for an extended example, see Reno 1995b). Weber identified patrimonialism as an outgrowth of "patriarchal authority," which he assumed to be the "natural" rule of an individual man over his household, including his wife or wives, children, and other dependents including slaves. This authority was seen as having no legal limits; the master of the family held absolute power over his subordinates (Weber 1978: 1006–9). Such a system, in which each household is constituted as a kind of ministate, could be extended when the "father" was accepted in a similar role over nonfamily dependents settled elsewhere, transforming the father into a ruler; this extension of familial loyalties to a larger sociopolitical unit is the essence of patrimonialism. The patrimonial state was the logical outcome of the growth of such institutions: "We shall speak of a 'patrimonial state' when the prince organizes his extrapatrimonial areas and political subjects—which is not discretionary and not enforced by physical coercion—just like the exercise of his patriarchal power. The majority of all great continental empires had a fairly strong patrimonial character until and even after the beginning of modern times" (Weber 1978: 1013). Clearly, Weber saw nothing inherently limiting or detrimental in this form of authority; he merely contrasted it with the legally defined bureaucratic structures (which he called "rational-legal authority") that arose later in Europe. Furthermore, Weber saw patrimonial authority as capable of holding together large, complex, multiethnic empires which could not operate on personalistic relations alone.

Contemporary political scientists, however, tend to insist that Weber's model applies to "small-scale, face to face types of traditional communities" (Hyden 2000: 18). Bratton and van de Walle believe that "His [Weber's] definition of patrimonialism may provide an accurate description of the political systems of small, isolated communities with rudimentary economies, including African chiefdoms in the precolonial era, and the practices of patrimonialism may persist at the local level in a number of different settings. . . . it is clear that some nations in the developing world, most notably in sub-Saharan Africa, retain in modified form many of the characteristics of patrimonial rule" (1997: 62).

Hence, patrimonial relations have come be defined as "natural" to Africa, and the differences between contemporary nation-states in Africa and those of the West are attributed to the continuation of these "archaic" systems into the present day. Neopatrimonialism is the "incorporation of patrimonial logic into bureaucratic structures," (Bratton and van de Walle 1997: 62), which are *supposed* to be characterized by legality, meritocracy, and transparency rather than by personalized and capricious ties. These rational-legal bureaucracies, furthermore, are assumed to be crucial in maintaining representational democracy, the regular competition between individuals for the right to represent "the people." Some authors make the specific connection between the supposedly patrimonial systems of the past and those of the present; Clapham, for example, has argued that the contemporary form in Africa exists because it most "corresponds to the normal forms of social organization in precolonial societies" (1985: 49).

There are several objections that can be made to this formulation. First, as seen in the above discussion, these scholars suggest that while patrimonialism is appropriate and workable in the context of a small village, it cannot be successfully adapted to the administration of larger, more complex territorial and political entities. Failed African states in the contemporary period, therefore, can be attributed to the anachronistic practices of earlier times; a kind of stubborn African refusal to "evolve" properly to more rational and efficient forms of government (Hyden 2000: 20). Here we see echoes of the "New Barbarism" discourse discussed earlier. This evolutionist discourse, directing attention *away* from analyzing the historical relations of extraction and accumulation between Africa and the West, continues to dominate discussions of African "governance," especially within multilateral donor institutions like the World Bank. What is the point of making loans to or investing in African countries, these officials wonder, if the money will disappear into the pockets of personalistic, patrimonial rulers rather than being transparently directed toward public goods or at least privately owned business enterprises? Patrimonial leaders are said to distribute resources to their followers as a means of ensuring their loyalty, rather than through rational, bureaucratic measures like open bidding. Yet since Weber himself saw patrimonialism as the basis of "great continental empires," there is no basis for reducing it to simple face-to-face relationships that have somehow been preserved into the present. It is certainly the case that Charles Taylor and a small circle of his cronies held a near monopoly on

Liberia's economy, but the reasons must be sought in the workings of contemporary global capitalism, not in the African past.

Second, it is certainly debatable whether or not Weber's ideal type of patrimonial authority is even appropriate to describe the complex trade systems, shifting alliances, and multiple forms of political organization that have been documented for Africa, even in the "stateless" forests of the Guinea Coast; for the most part, this has been asserted rather than demonstrated with ethnohistorical evidence. Even granted that Weber's model can provide some insights into nonbureaucratic forms of government, the whole analysis rests on a highly selective reading of what Weber has to say about the relationship between ruler and subject. For example, although Weber believes that patrimonialism emerges from the absolute authority of the male household head over his dependents, he also notes, "However, such a relationship, even if it constitutes at first a purely one-sided domination, always evolves the subject's claim to reciprocity, and this claim 'naturally' acquires social recognition as custom" (1978: 1010).

In other words, although patrimonial authority has, in theory, no legal limits, over time women, children, and other structural subordinates acquire publicly recognized rights, and these serve as a check on patrimonial power (1978: 1009). As these recognized rights become entrenched, part of the expectations people hold for each other, "the master's omnipotence toward the individual dependent is paralleled by his powerlessness in the face of the group. Thus arose almost everywhere a legally unstable, but in fact very stable order which diminished the area of the master's discretion in favor of traditional prescription" (1978: 1012). Somehow this aspect of patrimonialism has been excluded from the contemporary debate among political scientists about what is "wrong" with African governments, and yet it is Weber's description of the negotiation of mutual dependency that actually best accords with the ethnographic record. At the level of local administration, even village chiefs appointed by and supported by the power of the state are rarely allowed to behave autocratically without facing uprisings, resistance, and mass movements by their constituents (Mamdani 1996: 183–217). Local authorities should not bear the blame for national presidents whose criminal, dictatorial, and repressive rule is bolstered far more by the economic and political agendas of Western aid donors than by local constructions of legitimacy.

Of course, the notion that they are simply carrying out the "traditional duties of the chief" has been used by a range of despotic leaders to justify their actions, all reinforced by the scholarly authority of the patrimonialism thesis. It is important to note instances, however, when Africans themselves contest these claims to the prerogatives of "traditional authority." A recent example in Liberia occurred in October of 2002, when then-president Charles Taylor made just such a claim. Taylor is something of the exemplar of neopatrimonial African rulers: a man who came to power through relentless violence and systematically looted both the national coffers and the natural resources of Liberia. In the fall of 2002, rumors were circulating in Monrovia that Taylor was tiring of his official First Lady and intended to take another wife. When questioned by the press, Taylor asserted publicly that, in spite of having recently led a "Liberia for Jesus" campaign through his Baptist congregation, he was not only president but also a "traditional leader" and was therefore "entitled" to up to four wives at a time. He further claimed that if his current wife did not understand "this aspect of our culture," he would call elders from the rural areas to "instruct her." Taylor's comments unleashed a firestorm of protest from mainstream Christian groups, women's organizations, and ordinary citizens (*The Inquirer*, October 22, 2002). Everyone from the Association of Female Lawyers to the Liberian Rural Women's Initiative to the Catholic archbishop of Monrovia pointed out that, under Liberian law, Christians who have entered into church or statutory civil marriages are prohibited from taking another spouse. The president of the Association of Female Lawyers of Liberia stated, "It must be understood that polygamy is a part of our culture and that we do not intend to seek to abolish it, but both polygamy and monogamy cannot be practiced by a person at one and the same time" (*The News*, October 23, 2002). All the commentators explicitly rejected Taylor's claim that he was a "traditional ruler," either in his capacity as president of Liberia or in light of his clear identity as a "civilized" man and professed Christian. As will be described in Chapter 3, a binary discourse of "civilized" and "native" identity is enshrined in Liberian political life as well as in legal codes and daily practices (see also Moran 1990). Taylor's strategic deployment of traditionalism was not recognized by Liberians as politically legitimate, and they did not hesitate to say so, even in the face of a highly repressive state security system which ordinarily brooked little criticism of Taylor. Taylor himself, while never actually recanting his position, did not go through with his wedding plans and the matter was dropped from public discussion.

The blame for undemocratic, abusive leaders in Africa cannot be laid at the feet of "traditional" political institutions in village societies. This imaginary despotic African chief has been rejected by both rural and urban Liberians. Unfortunately, the obsession with secret hierarchies on the part of anthropologists and the insistence on patrimonialism, old and "neo," by the political scientists combine to leave us with a view of this region of Africa as hopelessly unsuitable for "democracy" or any system emphasizing broad participation and protection of individual rights.

In constructing his argument for the "religious" basis of violence in the Liberian civil conflict, Stephen Ellis relies on the work of anthropologists (including mine) to conclude that "Liberians believe" their traumatic recent past, future stability, and hopes for accountable leadership are controlled by an "invisible world of spirits," access to which is shrouded in secrecy (1999: 308–9). He argues that the Liberian state was able, in the twentieth century, to gather enough resources to coopt indigenous institutions and disregard or suppress their more democratic tendencies, resulting in a "tradition" of political autocracy (personal communication, 2004). Stripped of its subtlety and intentionally or not, this kind of argument plays directly into the hands of the New Barbarism theorists like Kaplan and Huntington.

I turn now to building the case for an alternative political discourse operating within this same region, a discourse derived from the practices of those simple, "uncivilized" Kwa-speakers of the southeast who have been understood as having acquired all their important institutions from the Mande speakers of the north. Can we find, in an examination of their political practices, an explanation for that surprising evaluation of a nineteenth-century missionary and, perhaps, a new definition of democracy?

In the rest of this chapter, I will identify some institutions present in Glebo communities of southeastern Liberia that provide structurally subordinate people, especially women and youth, with legitimate and recognized means of participation and expression. These institutions do not challenge the basis for their subordination, and even serve to reinforce it, while at the same time, they give individuals and groups an opportunity to make claims which must be heard. Although seemingly contradictory, a similar coexistence of structural hierarchy with guaranteed rights has been documented among Wolof-speaking Senegalese by Schaffer (1998). The Wolof term *yemale* denotes the idea that not everyone is of equal status, but that all should be treated *evenhandedly* (1998: 63). "The equality of *yemale*—and thus of *demokaraasi*—preserves hierarchies in age, gender, caste, and religious authority (just as [an American notion of] democracy preserves certain inequalities, such as those that differentiate Donald Trump and a secretary." (63). A very similar notion of "hierarchical egalitarianism" is described by Karlstrom for the Buganda of Uganda (1996). Obviously, a range of African societies as well as our own demonstrate that it is possible for democratic values to coexist with persistent, structural inequality.

I will also outline Glebo expectations of what constitutes meaningful and respectful relations with the national political center. I do this with the goal of trying to identify locally existing resources which may be available for the building of a new constitutional democracy in Liberia. I strive to avoid romanticizing; I do not wish to construct the Glebo as "traditional" or "more authentic" democrats in contrast with other groups in Liberia, but rather to show how their institutions and interpretations of their own politics and those of the nation-state contain principles of egalitarianism and provide opportunities for autonomous expression. Obviously, both these institutions and the ideas that support them have changed over time, most recently in a context of violent disruption and wartime displacement. Most of all, I do not want to be interpreted as arguing for some "different standard" of democratic practice to be applied only to Liberians, or Africans in general (see Kaplan 2000: 59–98, 119–25). Rather, I seek to be an ethnographer not just of the small-scale indigenous communities of Liberia but of the more "exotic" features and taken-for-granted assumptions about representational democracy in general.

Finally, I will show that violence is inextricably bound up with this very notion of egalitarianism and local autonomy. Again and again, Glebo people have gone to war against each other, against their neighbors, and against the national state. Violence may be enacted both materially and symbolically: in the outright killing and wounding of individuals or in causing their death or illness through sorcery. The capacity for violence is assumed to be an element of all human beings; women and even young children are not exempted. But violence, for the Glebo as for all other peoples, must be legitimated in discourse in order to justify the actions of its perpetrators. Commentators like Kaplan who see violence as a "natural" state to be contained by more or less "civilized" cultures have missed this crucial point. In all the many atrocities that were carried out in Liberia over the last two decades, no one, from Charles Taylor to the most obscure child soldier, believed they did not have to explain and justify their actions in cultural and moral terms (see Utas 2003: 119–67).

Turning again to the thorny problem of definitions, what features might we take as diagnostic of the presence of democracy in an African community? The literature provides a number of definitions grounded on the assumption of a constitutional state and a competitive "market" of political choices. A classic offering along these lines would be, "the democratic method is that institutional arrangement for arriving at political decisions in which individuals acquire the power to decide by means of a competitive struggle for the people's vote" (Schumpeter 1942: 269), which clearly conflates democracy with elections. A number of African scholars, finding such definitions culturally and historically too specific, have labored to identify a particular "African democracy," emphasizing "egalitarianism, participation, and the domestication of power" in contrast with the individualism of Schumpeter (Ake 2000: 178–79). The

Liberian scholars Wonkeryor, Forbes, Guseh, and Kieh have suggested the following: "a state of affairs in which people are empowered politically, economically, socially and culturally" (2000: 15).

While extremely broad, this kind of definition directs us toward an analysis of individual actors, operating within structured institutions and systems of meaning, seeking to make their voices heard. With this in mind, I turn to the Glebo, a Kwa (or Kruan) -speaking people of the southeastern coast of Liberia, who occupy an area of about thirty miles on either side of Cape Palmas (see Figure 1). Unlike the Wolof studied by Schaffer (1997), the Glebo have not incorporated a loan word into their language for democracy, but they have been represented in historical and contemporary accounts as having a political system that conforms to recognizably democratic principles.

Like other rural Liberians, most Glebo before the 1989 war practiced a mix of shifting, rain-fed rice cultivation and other cash-generating activities such as the sale of vegetables, sugar cane, tree crops, and natural latex. Their thirteen permanent clusters of towns between Fishtown Point and the Cavalla River are situated close to the shore, some on barrier beaches and brackish lagoons with water on both sides. These locations are excellent for people who were the apparent victors in a protracted struggle for access to the coast and its opportunities for trade with European ships. Glebo oral histories tell the story of their migration from the east and conflicts with the other groups they met along the way; a group known as "Eguerebo" were documented at Cape Palmas by the Portuguese explorer Pacheco Pereira around 1500, which may indicate their presence in the area from at least that time (Hair 1967: 257). Farmland, however, had to be located away from the beaches, and most people spent the majority of their time in "villages" occupied by a single extended family as much as twenty-five miles inland. Daily life for farm families was characterized by the constant traversing of different environmental zones: sandy beach and mangrove swamp, coastal savannah parkland, and secondary tropical forest.

Confusion is often generated by the use of the term "Grebo" to refer to a group of at least seven related languages, of which Glebo is one (Kurtz 1985: 2–3; see also Duitsman 1982–83). "Grebo tribe" was used administratively by the Republic of Liberia to refer to most of the inhabitants of Maryland County, lending to the people of the region an aura of ethnic solidarity that has never in fact existed. Even the term "Glebo" is problematic; the people in question consider themselves to belong to two *dakwe*, or confederacies of towns, called Nyomowe and Kuniwe and insist that they speak different "dialects" of the Glebo language. Eager to capitalize on local divisions, the Liberian government created separate "Paramount Chieftaincies" for Nyomowe and Kuniwe, which, adding to the confusion, were also designated as "clans." The last official census report in 1974 numbered the "Grebo" at about 20,000 people and eight percent of the national population (Liebenow 1987: 35); the Glebo (or "seaside Grebo") were probably between eight and ten thousand during the same period. During the civil war from 1989 to 1996, many fled to kinsfolk or refugee camps across the Cavalla River in Ivory Coast; it is unclear how many have returned.

The Episcopal missionary John Payne arrived at Cape Palmas in 1836 to join a struggling experiment in African American settlement which had begun only a few years earlier. The administrative unit which is now Maryland County, Liberia, originated as "Maryland in Liberia," a project of the Maryland State Colonization Society (for a recent history, see Hall 2003). In early nineteenth-century America, the state of Maryland occupied a curious position as a kind of border zone between the slave states of the south and the industrializing north. In 1810, over a third of its population was of African origin, and of these, over twenty percent were not enslaved (Martin 1968: 55). By 1830, 12 percent of Marylanders were "free people of color," who were seen as a threat by those still holding human property. The removal of such dangerous examples to Africa was an attractive idea to state lawmakers, and in 1826 they allocated $1000 to the American Colonization Society to support the colony at Monrovia, Liberia, founded in 1822. By 1831, frightened by the Nat Turner rebellion in nearby Virginia and discouraged by the slow rate of emigration from their own state, the Maryland Legislature decided to fund their own colony. Several Baltimore merchants were interested in Cape Palmas, a long established trading point for pepper and ivory, and a recruitment center for African maritime labor. After negotiating the "sale" of land from the local (Nyomowe) Glebo, a small colony was begun in 1833. From the beginning, missionaries from a number of American denominations arrived to serve the spiritual needs of the colonists and to convert the Glebo to Christianity (55–60). The Rev. (later bishop) John Payne represented the Protestant Episcopal Church of the United States.

So what exactly did John Payne mean by "the purest of democracies" when he lived among the Glebo of Cape Palmas in the 1830s and '40s? The quote comes from his journal entry of September 7, 1842, selections from which were published in the church publication, *The Spirit of Missions*. Given the context, in which he was describing Glebo governmental structures, it seems most likely that he was impressed by the checks and balances, the division of civil and religious authority, and the acknowledged role of people of all ages and genders in public life and decision-making. All individuals held membership in named, unranked patrilineal descent groups (*pane*), which allocated farmland and residential plots for houses. Age and gender were the primary means of stratification, although long experience with European traders along the coast was beginning to generate a pool of those with experience abroad and access to imported goods that later combined with mission education to create a category of "civilized natives." These people were employed by the missions and in the lower reaches of the colonial and early republican civil service (Moran 1990). Glebo town clusters had both a civil administrator (the chief or *wodo baa*) and a "high priest" (*bodio*), whose distinct duties were carried out with the advice of a council of elders representing each of the resident patrilineal kin groups. Following the familiar pattern of "dual sex" organizations common in West Africa (Okonjo 1976), a "women's chief" (*blo nyene*) and council of female elders had both a deliberative role and veto power over important decisions made by the men. Likewise, the *bodio's* counterpart was his wife, the *gyide*, who shared his ritual duties and the burdensome prohibitions which constrained every aspect of their lives. Younger men, organized into military units through age grades, also provided a check on the power of the older males. In particular, the age grade for adult married men, the *sidibo* or warriors, had its own internal officers or "war priests," the *tibawa* and *yibadio*.

The *sidibo*, or warriors, according to Martin's reading of the nineteenth century sources, seem to have had the most important governing functions, acting as lawmakers, judiciary, and enforcement officers in turn (Martin 1968: 19). Their primary responsibility, as the name implies, was the defense of the community and the cultural ideal of the warrior provided an elaborate and prestigious role central to the Glebo construction of masculinity (see Moran 1995). Yet the celebration of the warrior as a cultural ideal does not exclude women. Both men and women are referred to as warriors in contexts in which they must be brave and face pain and danger with courage. The funeral dances performed for elder men and women are called war dances, regardless of the gender of the deceased or of the dancers. These funeral ceremonies were said to have originated in the practice of men dancing before going into battle to "bury themselves" in case they should fall in the fight, but they have now become the defining life-cycle event for all adults. Even the years of actual war have not obliterated these ceremonies. When my foster father, an Episcopal priest and pillar of the civilized community, died in 1999, the family sent me photographs of his funeral. In one picture, his body lies in state, surrounded by the men of his *sidibo* age grade who are blowing on the traditional "war horns" or wooden trumpets. In another photo, the gathering at the graveside is shaded by a canopy made from a tarpaulin emblazoned with the letters UNHCR (United Nations High Commissioner on Refugees), a memento from their stay in refugee camps in Ivory Coast during the war. My foster family ensured that their father, the warrior-priest, was given a proper sendoff even in difficult times.

The fact that the status of warrior is not gender specific can also be seen in the transvestism of the male war dancer's costume, which combines elements of male and female clothing with natural leaves and organic material from the forest as well as items of Western manufacture. During the eighties, I observed costumes which incorporated inflatable beach balls, plastic Halloween masks, and baby dolls as well as symbols ranging from the Christian cross to the Liberian flag in a fantasy of combination and transgression. During the 1990s, and again during the battle for Monrovia of 2003, such unexpected attire worn by the NPFL rebels, and later by young fighters in all factions, attracted a great deal of attention from Western journalists. Interpreting the wigs and nightgowns worn by the fighters as evidence of primitive ignorance, superstition, or simply the desire for disguise, these observers misunderstood the local understandings of violence encoded in the warriors' dress. Courage and the willingness to use violence are seen as a legitimate response to protect one's community, fulfill one's social role, and even, perhaps, enhance one's standing. It requires, however, more than simple human action. Great violence and the strength and power needed to go to war must be channeled through extrahuman sources of power which reside elsewhere. The warrior, whether a young man of the *sidibo* age grade or a young woman in childbirth, is not him or herself, but a being between social and natural categories. This fluidity of the self has been interpreted by analysts like Ellis as a *loss* of personal responsibility and human agency, commonly seen in spirit possession (1999: 260, personal communication 2004). What is clear is that during the war, the ritual control over these powerful transformations once held by local elders was lost and appropriated by men like Charles Taylor.

War and the threat of attack seem to have been constants in the early nineteenth century and, according to Glebo oral and written accounts, were most common against close neighbors; Nyomowe and Kuniwe Glebo, in spite of close ties of kinship and intermarriage, were almost constantly at war during the mid-nineteenth century and into the twentieth (Wallace 1983; Martin 1968). Alliances were constantly shifting with a number of other coastal and interior groups of Grebo speakers, as well as with the American settlers at Cape Palmas and the missionaries who sometime acted as independent agents (Martin 1968: 192–96). Violence against neighboring people, affines, and even kin was seen as a legitimate response to instances of encroachment on fallow farmland, and also, in some cases, to unapproved elopements or insupportable insult. Success in war was also a means of upward mobility for young men, a route to reputation and respect that was matched only by equal success in the coastal labor market (see Brooks 1972).

The enthusiasm of the warriors, however, was checked by the women's council, which was composed of many inmarrying wives from other communities who might have kin in enemy towns. Without their cooperation and active support, war would be impossible, since they could potentially act as spies and saboteurs. The declaration of war, therefore, required that a case be made to the women that the cause was just. As late as 1983, my Glebo informants were emphatic that the *blo nyene*, whose title translates as "the whole earth woman" but was rendered as "the women's president" in English, had absolute veto power over any decision taken by the men. "What can they do if she says no? They can go up and down and make a lot of noise, but they can't do anything. She is the owner of the land." Violence might have been seen as integral to local political affairs, but it was certainly not unregulated.

Although positions like the *wodo baa, bodio, tibawa,* and *yibadio* "belonged" to specific patrilineages, successors to these offices were determined by the men's and women's councils from a pool of available candidates. Occupants of these offices could be deposed for misbehavior, and in one instance from a speech recorded by Payne, the positions themselves could possibly be reallocated to other lineages: "It does not follow that because the ancestor of one family was the most prominent man in the war by which we obtained the territory we occupy, that the headman of that family must ever be our chief. Who among us had not ancestors engaged in that war?" (Payne, quoted in Martin 1968: 19). This contrasts greatly with the careful use and manipulation of historical knowledge to preserve the position of high-ranking lineages documented for northern groups like the Kpelle, Gola, and Mende (Murphy 1980, 1981; Murphy and Bledsoe 1987; d'Azevedo 1962a). Decisions which affected the entire community were aired in an open forum, the *tapanu,* or assembly, as were serious conflicts between individuals, including accusations of intentional harm through sorcery. Secret societies dedicated to protecting the community against sorcery existed, but were not universal in their membership and did not have the initiatory functions of Poro and Sande to the north.

One thing that is striking about Payne's account is its similarity with the ethnography produced by the Liberian folklorist S. Jangaba Johnson in the 1950s (Johnson 1957) and with the surveys of inland Grebo-speaking peoples in the 1960s, indicating that these institutions and offices are present in very similar form throughout the southeast (see Kurtz 1985; McEvoy 1971). They were also present and functioning during my research in the early 1980s, meaning that they are relatively historically stable and apparently representative of the wider region. It is certainly possible that later authors "recycled" the older accounts, thereby producing the illusion of unchanging "tradition." Indeed, a Glebo author, Samuel Yede Wallace, relied heavily on earlier sources in a number of pamphlets on Glebo history and culture that he self-published during the 1970s and '80s (Wallace 1955, 1980, 1983). Yet I observed this structure in operation during the early 1980s and was introduced to the *wodo baa, bodio, blo nyene,* and *sidibo* leaders in numerous southeastern towns. As much as we have learned about the constructed nature of political authority, it is undeniable that people's expectations about legitimacy and the structures that carry it can be reproduced with astonishing continuity. While it would be logical to assume that the massive disruptions of the civil war years might have completely destroyed these institutions and weakened the values which supported them, the anthropologist Richard Nisbett, working on a village health project in the southeast in 1998, reports that the basic governance structure is still in place. Conducting participatory rural appraisals in seventeen communities on the boundaries of the Sapo National Forest, including Kru-, Sapo-, and Grebo-speaking peoples, Nisbett and his colleagues held town-wide meetings as well a separate sessions with men, women, and youth. His overall impression: "I was struck by the "democratic" nature of the dialog and of empowered females" (personal communication, 2002). These impressions were reinforced for Nisbett during a return trip in 2004. From 1842 to the present, outside observers have been remarkably consistent in their evaluation of the governing institutions of the Glebo and other Kwa speakers of the southeast.

There was much in Glebo government that Payne, as a mid-nineteenth century American, would have found similar to a New England town meeting, with the exception that women and young men were actually allowed to speak and had formal organizations that guaranteed their participation. It is also worth remembering that even during Payne's time, there was no consensus on the positive value of this "pure democracy." A later writer, George T. Fox, who used Payne's journal and those of other Americans to produce a biography of the missionary C. C. Hoffman, wrote in less flattering terms: "In all of these tribes there is, with a feeble hereditary element, the most rampant democracy. . . . The government is almost an unmitigated democracy, swayed by the impulses of malice, revenge, or covetousness according to circumstances; under such conditions, it were superfluous to add, there is little security for life, and still less for the accumulation or preservation of property" (1868: 187–88). In other words, Glebo egalitarianism was too "rampant" and "unmitigated" to make life easy or comfortable for the missionaries, who might have preferred to deal with a single (patrimonial?) strongman who could compel obedience. Indeed many accounts by foreigners of "unruly natives" imply the latter's distinct lack of tolerance for authoritarianism, a point that is also made by contemporary African theorists (see Monga 1996; Ake 2000). Yet Fox is also recognizing the inherent *violence in democracy*, the fact that personal autonomy and lack of hierarchy may come at the cost of personal security, as guaranteed by a despot. At a minimum, the data from all these sources and from my own field experience certainly contradict the charge of "traditional" patrimonialism and meet at least one of the formal criteria for democracy; that of institutions supporting broad participation in governance.

In the contemporary analytic discourse of political science, women's and youth organizations are generally relegated to "civil society" and seen as occupying a space outside of and supplemental to actual government. Payne recognized that for the Glebo, such structures *were* the government, along with the chief, high priest, councils of male and female elders, women's chief, and leaders of the men's age grades (see also Ake 2000: 180–82). This is *not* to say that all of these elements of government were considered to have equal power, or that all individuals had equal rights and privileges. Instead, this system deliberately allocates *different* and decidedly unequal forms of voice and redress to structural subordinates. This, I believe, is what Ake means by "the domestication of power" (178–79). Wonkeryor et al. point out, however, that forms of democracy supposedly grounded on the equivalence of individuals can subvert principles of equal participation, as in the United States when electoral majorities allow the suppression of racialized minorities (2000: 17; see also Guinier 1994). I will return to this point below.

But surely democracy is as much a set of values and attitudes as a set of governmental structures. Payne also recognized in 1845, as I did in the 1980s, that a strong sense of individual personal autonomy is held in high value in Glebo communities. Everyone, from a newborn infant to the most frail elder, is understood as having individual desires, plans, and intentions, not all of which may be benevolent or innocuous. It is important here to differentiate, following Charles Piot (1999), between *autonomy* as I am using it in this discussion and Western notions of *individualism*. Piot is justly critical of "rational choice" models which assume that an "Enlightenment-capitalist cosmology" (1999: 14) constitutes a human universal. Piot notes that theories from Durkheimian functionalism to Bourdieu's practice approach are premised on selfcontained, maximizing, strategizing actors, busily negotiating (for themselves) the binary opposition of structure and agency (15–16; see also Bledsoe 1980). Opposed to such formulations are another set of understandings of "African persons" which emphasize mutual dependency, relationality, and sociality (see Riesman 1992; Gottlieb 1998, 2004; Jackson and Karp 1990). "Not only is the self in these societies tied to other human beings; it is also diffusely spread into the nonhuman world of spirits and ancestors. . . . All of these other beings influence and have intentionality toward the individual, and vice versa. A person may also use these beings, or their powers and magical properties, to amplify his or her own powers and affect his or her relations with other humans" (Piot 1999: 19). The power of a person thus comes not from within a bounded entity defined by the biological limits of the organism, but from the web of relationships in which any individual is constituted.

The difficulty with posing alternative conceptions of generalized "African personhood," as Piot notes, is the potential for "orientalist othering." To suggest that Africans are nonindividualistic and communitarian or that they are incapable of seeing themselves as disconnected from others is to fall, once again, into the Kaplan-Huntington position that "cultural difference" is essential, enduring, and unchangeable. It would also seem to make a powerful argument for why Africans are ineligible for Western-style democracy. Yet Piot argues convincingly, "Surely it is possible to proffer a more nuanced—post-orientalist view that would not regard all perceived differences as equally othering and would not see similarities and differences as necessarily mutually exclusive" (20–21). Below, I will suggest how personal power is indeed constructed for the Glebo, and how this understanding is linked to connections with occult forces. This idea will be further explored in Chapter 4.

Glebo describe occult power or *we*, glossed in English as "witch" or "medicine," as a natural form of power or energy inherent in all living things. In terms of human social relations, it is the ultimate leveler; although older men and women are assumed to have greater occult power simply by virtue of age and experience, anyone with a "strong heart" is capable of bringing harm to others through sickness or accident (for more on the intentionality of infants among the Beng of the Ivory Coast, see Gottleib 2003). The most powerful witches are those who have ritually killed and "eaten" another human being, usually in concert with others who form a "society" for enhanced power. In much of the literature on West Africa, the use of this power has been framed as antisocial individualism run amok. Ferme, writing of the Mende of Sierra Leone, argues that

Individual autonomy and independence threaten these larger units [kin groups, farming households] with infertile and unproductive splits. . . . Those who are on their own are liable to be suspected of antisocial behavior, such as witchcraft. But it is not only potential dependents, those who are "for someone," who can become ostracized for showing too much autonomy. Big people (*kpakoisia*) who are very successful in farming, politics, or business are liable to be equally suspect, particularly if there is a perception that they do not use their wealth and status to help dependents and instead seek only their own profit. Thus the system is one of thorough interdependence, albeit within a hierarchical social order. (2001: 110)

Yet the "idiom of hierarchy," according to Ferme, is constantly being undermined by the actual autonomous activity of people at all levels and by the history of reversals in fortune and patronage that is commonly known to all. Although material resources are supposed to be distributed through systems of rank, age, and gender stratification, underlying everything is the awareness of occult power and personal agency attributed to *all* living humans. The knowledge that *anyone* may be more powerful than they seem on the surface is the basis of this ultimate egalitarian value. Although the Kwa-speaking peoples of the southeast are, as we have seen, less hierarchically organized than the northern peoples, they participate in the same ongoing sense of unease; one's own family, the very people on whom one should depend the most, are also the most likely to be insulted or hurt by one's behavior. The Glebo proverb, "if the house will not sell you, the street cannot buy you," recognizes the contradictory emotions of love, loyalty, anger and revenge circulating in every household.

Too many Western journalists have attributed the extreme violence against civilians in the Liberian and Sierra Leone wars to a presumed "lack of regard for human life." I suggest that the ruthless killing of men, women, children, old and young was not because they were seen as helpless and worthless but rather precisely because any human being, despite his or her ostensible place in the social order, is a potential conduit for great power. Here we see the mutually embedded constructions of democracy and violence; if all are potentially equally powerful, then all are equally dangerous. There can be no "noncombatants" in a war in which not all the weapons can be seen. Indigenous institutions recognize this by providing outlets and means of expression for structural subordinates precisely so they will not turn to occult means for self-protection and advancement. Rural Liberians do not need to be instructed on the "value of individual life" by Western human rights consultants, but they do need national institutions, like the local ones, that work to balance individual autonomy with the protection of communal social life.

It is undeniable that the strong sense of individual agency outlined above exists *in the absence* of any expectation that all agents are functionally equivalent or equal. Glebo ideologies of value are explicit in ranking men over women and elders over youth; these systems even merge in statements like "men are always older than women," as I was advised in the course of a lecture on why I should always defer to my husband. But structural inequality is mitigated through *institutionalized* practices whereby subordinates can act collectively and sometimes individually to air grievances, bring pressure on decisionmakers, and alter their situations. Below I provide two examples of how this works in practice.

One morning during my fieldwork in 1983 I witnessed a mass protest by over 240 rural women from an interior Grebo-speaking *duko*. It was early, and like most everyone else in the Glebo community of Hoffman Station (an old "mission town" attached to the Nyomowe "capital" of Gbenelu), I was in the middle of breakfast. Crouched on a low stool with my bowl of boiled cassava and a sauce of last night's palm butter, I was startled to hear the ringing of brass handbells and blowing of police whistles suddenly coming from behind me. These "traditional" instruments, introduced by European sailors in the nineteenth century, are associated with the women's council of elders, the *blo nyene*, and the "women's war dance" which is performed for the funeral of a "fully grown" woman (one who has reached the age of fifty). But there was no war dance scheduled for that day; indeed, it was not the season for "false burials," which usually take place after the rice harvest between November and January. Hearing these instruments outside their proper ritual and political context was highly unusual. As I sat open-mouthed on my stool, approximately 240 women walked right past me (I tried to count), single file, on their way to see the Nyomowe paramount chief, who lived across the yard. "They are from Nyambo," hissed my foster mother, recognizing some of her husband's kinswomen in the line. She was assuming that they would be eating with us and staying the night, and was already worried about having enough food on hand to entertain them properly as a "wife," or subordinate to their position of husband's "sisters."

The paramount chief was clearly as surprised as the rest of us, but he received the women graciously and made a big show about commandeering every chair in the neighborhood as well as canvassing all close-by houses for kola nuts in order to welcome them respectfully. The process of getting them settled took almost an hour, during which time the large crowd that had gathered speculated madly about what could have brought these women from their homes and farms more than twenty miles to the north. "Why have they come?" I asked my foster mother. "It must be trouble," was her reply, and others in the crowd began to tell me stories of mass marches by women in the past. It seemed the father of the present paramount chief, when he was *wodo baa* of another Nyomowe town, had collectively insulted all the women in the community by implying that they were killing each other's children through witchcraft. All the adult women marched out of town and took refuge with another chief, leaving the men to cook, carry water, and generally fend for themselves. "You couldn't find one little girl in that town!" one woman told me gleefully. Eventually, the chief had to go several times to the other town to apologize and convince the women to come back. It took "many cows," ritually slaughtered and used for a big feast for the women, before they would consent to return (see Moran 1989). The Liberian folklorist Johnson also recorded examples of mass marches by women in defense of their honor and accepted role in decisionmaking (1957). In some of these examples, there seems to be a direct link between this strategy and the veto power described for the *blo nyene*, with collective action as the ultimate sanction if her decision is challenged.

In this case, the women were using an institutionalized form for protecting their rights in the local arena to address concerns with national policy. Although they stopped with the paramount chief as a courtesy, he was not the object of their march. They were on their way to see the Maryland County superintendent, a military appointee, to complain about the reinstitution of a head tax on rural people which had just been announced. The chief, who was clearly relieved that it all had nothing to do with him, acknowledged the legitimacy of their right to make their sentiments known to the national government. Likewise the mayor of Harper city, another military man who received them in lieu of the absent superintendent, acknowledged the form of their protest while warning that they were violating the military government's ban on "political activities," then still in effect. They were sternly advised to go home and "look for the money" for their taxes, and to channel all future petitions through their paramount chief, as their local representative to the government.

Accounts of mass boycotts and strikes by women abound in the literature on West Africa; from Sierra Leone to Cameroon to Nigeria, the pattern of women taking collective action in defense of their rights is well documented (Ardener 1975; Ifeka-Moller 1975; Van Allen 1972, 1976 among others). The fact that informants described for me detailed rituals and exchanges which were required to end the action, and that these means were adapted to anticolonial struggles in Nigeria and elsewhere, argues that these are not spontaneous acts of resistance but institutionalized and highly scripted means of expression. Yet, precisely because women are never properly "older than men," they must act collectively in order to counter the power of a political hierarchy in which they are junior partners. They have a voice, but not an equal voice, and the national government, officially recognizing only a single set of supposedly gender-neutral "representatives," refused to acknowledge the validity of their claim by charging them with violating the ban on "political activities." Yet this in itself is telling, since the women's march was certainly understood as political in nature. In each venue where they made their case, the Nyambo women were treated with respect and onlookers agreed that they had a right to speak *as women.*

The second example concerns a sorcery accusation brought against a young man living with his relatives in Gbenelu. Several children in the household had died in quick succession and the family was anxious to find the cause. After several days of circulating rumors, a *tapanu,* or gathering of the entire town, was convened and the young man formally charged. After several attempts at denial, he confessed, but used the occasion to deliver a long oration about his wrongs at the hands of his relatives. He worked for them on their farm and in return they had promised him new clothes and in particular, a long-sleeved shirt, but now the harvest was in and they had not rewarded him. He had further complaints about the quality of the food he was given and the hardship of his labor. The entire community listened and agreed that he had a point; he had been badly treated and it was not surprising that he had resorted to sorcery. He was severely lectured on the immorality of taking things into his own hands; he should properly have complained to the "big people" in town, the chiefs and the elders, who would have protected his interests. He was told further that if there were any more "trouble" in the family or indeed in the town, he would be held responsible. His relatives were told to attend more carefully to his needs in the future and, in particular, to get him the long-sleeved shirt. All parties then participated in a reconciliation ceremony.

One again, a structural subordinate was able to use an existing institution to express his agency and assert his rights, this time as an individual. Note however, that his claim was phrased in terms of the *negligence of others in fulfilling their responsibilities to him*, not in his lack of freedom to make his own choices. One may think he should not have had to confess to witchcraft in order to be paid for his labor, but at least his *right to speak* and to publicize his feelings of exploitation was recognized by all as a powerful claim on the community. Caroline Bledsoe has written on the belief of Mende parents that their children must suffer deprivation, often as fostered "servants" in other households, in order to grow into disciplined, successful adults who will make a contribution to their family and community (1990). Mats Utas, likewise, has discussed the violence experienced by young people in homes and schools before the war which led some to "enjoy themselves" as combatants with scores to settle (2003: 123–38). That suffering, however, while an accepted part of a young person's education and training, is not unchecked or unregulated. Community norms insist that a child who has been placed with a distant family in order to attend school cannot be removed from the educational system and used simply as unpaid labor (see Moran 1992). Likewise, the failure of the family in this case to deliver on the promise of the long-sleeved shirt was viewed as a serious lapse that opened them to attack by sorcery. Reconciliation ceremonies such as the one I witnessed in this case have reportedly been used to reintegrate ex-combatants into rural communities, even those known to have committed terrible atrocities (Nisbett, personal communication, 2002; Utas 2003: 238). The logic of a "diffuse, unbounded selfhood" (Piot 1999: 21) is one that allows for the possibility of reform and forgiveness, one which assumes that those who have turned to violence (including sorcery) as a form of protest can still be heard and their concerns addressed. The young man who admitted killing children through sorcery in his anger and resentment could still mature into a responsible, respectable adult, although one whom others might think twice about angering in the future. The excombatants in the civil war who returned to their home communities in Sinoe County "had committed crimes in the area, even direct assaults on family and kin, 'but they are our sons and daughters, so we have to forgive them'" (Utas 2003: 238).

Several times during the military government of Samuel Doe, student leaders at the University of Liberia and other institutions were jailed, beaten, and threatened with execution. In each instance, the Market Women's Association in Monrovia rose to their defense, once threatening to shut down the food supply of the entire city if "our children" were harmed. In an interview with a former student leader, conducted in 1993, I was told that "Without these women, we would be dead. They called us their children, you know? They said to the government, 'What? We go in the market and work so hard to keep our children in school and now you want to kill them?'"

I suspect that the well-known tendency of market women's associations to act collectively in the defense of imprisoned student leaders has something to do with the recognition of common cause among structural subordinates and of the need to support each other's right to participate in the decisionmaking process. Obviously, these are not practices that can be codified by law or written into a constitution. Equally obviously, structural subordinates do not always support each other and indeed can often be pitted against each other by manipulative political strategies. However, these alliances, where they exist, should be recognized as aspects of indigenous democratic institutions and as essentially governmental structures, designed to preserve the rights of all in a context in which strictly *equal* rights are not recognized.

Given the alternative democratic tradition I have outlined above, what is it that rural people in the southeast expect from national leaders, whether they have voted for them or not? In November of 1983 the head of state, Samuel Doe, arrived in Cape Palmas to celebrate a national holiday, the birthday of long-term president W. V. S. Tubman. Tubman was a "native son" of Maryland County, the first Liberian president who was not a member of one of the elite Monrovia families, and in spite of the fact that Doe's small band of enlisted men had overthrown his successor and the rule of his single party, Tubman's memory was still widely revered. It was only a month, however, after an alleged coup attempt that sent Doe's most serious rival, Thomas Quiwonkpa, into exile; it was widely speculated that Doe would never leave the relative safety of Monrovia for the southeast. But come he did, bringing with him a large military contingent and a great deal of heavy weaponry. The soldiers, nervous and edgy, harassed the local people and generated a great deal of resentment during the days that Doe was in residence. The only consolation was that the city of Harper and its surrounding communities benefited from twenty-four-hour-a-day electrical current for those few days, the first anyone could remember in years.

At a public development event at Harper City Hall, Doe was scheduled to be welcomed by the two local paramount chiefs representing Nyomowe and Kuniwe Glebo. While all the other local officials, representing the government itself and the Harper "civilized" community, were flattering and obsequious, one of the "native" chiefs launched into a scathing critique of Doe and his policies, centering on land appropriations for concession agriculture that threatened the Glebo economic base. He imperiously informed Doe that he (Doe) was far from perfect and had made plenty of mistakes so far. Nevertheless, he promised him protection while in Glebo territory and assured him, "nothing will happen to you here." Although he delivered his speech in Glebo and used the place name "Gbenelu" in referring to the territory under his jurisdiction, the educated Glebo man translating his words into English consistently rendered "Gbenelu" as "Maryland County," to which the neither the chief, who was perfectly fluent in English, nor Doe, whose first language was the closely related Krahn, objected. In essence, the chief and his translator collaborated to represent *him* as the legitimate political authority in Maryland County, while the government-appointed county superintendent sat on the stage with the other officials. No one, from either the Monrovia party or the local hierarchy, contradicted this claim. Doe himself took the tonguelashing with surprising meekness.

When I commented later that the chief was quite brave to criticize Doe, especially with all those armed soldiers standing around, people said, "Humph, that was nothing." They proceeded to recount a barrage of stories about the rather highhanded treatment of government officials by local leaders, telling with particular relish a tale about Kla, the old Kuniwe chief. Sometime in the 1970s, Tubman's successor, President William Tolbert, promised to visit the capital of the Kuniwe *dako* on one of his tours of the southeast. The chief organized a reception, the food was prepared, the "war dancers" were in their costumes, and the drummers were ready, but Tolbert did not arrive as planned. Hearing that the president had decided to visit another town instead, old Kla went physically to get him, took him by the arm, and said, "Small boy like you? I should come to you? I who could born you twice? You must come to me!" According to the story, Tolbert went obediently to his prepared reception and apologized profusely. Everyone agreed that this was just how it should be.

*   *   *

It does not really matter if the story about old Kla and President Tolbert is a "true" account of what really happened. What is reflected in these stories are people's expectations of their relationship with the national center and of the treatment they deserve as citizens. They clearly see this relationship as not limited to participation in elections. They believe they have the right to dissent and to criticize, exercised by both the chief in his remarks to Samuel Doe and the women who marched against the head tax. They believe they have the right to courtesy and respect and to be treated as equals, as illustrated in the story from the Tolbert era. Furthermore, they expect the criteria by which they allocate prestige and authority, principally relative age, to operate on the national as well as local level, as Kla reminded Tolbert that he could "born you twice." This principle was also clearly operating in the scolding meted out to Samuel Doe, then in his late twenties, by the Nyomowe paramount chief, an imposing man in his fifties, and in the head of state's mild reaction to his speech.

These are not the actions of people who are fatalistic, clientalistic, mystified by hierarchies of secrecy, or utterly dominated by "religious thinking." Indeed, their parents and grandparents resisted incorporation into the Liberian state militarily as recently as the 1930s, with enormous casualties, summary executions of leaders, and wide-scale population displacement, both internally and to neighboring countries like Ivory Coast and Ghana. Glebo people are willing to turn to violence in defense of the rights they believe they have, as individuals who have been cheated or insulted and use occult power to gain the attention of their superiors, or collectively in overt, organized activities like protest marches and warfare. No one has to teach them about what it means to be "empowered politically, economically, socially, and culturally." Rural Glebo fully understand that, in their experience, violence is not the opposite of democracy, but an integral aspect of it. As I will argue in the conclusion, these understandings constitute valuable resources which can be used in the formation of a new Liberian polity in the postwar era.

Chapter 2
Contested Histories

Few other nations in Africa have been so relentlessly represented as the victim of their own "peculiar" history as Liberia (for a classic example, see Tim Weiner, "Of Liberia's Many Sorrows, and Their Roots," *New York Times,* September 3, 2003). Indeed, many other African countries are viewed as having little history at all, beyond the dates when they were "conquered" by European powers and, again, the dates they gained independence. Liberia's unusually early founding as a national state, its "preemptive" declaration of independence in 1847, and its representation as the prime example of "black misrule" in Africa are all cited as root causes of its twentieth-century conflicts. The ubiquitous phrase "founded by freed slaves from the United States" appears in every newspaper article and most scholarly accounts of Liberian affairs. In fact, as pointed out in Chapter 1, this phrase is not really accurate. At a conference several years ago, a prominent Liberian academic complained bitterly, "we don't belong in the slave section, we have to get out the slave section" of the history books. She referred to the fact that Liberia was never intended by its real founders, the wealthy white members of the American Colonization Society, as a solution to the problem of slavery. Rather, it was a solution to the problem of free people of color, whose very existence slave owners found so threatening. Yet the stigma of slave origins continues to cling to Liberia, just as it does to those African Americans who chose to stay in the Western Hemisphere.

This is a very different role for slavery in the structuring of historical memory from that described for Sierra Leone by Rosalind Shaw (2002). In her rich analysis, Shaw argues that, although the Temne people of Sierra Leone were not as deeply affected by the Atlantic slave trade as some other populations along the West African coast, "the fact that warfare, raiding, and the knowledge that bodies could become commodities in exchange for wealth formed part of the everyday conditions of life for over four centuries was surely insidious in itself" (2002: 41). Using the writings of early European explorers as well as her work with contemporary

Temne diviners, Shaw demonstrates how the local spirits, who figure prominently in Temne narratives, were transformed from "close neighbors into external marauders" (54). Towns became fortified stockades, witchcraft accusations a means to wealth through the sale of the accused, and cannibalism associated with accumulation, whiteness, ships, and the sea (60, 213–18, 227–30). The Temne experience of incorporation into the Atlantic world provides the template through which future ruptures, including British colonialism and postcolonial political corruption, are understood and interpreted by contemporary Sierra Leonians. "Memories of the violence of Atlantic and colonial modernity are, I suggest, 'burned into' nondiscursive memories that structure the agency of postcolonial subjects as they experience the opacity and dangers of national politics and reflect upon the opportunities the modern state provides for its own forms of extraction" (262).

This chapter addresses the ways that local Liberians understand their relationship to the current state in terms of a violent past. I argue that they recognize their own representation in the historical narratives that have been constructed by national elites and work to "correct" or revise versions of history that diminish their agency and status as independent peoples. The Glebo of Cape Palmas use historical narratives and interpretations of the local landscape to make claims for democratic participation, claims which they insist the state must pay attention to.

Of course, even the most active subjects do not have free rein to construct any version of the past that they would like. Arjun Appadurai (1981) has argued that all societies have rules governing the debatability of the past to ensure that history is not purely an invention. Material remains provide one check on the creativity and inventiveness of those who would chronicle the past: "What happened leaves traces, some of which are quite concrete—buildings, dead bodies, censuses, monuments, diaries, political boundaries—that limit the range and significance of any historical narrative" (Trouillot 1995: 29).

In what follows, I trace the themes of violence and democracy in the historical landscape of Cape Palmas and the attempts of its residents, Glebo and settler alike, to inscribe it with competing significances. Michel-Rolf Trouillot reminds us that "Human beings participate in history both as actors and as narrators. . . . In vernacular use, history means both the facts of the matter and a narrative about those facts, both "what happened" and "that which is said to have happened." The first meaning places the emphasis on the sociohistorical process, the second on our knowledge of that process or on a story about that process" (1995: 2). I will not recount in detail here the "official" national history, taught for many years in Liberian schools, which depicted the struggle of the "pioneer fathers" against the benighted savages of Africa as they strove to bring the light of civilization to the wilderness (for example, see Hen-ries 1966). Likewise, I will not trace the careful work of several Liberian scholars who have critiqued the standard historiography of Liberia as a "morality play" in which "simple natives" were deceived and exploited by "black colonialists" who had learned nothing from their own experience of oppression but how to impose it on others (Burrows 1989a; Liberty 2001: 37–43). Rather, I will examine how the Glebo have rejected both of these narratives in favor of one that offers a different model of settler/native relations; one which makes claims for equal status and mutual respect similar to those demanded by old Kla in his encounter with Pres-ident Tolbert. The Glebo version of history belies the sharp distinction between settler and native that structures so many of the other accounts, and presents a complex picture of numerous canny, strategizing groups and their individual leaders, struggling to manage conflicting interests and loyalties.

In Liberia, the materiality of history is literally scattered all over the landscape. In the coastal areas like the region around Harper city in Maryland County, one frequently encounters permanent historical mon-uments which have been erected to celebrate the "official" version of national history. These recount the exploits of the American "pioneers," heroes of a narrative with obvious roots in the saga of the European dis-covery of the New World. Liberia's very name, derived from "liberty," tells the story of its founding, as do numerous other place names like Provi-dence Island, Monrovia (from U.S. President James Monroe), Bunker Hill, Philadelphia, and Baltimore Avenue, as well as Maryland County itself. Missionary churches, still active or ruined and abandoned, replicate the familiar ecclesiastical architecture of the West, while domestic struc-tures also arise from prototypes in the American South (see Holsoe et al. 1988). In indigenous communities remote from Monrovia influence, the landscape bears traces of another, less permanently marked past for those who can read them. Patterns of vegetation reveal the location of former farms and towns, while great cotton trees, large rock formations, and other natural features are remembered as sites of great events (see also Ferme 2001: 25–26). Ornate cement graves, raised above the surface of the earth, mark the lives of chiefs and wealthy people, while poorer folk are memorialized only by almost imperceptible depressions in the soil.

How does this landscape, and its interpretation within intentionally historical narratives, reveal the twin themes of violence and democracy which, I have argued, are at the core of Liberians' understanding of themselves and their politics? As an example, I turn to one particular historical relic and its local interpretations. Rising incongruously from the lush vegetation on a steep slope above the sea, a small but elaborate cement monument commemorates a moment in the history of Maryland

County, Liberia. Erected in 1957, the monument honors the centennial of the admission of Maryland in Liberia, formerly a colony of the Maryland (USA) Colonization Society and, briefly, an independent nation, into the Republic of Liberia as its fifth county in 1857. In 1982, when I photographed it (see Figures 2–6), the monument and the small park surrounding it had almost disappeared in the overgrown bush. Shaped like an obelisk with an open pavilion in the center containing two statues locked in an embrace, the monument embodies a mid-twentieth-century construction of nineteenth-century events and the many contradictions and ironies of African repatriation, nation-building, and local incorporation into the state.

The iconography of the monument almost perfectly encompasses the themes of violence and democracy in Liberian history. One side depicts in bas relief a scene of violent confrontation, with the text, "Natives Combat with Pioneers" (Figure 6). Two figures are shown, differentiated by flaking blue and brown paint, engaged in battle. Another side shows a scene of peaceful negotiation between equals: "Natives and Pioneers in Peace Conference" (Figure 5). The names of those present at the early negotiations, both settlers and Glebo, are inscribed beneath the figures. On the third side, profile busts of Stephen A. Benson, the Liberian President in 1857, and his counterpart one hundred years later, William V. S. Tubman, are linked by a garland below the words "Maryland Admission Centenary Monument" (Figure 4). Tubman, a "native son" of Maryland County and the longest-serving president in Liberia's history, is connected through time and place to the "pioneers" who founded the nation state. Tubman is also associated with the "unification policy" which attempted to address the settler/indigenous division by extending full citizenship to all "indigenes" who could prove that they owned a hut and paid taxes on it (Sawyer 1992: 207). In 1954, only a few years before the monument was erected, Tubman held the first of three "national unification councils" in his home town of Harper. Rural leaders from all over the country attended the conference, at which Tubman called for an end to class and ethnic divisions. "Although the Harper meeting did not accomplish any tangible transformation, it provided an enormous psychological boost for a society troubled by ethnic problems" (208).

On the fourth side of the monument, the names of the prominent local men of Maryland County who served on the 1957 Centenary committee are listed, inscribing them into history with the "pioneers," "natives," and presidents. These are, presumably, the local elite "authors" of the monument, who gave final approval to its design and texts. Above the four-sided base of the monument, two figures embrace in the small pavilion which holds up the top section of the obelisk. From up close, they are both clearly male, although one wears Western men's attire and

Figure 2. Maryland Centenary Monument. Photograph by the author.

Figure 3. Figures in the Maryland Centenary Monument. Photograph by the author.

Figure 4. Portraits of S. A. Benson and W. V. S. Tubman, Maryland Centenary Monument. Photograph by the author.

Figure 5. "Natives and Pioneers in Peace Conference," Maryland Centenary Monument. Photograph by the author.

Figure 6. "Natives Combat with Pioneers," Maryland Centenary Monument. Photograph by the author.

the other a wrap-around cloth associated with the ceremonial dress of "native" men. For those versed in the "official" version of Liberian history, the statues depict the reunion of African brothers, one "civilized" and the other "native," separated by the slave trade but now brought together in the pursuit of national unity. Yet when I asked my Glebo friends and informants, they told me the statues were of "President Tubman and his wife."

To be fair, there are literally dozens of statues of Tubman and members of his family, including his wife and his mother, scattered around Harper and its immediate vicinity. Given that Tubman was the first non-Monrovian to hold the national presidency, that he generously directed development and infrastructural support to his home region, and that he is closely identified with Maryland County (and vice versa), it is not surprising that local people might view the monument in these terms. It had been, after all, almost thirty years since the centennial and the monument was in an out-of-the-way location, neglected and overgrown. Yet even when I pointed out that the pictures around the sides of the obelisk depicted events of the early nineteenth century and mentioned that the figure wearing a skirt still seemed to be a man, my friends just shrugged. The date was 1957, and that was "Tubman time," so it *must* be Tubman. "And his wife kind of looked like a man."

Is this interpretation of the monument an "alternative" account of history or simply misinformation? At the time of my fieldwork, only two years after the military coup that toppled the True Whig Party of the "pioneers," was the settler history of Maryland County already being reframed? Certainly, the neglect and disrepair of the monument, even its location on the high promontory of Cape Palmas, contributed to an almost archaeological sense that one was observing the ruins of a lost civilization. Once the "up Cape" section of the city of Harper had been the center and symbol of Americo-Liberian power in Maryland County. The African American settlers who arrived with their white sponsors in 1834 situated themselves on the location of an existing Glebo community on a high bluff overlooking the small harbor. After the colony became independent from the Maryland state organization in 1854, the settlers forced the Glebo to move to lower ground across the river (Martin 1968: 194–97; Hall 2003). It was the counterattack by the displaced Glebo and their interior allies that forced the settlers to call on their neighbor to the north, the Republic of Liberia, for help. In return for Liberian military assistance, the tiny independent nation of Maryland was annexed to the republic, the event commemorated by the centennial monument.

The city of Harper eventually spread down the hill and along the protected beach of a brackish lagoon, but the cluster of official buildings occupying the high ground continued to dominate the landscape. By the early nineteen eighties, most of the public buildings were deserted, including the old hospital, orphan asylum, Masonic temple, lighthouse, and even the "Maryland Mansion," an exact replica of the old Executive Mansion in Monrovia built by President Tubman as his official residence in his home town. Apart from a few elderly residents and some expatriate development workers and Peace Corps volunteers renting rooms in the deteriorating buildings, no one lived on the "up Cape"; there was no street life, no sidewalk market vendors, no noisy gangs of children as in other parts of Harper. As I walked the empty streets and photographed the decaying buildings, including the Maryland Centenary Monument, there was only an eerie silence in which my footsteps echoed on what had been impeccably paved sidewalks, now cracked and overgrown by vegetation. The small landscaped park which had once surrounded the monument, with the remains of a hillside amphitheater and cement lecterns which had presumably held explanatory text, was a ghostly reminder of a public life and social order that no longer existed in the aftermath of the 1980 military coup.

Rosalind Shaw has argued that the slave trade provides an underlying narrative and context for contemporary Sierra Leonian interpretations of everything from electoral politics to Temne divination (2002). She crafts a careful and subtle argument, reminding us that it is too simple to view competing historical accounts as merely serving the practical interests of present actors (2002: 12). I argue that in Liberia, the encounter between "returning" African Americans and the indigenous inhabitants of the Guinea Coast provides a similar "template" for the analysis of contemporary events for elites and scholars, but *not* for the local people of Cape Palmas. This local understanding of the monument, which reinscribes the climactic meeting of settler and indigene as "President Tubman and his wife," explicitly rejects the "morality play" which reduces the Glebo to either hapless victims or naturalized savages. The significant time frame shifts through a process of foreshortening from the early nineteenth century to the mid-twentieth; from the founding of the nation to the moment when indigenous people were first promised citizenship and full democratic participation. This kind of chronological collapse is, as we shall see, quite common in African oral histories. For the Glebo of Cape Palmas, the struggle depicted on the monument, between the attraction and danger of externally imposed political authority and its associated systems of meaning (coded as civilization, modernity, democracy, and national unity), is a problem of the 1940s and '50s, not the 1830s.

Scholars attempting to interpret local histories in their own terms have frequently encountered chronological shifts like the one described above, particularly when oral accounts seem to conform to a structure other than the linear model of Western history. In contrast with the sequence of discrete events following each other through time, non-Western histories are often characterized as cyclical, possibly taking their shape from agricultural cycles, the sequence of human generations, or even the grammatical structure of some languages (for example, Geertz 1973b: 370–79; Lee 1977, among others). Warren d'Azevedo, on the other hand, has argued that knowledge about the past and the discursive style in which it is represented is highly contextual, producing different kinds of accounts, depending on the circumstance, in the same society (1962a). Some contexts, particularly legal and political ones, require the rearrangement of historical knowledge into linear sequences, while others do not. In examining oral accounts of the Gola of northern Liberia, d'Azevedo disputes the notion that "a sense of historical time in the tribal cultures of the region was a product of European intrusion and dominations; rather it might be said that these later events intensified the process of objectification of time-perspective which was inherent in the conditions which defined the early interrelations of [Guinea Coast] peoples" (1962: 33).

Building on this idea that the structure of African historical accounts is a product of inter-*African* relations, rather than a product of contact with Western ways of thinking, Igor Kopytoff offered a model of frontier process which relocated the production of historical narratives while maintaining the emphasis on circularity. Kopytoff argues that continent-wide patterns in oral histories, origin tales, and narratives of wandering and migration must be attributable to "the participation of all these societies in a common culture-historical stream in which similar historically-given features have interacted functionally in similar ways" (1987: 16).

To condense Kopytoffs' argument radically, the historical "cycle" proceeds as follows. (1) African societies, both state and nonstate, share an internal dynamic which periodically and often violently ejects people out of their communities and polities, what Kopytoff calls "the systemic production of frontiersmen." (2) Those who are ejected experience this disengagement as *groups* rather than as individuals. (3) The definition of the frontier, or margin of the ejected group's polity, is a political one. "To the immigrant settlers it represented an institutional vacuum, although it usually contained other organized groups with which the settlers had to deal" (16). (4) Some immigrant groups join the existing polities they encounter, while others attempt to build their own, using models of legitimate social order they bring with them. (5) While the kin group provides the initial model of integration for the settlers, survival on the frontier lies in numbers. Dependents and adherents are incorporated by means of pseudokinship, although genealogical knowledge is often retained as a political resource by the dominant group and remains a contested arena. (6) If the "emergent polity" is successful and grows in size, kinship as an integrative idiom is abandoned for one stressing the interdependence of leaders and followers (described elsewhere, as we have seen, as "patrimonialism"). (7) The political authority of the leaders rests on their being "first comers," but often this principle must be qualified when the de facto elites are actually a latecoming immigrant group. This is accomplished by "deculturing" the previous inhabitants so the present leaders can claim to be the first to have brought "civilized" life to a particular area. (8) Ideological tensions between the "patrimonial model" (borrowing from Weber) of the original settlers' first frontier hamlet and the actual independence of the followers (who can, if dissatisfied, migrate elsewhere) produce the characteristic African institution of the "divine king" or priest-king. (9) As a consequence, the polity begins to place more emphasis on the integrative effects of royal ritual. (10) In order to gain legitimacy in the *regional* context, the emerging polity must draw on "values, traditions, and legitimizing themes widely shared in the region" thus accounting for regional continuity in spite of local variation (17; this kind of regional, interactive approach was pioneered much earlier by d'Azevedo 1962b). (11) Finally, the new polity may stabilize and begin to expand at the expense of its neighbors, or dissolve due to internal stresses or the predations of more successful polities or metropoles. "In this, too, it played a role in the political ecology of the frontier, which systemically generated small polities, endowed them with a frontier-conditioned political culture, and reinjected them into the regional system" (17).

Kopytoff's model is, as he says, designed for the *internal* African frontier, as a description of precolonial African political relations. He offers it as a corrective both to static accounts of unchanging "tribal" identities and to evolutionary theories that "see small polities as arising out of some hypothetical archaic bands" (3). Rather, Kopytoff argues that centralized states and frontier communities produce each other in a dialectical process. African oral histories and origin tales which display a circular and repetitious narrative structure may thus be seen as fairly faithful representations of past and ongoing events. The model also gives us an interesting perspective on how the arrival of the American settlers must have looked to the Glebo; not as a unique, defining moment inaugurating a radical shift in local events, but as simply a new group on the scene, pushed out of their old territory and trying to make claims for legitimacy on the basis of their socalled "superior culture." The Glebo saw the settlers as participants in the same system that had led them to settle along the southern Liberian coast, and their attempts to recruit both the African American colonists and the white missionaries who accompanied them into local conflicts and patron-client arrangements testify to this (Martin 1968).

One interesting feature of the written accounts of Glebo history, which appear to describe a classic case of Kopytoff's frontier process, is that they contain a distinctly precise and linear chronology. Literacy in both English and Glebo has been a point of pride in the southeast for well over one hundred years, and a number of historical texts have been produced by indigenous writers (Ingemann and Duitsman 1976: 128). One of the more prolific authors was Samuel Yede Wallace of Hoffman Station, Cape Palmas, who was born to immigrant Glebo parents in Lagos, Nigeria, in 1902. Educated in Ghana in the 1910s, he learned to read and write Asanti as well as English and later continued his studies at Cuttington College back home in Cape Palmas in the twenties (Wallace 1983: 1, 16, 28). In the 1950s he began writing historical pamphlets in Glebo and English, which he had privately printed in Lagos and Monrovia. As sources, he undoubtedly drew upon both oral traditions and the work of earlier Glebo historians such as S. W. Seaton, who had published "Migrations of the Grebo Tribes from the East" in a local newspaper, the *Cape Palmas Record*, in 1899 (Martin 1968: 39; for similar work on Kru historical narratives, see Tonkin 1988, 1992; Davis 1976). Wallace's "Historical Lights of Gedebo or Glebo (Yesterday and Today Glebo)" was printed in Harper in 1955 (shortly before the erection of the centennial monument) and was one of the sources for Liberian ethnographer S. Jangaba Johnson's *Traditional History and Folklore of the Glebo Tribe*, published by the Bureau of Folkways, Republic of Liberia, in 1957. Both Wallace and Johnson also drew on earlier accounts by European and American missionaries, including J. L. Wilson's *Western African* (1856), and the linguistic work of Bishop Auer in the 1870s (Martin 1968: 39).

Wallace and Johnson have both achieved the status of "standard sources" and are cited repeatedly by later scholars. In the 1960s, Wallace worked with the U.S. Peace Corps Training Program in Boston and later with linguists at the University of Liberia to standardize the Glebo orthography developed by Bishop Auer in the nineteenth century. He continued to produce historical accounts, including a revised and updated "Complete History of Yesterday and Today Grebo" (1980, still an unpublished manuscript in 1983), and a series of "Grebo Comparative Primers" which he hoped would be adopted for teaching Glebo children to read and write in their own language in the public schools. When I knew him, he was the elderly head of a large but impoverished family, living on a small and irregular government pension, but still writing and looking for funds to publish his pamphlets. He died during the early years of the civil war.

One of the more striking aspects of Wallace's accounts, and one that appears in all subsequent work based on his, is the precise dates which punctuate the familiar stories of frontier migration and conflict with other groups. Wallace alone is not responsible for these dates, since they occur in oral versions of the origin tale as well. The people who became the coastal Glebo are said to have originated in the Krahn area of the interior, driven out by strangers encroaching on their land and tapping their wine palm trees. Eventually, the strangers joined with other local groups in expelling the Glebo, then known as Gbobo, from their territory. According to Wallace, this event occurred in the year 1699 (1980: 17). By 1700, the Gbobo had migrated south to the Atlantic coast at Bereby in present-day Ivory Coast, joining a people they called the Muniwe. They were originally welcomed, but desired a land of their own not under Muniwe domination and, following the advice of a wide-ranging hunter, decided to move north and west, up the coast to Cape Palmas. Stealing the canoes of the Muniwe, they set off, although many canoes capsized and some groups were discouraged and turned back. Those who survived reached Cape Palmas, according to Wallace, on June 4, 1701, and re-named themselves "Glebo" because they had "climbed the waves" as the *gle* monkey climbs trees (25–26, 39).

A series of wars with groups already occupying the area and with the Muniwe, who came after their stolen canoes, followed, and the Glebo were unable to establish real control until 1704. Wallace gives precise dates for the founding of each of the contemporary Glebo settlements along the coast: April of 1704 for the ritual center of Taake, 1705 for the rebuilding of the original Cape settlement, Gbenelu, after it was destroyed in a Muniwe attack, Puduke in 1709, Seede in 1715, Yaake, 1720, Glebogbade, 1726, Blegye, 1735, Gbede, the southernmost town, 1794, and Waa, the northernmost outpost, 1795. The colonization of about thirty miles of coastline, with its valuable access to European trade, was accomplished in a little less than one hundred years.

Aside from the precise chronology, the Wallace account fits the typical pattern of origin tales described by Kopytoff as a product of the frontier experience: the extended wanderings, the threats of incorporation by other groups such as the Muniwe, the struggle with previous inhabitants, internal factions resulting in splitoff communities, the appearance of powerful and dangerous warriors who are incorporated through marriage, and so on. The same motifs appear in an origin tale collected and translated by Wallace from elders of an interior Grebo-speaking group in the 1970s, but without the specific dates (1983, unpublished manuscript).

It is certainly easy to assume that Wallace's Glebo chronology is a later insertion into oral traditions, and while widely cited, it has also been widely disputed. Jane Martin suggests that other evidence places a people called Glebo on the Cape several centuries earlier than the accounts claim (1968: 41). Around 1500, the Portuguese explorer Pacheco Pereira Duarte described the people of Cape Palmas as "Eguerebo" (Hair 1967:

257) and in 1614 Levinus Hulsius, a German geographer, referred to them as the "Gruvo" (Johnston 1906: 85, n. 1). Ronald Davis reports that fifteenth-century European ships purchased provisions from the people of Cape Palmas (1968), and the southern coast town of Blegye or Graway (the founding of which Wallace dates to 1735) appears on late sixteenth and early seventeenth century maps as Croua, Growa, and Gruway (Martin 1968: 41). Martin links the arrival of the Glebo on the coast to the "Mane Invasions" (citing Walter Rodney 1967) of Sierra Leone in the mid-sixteenth century, suggesting that the first groups may have arrived on the coast at this time, later to be joined by newcomers fleeing the movements of the Baoule to the east (Martin 1968: 42). She further speculates that the structural division of ritual and civil authority in Glebo towns may be a result of successive migrations, with the *wodo baa*, or town chief, representing the clans which arrived early and the high priest, or *bodio*, "a more recent official imposed by new migratory people. The rituals of war, so important to the Glebo of the nineteenth century, may also show some correspondence with the customs of invading groups" (42–43). Here we seem to have a perfect example of the process of small polity generation, formation, and consolidation described by Kopytoff.

As to why the Glebo historical account should contain a chronology which begins in the eighteenth century, we must remember both the tendency to foreshorten time, as demonstrated in the interpretation of the centennial monument, and the increasing presence of European ships on the coast at precisely this period. Ancestors of the present Glebo may have been in the region earlier, but moved, literally onto the beaches, around 1700 in order to secure their position in the coastal trade. Both Wallace's account and one given to the linguist Gordon Innes in London by J. Y. Dennis, a Glebo at the School of Oriental and African Studies in 1955–57, mention that when the Glebo came ashore at Cape Palmas, they found a "slave ship" at anchor off the coast, captained by a man named Bostman (Wallace 1980: 26, Innes 1966: 142). Presumably, this is William Bosman, whose *A New and Accurate Description of the Coast of Guinea* (London, 1721), is a standard source, one that Wallace surely had access to. Martin notes, however, that the account of Cape Palmas in Bosman's book was actually written by a John Snoek, and dated January 2, 1701. Richard Burton wrote in 1863 that the Glebo of that time claimed there had been a slave factory or "foreign house" on the Cape when they arrived, and Martin suggests that the Bosman slave ship story may be "a later variant on an earlier tradition" (1968: 40 n. 83). In any case, it ties the Glebo chronicle to the recorded presence of Europeans in the area.

What this accomplishes is an assertion that the Glebo and the Europeans arrived simultaneously. What Kopytoff calls "the importance of being first" can be established, as Murphy has shown, in numerous ways.

One can be the first to build a house, to establish a ritual center, or to form a treaty with an outside power (Murphy 1988: 1). In tying their chronology to the recorded European "history" of the early eighteenth century, the Glebo make certain claims about international contacts and access to imported Western products which predate the arrival of the African-American settlers in 1834. Since Glebo men began to participate in the coastal system of migratory wage labor aboard European ships around the mid-1700s (the "Kruman" phenomenon documented by Brooks 1972, see also Frost 1999), their history and that of Europeans were further entwined (Martin 1982). In resisting the alleged cultural superiority of the American settlers, this eighteenth-century history became a strategic resource in the Glebo attempt to define their own version of "civilization," one that could not be understood as the exclusive property of the American settlers.

In the early nineteenth century, Cape Palmas was colonized as an independent project of the Maryland State Colonization Society, a chapter of the American Colonization Society which had begun settling free black Americans two hundred miles up the coast at Monrovia in 1822. The state of Maryland had an unusually enthusiastic chapter, due to having the highest percentage of free people of color in the nation (by 1830, 12 percent of the state's population) (Martin 1968: 55). The Maryland settlement was one of a series of independent ministates along the coast which were later consolidated into the Republic of Liberia.

On February 14, 1834, Dr. James Hall, the colonial agent, arrived with the first group of seventeen Maryland settlers (Martin 1968: 74). Their first town, Harper, was unique among Liberian coastal settlements in that it was built right in the middle of a preexisting indigenous community of between 1500 and 2000 Glebo; the original landing place of Gbenelu (Fox 1868: 177). The treaty of 1834, memorialized on the centennial monument, was signed by Hall and by elders and leaders representing just one section of the local Glebo. The treaty provided for the "sale" of land to the colonists and promised schools and teachers for both settler and Glebo children. Since the Maryland Colonization Society did not have the funds to fulfill this obligation, they invited the American Board of Foreign Missions to take over all educational matters and granted them land in the colony in return (Earp 1941: 367). According to the written histories of mission activity in Cape Palmas, including the accounts produced by the early missionaries themselves, two Presbyterian clergymen accompanied the original band of colonists in 1834. The first mission station of the Protestant Episcopal Church, which was to have the greatest success in converting, educating and "civilizing" the Glebo, was established in December of 1835 (Fox 1868: 181; Earp 1941: 368; Martin 1968: 73, 127).

Perhaps not surprisingly, the Glebo version of these same events is a bit different. Wallace dates the establishment of the Episcopal mission at Gbede, on the Cavalla River, to 1830 (1980: 74). Other oral accounts given by Glebo clergy confirm this, and I was given this date by the Glebo catechist at Gbede when touring the old stone church, which was still standing in 1983. Wallace further states that, in their initial meeting with the representative of the colonization society (who is identified only as the "captain of a slave ship"), the Glebo demanded "education and the Christian religion for their children" in exchange for allowing the colonists to settle among them (73). Wallace states explicitly, "The missionaries therefore came out at the request and invitation of the Glebo and before the arrival of the immigrants" (73).

What does this revised history accomplish for the Glebo? Most importantly, it gives them a prior claim on the values, standards, and lifestyles which became elaborated into the concept of "civilization." By denying that civilization was "brought" by the colonists, the Glebo ideologically resist incorporation into the Liberian state as mere "natives" and subordinates to the more culturally sophisticated settlers. While the colonists adopted the American narrative of "pioneer fathers," bringing light to the darkness of Africa and civilization to their "benighted brethren," the Glebo assert that they had already recognized and taken steps to acquire this complex of valued symbolic capital, including literacy, Western education, and Christianity. They position themselves as equal agents and partners in the historical encounter, the foundation of their insistence on democratic relations with the central government in the years to come.

Furthermore, the account of the treaty between the Glebo officials and the "captain of the slave ship" leaves a reduced role for the settlers, who are relegated to little more than the "slaves" on board. The real protagonists are the Glebo and the white ACS officials, who must carefully negotiate their positions as equal parties to the transaction. An incident from Wallace's narrative of the initial meeting between the Glebo and the colonial agent illustrates this point. When the "captain" was introduced to the *bodio*, or high priest, and elders of Gbenelu, he presented them with three men, one very black, one light brown, and one very light. The *bodio* commented that the first was much like them (the Glebo), the second "like an Arab," and the third "like a white man." The captain explained the differences in skin color by the amount of time these individuals had been in America, claiming that the weather there had "bleached" them. The *bodio* replied that, if this was the case, why had not their own weather the power to turn white men black, since some European traders that he knew had been working the coast for forty years? And so, Wallace concludes, "he caught the captain in a lie" (1980: 67–70).

While one point of this story may be that the captain's lie was only the first of many, what the bodio *really* caught him at was condescension, assuming the Glebo to be unsophisticated country folks with little experience beyond their own region. On the contrary, by 1834, many Glebo men were widely traveled and worldly, and up to half of them spoke some English or other European languages (Martin 1968: 84). Several of the leaders of Gbenelu had lived in the Freetown colony in Sierra Leone, and a few had been to London in the course of their shipboard life. Over the next few decades, a community of "civilized Glebo" emerged, part of a growing West African Anglophone coastal intelligentsia which included their counterparts in Sierra Leone, the Gold Coast, and Nigeria. Never fully incorporated into the Americo-Liberian elite and differentiated but still identified with their Glebo "native" kin, they found employment in the mission schools, courts, and small businesses of the growing regional center of Harper. Yet the American colonists were quick to reject any claims to equal status and referred even to highly educated Glebo as "native dogs" (Martin 1968: 267). The Episcopal congregation at Harper refused to seat Glebo converts in their church and insisted on segregated houses of worship (220). In spite of the colonists' hostility, the local mission town of Hoffman Station, founded by an educated Glebo man, N. S. Harris, in 1852, rapidly became the center for "civilized Glebo" in the region (Martin 1968: 189–90; Moran 1990).

It is therefore not surprising that Glebo historians, drawing on a rich oral tradition of frontier political processes and highly sensitive to "the importance of being first," yet at the same time aware of the rhetorical uses of sequential chronology in establishing legitimacy in Western discourse (see Alonso 1988: 36), should have injected an eighteenth- and nineteenth-century "timeline" into their accounts. In this way, they were able to legitimate their own model of civilization and assert its independence from that of the settlers. Wallace's history continues, congruent with other written accounts, to detail the numerous nineteenth- and twentieth-century wars between the Glebo sections, the American settlers, and the national government. The Glebo appropriation of colonial history challenges the domination of the local settler elite and disputes their claim to have "brought civilization" to the wilderness and thus, the basis of their claim legitimately to dominate the Glebo.

As Kopytoff reminds us, disputes about "what happened when" are rarely "about chronology per se but about chronology as an indication of seniority, not about who brought in what crop but about what this says about civilization. . . . In brief, the arguments [are] not about history as raw events but about the meaning of events for a history that sanctions political relations" (1987: 60). Or, as Murphy puts it, "claiming 'founder' status thus relies on the power to define one's cultural order as superior and therefore first" (1988: 2).

Until the military coup of 1980, the power to produce "official" Liberian history lay securely in the hands of settler-descended elite, who produced the texts used in schools and universities and who represented the nation to international scholars. These contained a different frontier story, modeled after the American experience. The Liberian national motto, "The Love of Liberty Brought Us Here," clearly did not recognize the presence of anyone of consequence "here" before 1822. It is in this light that the writings of Samuel Yede Wallace and his literate Glebo predecessors must be viewed as an act of resistance. But such projects are a strategy for gaining control not only of the past, but of the future as well.

Murphy has described the efforts of two rival "houses" among the Mende of Sierra Leone to produce written histories of a dispute over succession to the paramount chieftaincy in their area (1988: 3–4). Analyzing the careful archival work being done by a member of the family currently *out* of power, Murphy notes, "Despite the political strength of the Farma house, E. J. Quee still privately and quietly compiles his case from the evidence of written texts which could justify the fall of the Farma house if the Quee house had the necessary political backing from local and national-level forces" (13). In a like manner, Glebo historians have been "privately and quietly" compiling written evidence to support their claim to a nonsettler standard of civilization. At the same time, the narrative of frontier political process remains the subtext on which the new chronology is built.

* * *

The Maryland Centenary monument and the Glebo history of Samuel Wallace contain both converging and diverging narratives of local and national history in Liberia. If the Atlantic slave trade provides the underlying text for contemporary Sierra Leone, as argued by Shaw, it is clear that the settler/native encounter provides the dominant "master narrative" for Liberia. Indigenous groups wishing to contest this narrative must marshal their historical and chronological evidence and "see" a twentieth-century First Lady in the statue of a nineteenth-century Glebo man. The Maryland monument neatly encapsulates the twin themes of violence ("Natives Combat with Pioneers") and democracy ("Natives and Pioneers in Peace talks"), as does Wallace's tale of frontier struggles and the rejection of second-class status. Both of these "texts" share points of value as well; the perceived advantages of literacy, Christianity, and the reverence for Tubman, who at least made a show of bringing settlers and natives together. Glebo accounts of the monument and their written histories are not just an "alternative" reading but a politically situated reworking

of national themes. Even as they actively resisted externally imposed polit
ical control, local people also incorporated and "naturalized" the meanings of terms like "civilization," claiming them for their own by rooting
them in their own historical narratives. The very bodies of knowledge and
practices that they claimed to have recognized before the settlers' arrival
are now merged with a discourse of "modernity" and "development." In
the next chapter, I turn to the struggle to bring the nineteenth-century
meaning of civilization into the present, and the debates which were
sparked by the military coup of 1980 and the rise to power of Liberia's
first indigenous president, Samuel K. Doe.

Chapter 3
Civilization and the Liberian Nation

When the young, rurally recruited fighters of Charles Taylor's NPFL entered Monrovia in the summer of 1990, it was the first time that many of them had seen their capital city. Ellis writes that these young men reserved particularly vicious retribution for members of their own ethnic groups who were long-term city residents, because "they regarded anyone who had lived in Monrovia for too long as having betrayed the moral values of the village" (1999: 117). The violence unleashed by the civil war is framed in this account and others as a conflict over which set of moral values, those of the decadent, Westernized metropolis (and by implication, those of the Americo-Liberian elite) or those of "the village," would characterize the nation as a whole. Like the radical disjuncture postulated between settler and native, this analysis assumes that the lines dividing various sectors of prewar Liberian society were sharp and unambiguous. The violence and upheaval of the civil war have, as we have seen, been blamed on the historical encounter between indigenous Africans and American colonists, but this dichotomy is also projected onto the present as a divide between "rural" and "urban" (or traditional/modern, civilized/native, country/kwi, and other locally used terms of contrast). The lack of a fully modern national sense of self, or Liberian national identity, is likewise invoked to explain the war, whether this is ultimately blamed on Americo-Liberian venality or on stubbornly "tribal" loyalties. What is lost in this dichotomous construction is the fact that neither modernity nor "the moral values of the village" are exclusively located in either the city or countryside (see Piot 1999; Gupta and Ferguson 1997, Ferguson 1999, see also Williams 1973). Rather, rural backwaters like Cape Palmas and urban centers like Monrovia are linked not only by the constant stream of people and goods which flows between them, but also by participation in the same struggles over the meanings of place and identity. The following three chapters all address the ways in which these struggles were ongoing in both rural and urban contexts in Liberia in the period before the civil war.

In most of the scholarly literature on Africa, nationalism is contrasted, either explicitly or implicitly, with ethnicity or "tribalism." There is a curiously unexamined evolutionism to this view, as if ethnicity was an historically earlier, more "traditional," and certainly more deeply felt form of group identity. Commitment to the nation is defined as "modern," and its failure to supersede and replace other attachments becomes the source of much concern. Even though many supposedly "primordial" tribal identities have been shown to be of recent origin and to have strategic political uses (see especially Ranger 1983: 248–49), the binary opposition "nationalism/ethnicity" still drives much analysis of the state in Africa. This chapter examines the often unspoken association between nationalism and modernity or, to use the favored term in Liberia, "civilization."

Civilized Liberians have been understood to owe their primary allegiance to the nation-state, while natives privilege the ties of "tribal" or ethnic affiliation. But as we have seen for the Glebo of Cape Palmas, the term "civilized" incorporates other meanings and values which make, at best, for an uneasy and contradictory association with a nationalism grounded in identification with the settler elite. Officially and unofficially, having two categories of citizens raises questions of loyalty, identity, and democratic rights. For example, the Liberian legal system had, for more than a century, allowed some minor crimes to be tried by native chiefs when the parties involved were considered natives. The same crimes, committed by civilized persons, were tried in statutory courts with a system of procedures and penalties based on Anglo-American law. Some individuals have been known to try their luck in a statutory court, then redefine themselves as native and seek a more favorable outcome elsewhere (or vice versa). Obviously, these categorical identities are more flexible and situational in practice than in the often rigid definitions of Western analysts.

Similarly, men and women, both "native" and "civilized," seem to stand in different positions as citizens in Liberia and elsewhere. The state, as a bureaucratic structure, and the nation, as an imagined collectivity, require and impose differently gendered subjectivities. I argue that it is with the addition of a gendered analysis that the contradictions of nationalist discourse and its relationship to civilization in Liberia are most thoroughly exposed and the ambivalences surrounding both are made visible. The difficulty and ambiguity of assimilating civilized, modern, *female* citizens into existing discourses of the nation have been noted in a variety of times and places. Here, I analyze both a rural community and a selected group of images of these women from a major Monrovia newspaper in the early 1980s.

While I lived in Liberia conducting research in Cape Palmas, I was aware that these terms transcended purely local usage and were part of a broader discourse of class, status, and identity in the country as a whole. An extensive literature exists addressing the rural and urban implications of these conceptions for understanding upward mobility, capitalist penetration, and the mystification of class and ethnic relationships in Liberia (Brown 1982; Frankel 1964; Tonkin 1979, 1980, 1981). All these authors noted that to be civilized, both in rural Liberia and among recent migrants to Monrovia, was to be in a highly valued position, one that implied both moral and material advantage over natives.

In the course of my ethnographic research, I collected national newspaper accounts relating to Liberian women. I subscribed by mail to the *Daily Observer*, the major independent paper in Monrovia. Over a period of fifteen months, I was able to accumulate an extensive clipping file. On my occasional trips to Monrovia I collected additional publications and discussed them with colleagues at the University of Liberia as well as with friends back in Maryland County. Newspapers and other textual materials have provided anthropologists with a rich source of evidence for the analysis of gender and nationalism in contemporary Africa. Classic studies by Little (1973, 1980) and Schuster (1979) emphasized the scapegoating of urban women in African newspapers as sexually uncontrolled, spiritually dangerous, and most importantly, *unpatriotic* parasites or folk devils (Schuster 1979: 140–53). More recent work by Bastian (1993, 1995) on the popular press in Nigeria provides a wonderfully nuanced account of the ambivalence surrounding modernity and urban life and its representation in highly gendered narratives about the bodies of men and women. In addition to documenting shifting views of gender, however, Akhil Gupta has argued that "In the study of translocal phenomena such as 'the state,' newspapers contribute to the raw material necessary for a 'thick' description. . . . Obviously, perceiving them as having a privileged relation to the truth of social life is naive; they have much to offer us, however, when seen as a major discursive form through which daily life is narrativized and collectivities imagined" (1995: 385). No more than do our own, African newspapers do not simply reflect ongoing social life. Rather, they are one way in which that life is constructed, given meaning, contested, and changed. The imagining of collectivities, whether these are based on gender, ethnicity, or common membership in the nation, is never finished; it is in a constant state of negotiation and struggle. The analysis of newspapers can help us capture specific moments in this process, but we must be careful to avoid investing them (or indeed, any text) with too much stability over time.

In examining a series of cartoon images of "civilized" women in Monrovia from the early 1980s, I was intrigued to find many of the same negative, scapegoating motifs described by analysts of other African countries.

I found this curious, because the understanding of civilization as a positive and desirable status for women seemed so overwhelming at the site of my rural fieldwork. Urban civilized women were often pictured as greedy, sexually uncontrolled parasites who diverted men from their responsibilities and impeded the progress of national development. Yet it is clear that the cartoons represent a critique not only of urban women, but of the military government during a period when press censorship made open opposition impossible. It is important to note that these images date from the early years of Liberia's first military government; a time when the head of state, Samuel K. Doe, was a young master sergeant with a tenth grade education. I suggest that the negative image of urban civilized women masked a critique of Doe and his pretensions to civilized status. In 1985, Doe became president of the Republic of Liberia in what was clearly a fraudulent election. In 1989, armed opposition to his repressive and corrupt rule began, leading ultimately to the protracted civil war in which about 200,000 Liberians lost their lives. These images date to the historical moment before the collapse of the state, when many possibilities seemed open and the definition of the nation and its citizens appeared unusually fluid. The cartoons reflect this sense of uncertainty in that they are neither consistent nor univocal. Rather, they seem to contain contradictory messages which can be read in multiple ways.

Gender and sexuality have been implicated in the construction of competing nationalist and subnational identities by a number of scholars across the disciplines (see Anthias and Yuval-Davis 1989; Parker et al. 1992; Enloe 1988, 1993, 1995; Mayer 2000). It is clear from this research that the construction of citizens of either gender is an on-going and often contested project for any nation state. For my purposes here, I would like to make three points about this relationship. First, both gender and nationalism represent categorical identities that are easily *naturalized* and *essentialized*. As Anderson has noted, in the modern world everyone must "have'" a nationality just as they "have" a gender (1991: 14). Such naturalization increases the emotional investment individuals bring to defending or challenging these identities and increases the political stakes for everyone. Second, both gender and nationalism are tied to the highly charged issue of *reproduction*, from the level of individual human bodies all the way to the continuation of "the people" however defined. This association between biological and social reproduction in turn can increase the level of tension and potential conflict between women and men over such issues as sexual autonomy, mobility, and economic independence. Enloe has noted that "It is precisely because sexuality, reproduction, and child rearing acquire such strategic importance with the rise of nationalism that many nationalist men become newly aware of their need to exert control over their community's women" (1995: 22). Third, both gender and nationalism, while locally defined and enacted, are situated within global processes of *commodification* and *identity production*. Local constructions are in at least implicit dialogue with globalized media images of masculinity, femininity, and "national culture" as they are represented in popular forms like movies, music, beauty pageants, and television shows, increasingly available in even the most remote locations. Whether this engagement takes the form of resistance ("*Our* women are not like those loose Western women in the films") or emulation ("In order for the nation to be modern and progressive, our women must abandon their backward ways"), it is usually signaled by specific items of clothing or material culture. As these items circulate globally, they become markers of identification with or resistance to the "modern" nation state. All three of these dynamic points of intersection, the tendency toward *naturalization*, the association with *reproduction*, and the situatedness within globally circulating systems of *commodities*, are visible in the cartoon images to be discussed below.

In his masterful, multipart article, "A Tribal Reaction to Nationalism" (1969–70), Warren d'Azevedo uses the term "nationalism" to describe, "almost one hundred and fifty years of slow insistent absorption of a heterogeneous population into a national entity" of Liberia (1969: 4; see also Martin 1969). The American settlers, who never constituted more than two or three percent of the total population, used a combination of military conquest, trading partnerships, strategic marriages, and adoptions to create links with rural indigenous elites, and ideological constructions of their own version of manifest destiny to maintain their political and economic dominance, until their government was toppled by the military coup in 1980. Liberian nationalism, therefore, has always been, in the terms used by Benedict Anderson, "official" (1991: 86) in that it is a projection of the state; no sense of nationhood predates the arrival of the settler minority. This official nationalism was closely tied to such identifying markers as literacy, fluency in English (the national language), employment in the wage sector, at least nominal membership in a Christian church, residence in urban areas, especially Monrovia, and the accumulation of Western products; in other words, with "civilization" as defined by the American settlers. The settlers and their sponsors in the American Colonization Society imagined Liberia as an outpost of Christianity, democracy, and Euro-American capitalism on the "Dark Continent."

As we have seen in the previous chapter, that vision was not simply accepted by the indigenous people, for whom until quite recently other forms of personal and group identity were more central than a sense of "being Liberian." Although the lack of a color bar between the colonizers and the colonized allowed many individuals to pass into the elite through marriage, adoption, and patronage, most maintained a geographically defined affiliation. Rather than tribe or ethnic group, however, these local identities were built around either small clusters of towns with their accompanying farmlands (in the south and east) or loosely structured, often multiethnic and multilingual chiefdoms (in the north and west). Unlike the isolated ethnic villagers of Africanist stereotypes, many indigenous Liberians in the eighteenth, nineteenth, and early twentieth centuries had extensive knowledge of and interactions with other peoples, including traders from the northern savannahs and Europeans along the coast. They were aware of a variety of ways of being civilized and acquired many civilized traits, including proficiency in European languages and access to Western commodities, without the mediation of the settlers (see Frankel 1964; Tonkin 1979). The official nationalism of the settlers only began to take on salience in the post-World War II period, when a booming economy based on the export of iron ore and rubber encouraged permanent labor migration and the spread of schools and other state institutions in the interior.

Various attempts were made to extend the official nationalism of the state symbolically to the indigenous people. W. V. S. Tubman's Unification Policy, discussed in the previous chapter, extended both the franchise and the symbolism of the state much further into rural communities. It was not uncommon in the 1980s to see, even in very isolated rural parts of Maryland County, the public rooms of local chiefs decorated with photographs of Tubman, often in association with other leaders of his time, like John F. Kennedy. Tubman's successor William Tolbert had continued this practice, as did Samuel Doe, so a veritable gallery of portraits became the overt symbol of the rural chief's authority. Each chief, as well as local justices of the peace and the "chairmen" who served as local authorities in civilized townships, was also issued a Liberian flag, which was dutifully raised and lowered at sunrise and sunset each day. At the moment the flag began to move up the flagpole, a whistle was blown and all passersby literally froze in their tracks. Everyone was required to stand still in respectful silence as the flag was lowered or raised, on penalty of a fine or even a beating. I myself was "caught" and let go with a stern warning on more than one occasion for absentmindedly continuing to walk by during the flag ceremony. Flag Day, a national holiday, was celebrated with annual parades of school children, military units, and other organized groups including market women's associations. July 26, Liberian Independence Day, was likewise celebrated with the appearance of "country devils," or masked figures from the indigenous repertoire. In a stroke of genius, Tubman made his own birthday a national holiday, which continued to be celebrated long after his death, especially in Cape Palmas. This will be discussed in greater depth in Chapter 5.

Official nationalism in Liberia was thrown into question with the 1980 coup. The new military leaders, young men from a variety of indigenous backgrounds and with modest levels of formal education, were faced with redefining the nation-state they had just acquired by force in a way that would both justify and celebrate their own actions. Ordinary Liberians, of both indigenous and settler origins, suddenly found new possibilities open to them in both government and the private sector, as many in the former ruling class became political refugees abroad. The influx of moderately educated people of indigenous descent, who could never have hoped to rise so far under settler dominance, into government ministries and other state institutions created for many new questions of national identity. Should the new government construct itself in class, ethnic, and/or universalizing terms? Should one ethnolinguistic group, out of more than sixteen recognized "tribes," be elevated to represent the totality and if so, which one? Without the settler class in control, was Liberia still a civilized nation? Was it now a more authentic African one? These issues were of evident concern to both urban and rural Liberians during my fieldwork in 1982–83.

As outlined above, Liberia's peculiar history of American settlement and early independence resulted in a conception of civilization with clear roots in the nineteenth century. Although originally describing the cultural differences between African-American settlers and indigenous people, the term "civilized" came to be used locally to include educated, well-employed, and/or Westernized sophisticates of all backgrounds. Neither an ethnic category nor a class fraction, civilized Liberians may best be understood as sharing "status honor" in the Weberian sense (Moran 1990). Each of Liberia's indigenous ethnic groups developed its own sector of civilized natives whose connections to noncivilized kin and friends (and sometimes spouses) take a variety of forms. As we have seen in the previous chapter, the civilized Glebo of Cape Palmas trace their origin to the Episcopal missionaries they claim preceded the American settlers to the region. By the mid-nineteenth century, separate civilized towns of educated converts to Christianity had sprung up all along the coast, by their very presence challenging the settlers' claim of cultural superiority (Frankel 1964; Tonkin 1979).

In all its specific, local manifestations, civilization includes explicit lifestyle and behavioral standards of dress, personal hygiene, and home decoration as well as a commitment to civilizing institutions like churches, schools, and state bureaucracies. All analysts (and, as Tonkin notes, every writer on Liberia in the twentieth century has felt compelled to discuss this concept) have emphasized the positive, moral aspect of the term (see Frankel 1964; Tonkin 1981; Moran 1992). In the case of civilized natives like the Glebo, this moral loading has constituted an implicit critique of Liberia's long history of political dominance from Monrovia. By claiming that they could be *both* civilized and native, Western-educated Glebo presented a challenge to the more common route toward upward mobility: absorption into the settler group through adoption and the construction of a fictive genealogy which denied native origins. The American settlers, like European colonialists elsewhere, based their claims to the right to administer natives on the objective fact of their superior culture. Unlike Europeans, however, they could not ground these claims in an explicitly racial hierarchy. The settlers had no choice but to work within a discourse of civilization as acquired rather than innate, but this presented problems of how to regulate access to the institutions which could confer civilized status.

As an ideological construct, civilization never completely masked the realities of the Liberian class structure (see Brown 1982). It was possible, however, for indigenous people who chose to maintain their local identities to invoke simultaneously the moral, universalizing aspects of being civilized. Civilized Glebo who suffered discrimination and segregation in housing and employment at the hands of the settlers could still hold themselves up as models of "true" civilization for both their native kin and the local settler power structure. Like the restructured historical chronologies discussed in the last chapter, the Glebo symbolically contested the misuse of state power by the settlers, even as they recognized they could not fully contest that power in a material sense.

The gender dimension of achieving civilized status has historically been a point of conflict for native aspirants. In theory, hard work, the acquisition of educational credentials, and a well-paying job in the cash sector should confer civilized status on anyone. It is, however, the moral, positive aspect of the term as it is deployed locally which may be called into question when the person designated as civilized is female. The implications of civilization, depending as they do on access to an income from the wage sector, have historically been fraught with contradictions for women. Among Liberia's indigenous populations, cultural constructions of femininity cast native women as breadwinners. Under a "female farming" regime of shifting dry rice cultivation, women work on land that belongs patrilineally to their husbands, brothers, or fathers. Although an individual woman may achieve significant levels of independence, the ideal dictates that she direct her economic energies toward the support of her children, not to personal consumption. Financial independence for native women is an aspect of their obligations to kin and household, not a route to competition with men.

Civilized women, in contrast, are defined by the fact that they do *not* participate in farm labor. Defined by the missionaries as "not strong" enough for strenuous work, civilized women were ideally to be dependent housewives, fully occupied with the care of home, children, and other household members such as servants and foster children. Through their daily domestic practice, including the laborious care of such status markers as clean, well-pressed Western-style clothing (especially children's school uniforms), these women both produce and reproduce the status honor of the entire household as well as the next generation of civilized people (Moran 1990, 1992). The accumulation and display of Western commodities, not to mention the typical dependence on government payrolls, symbolizes the integration of civilized natives into national Liberian life, even when such people maintain residence outside the capital city in towns and villages to which they have patrilineal affiliation.

Civilized status is not formally assigned; like Weber's view of status honor, it is the consensus of the community which determines who is or is not civilized. While I never heard of a man being involuntarily stripped of civilized status once it was attained, women are in a more vulnerable position. A woman can lose her status as civilized by engaging in the "wrong" type of work, such as subsistence farming or public marketing, precisely the productive and cash-generating activities associated with native women. The shift in status is signaled by a change in clothing from the Western-style dress, worn only by civilized women, to the wrap-around cloths or "lappas" (which may be worn by a woman in any social category, but are especially associated with native women). So strong is this connection between clothing style and communally recognized status that gossip about women who "used to be civilized" but had, out of necessity, "tied lappa and made market," was common in the strained economic times of the early 1980s. For example, my civilized Glebo foster mother was planning to visit a young kinswoman whom she had raised in her home and who had gone to live with her husband in Ivory Coast. Before the trip, my foster mother received word that the young woman's husband had lost his job. Stranded in a foreign country, this young educated woman had begun selling in the public market place to support them both; as a consequence, she was no longer civilized. My foster mother decided to postpone her trip, because to see the young woman wearing lappas would "embarrass them both too much." She hoped that the loss of status would be a temporary one, but knew that some women spent many years as natives who "used to be civilized." The shift in dress symbolized the differential experience of civilized status for women and for men.

The constraints that civilized women seemed willing to endure in return for prestige were enforced by the sanctions usually found in small, face-to-face communities: gossip, exclusion, loss of reputation and respect. The prestige of civilized status was further enhanced by such local institutions as the Christian churches and their affiliated women's clubs and organizations open only to civilized women. The clergy and lay leaders in the Cape Palmas Episcopal church have been entirely Glebo since the turn of the century, so the church, like the concept of civilization, may be said to be a thoroughly Glebo institution.

In the six Glebo communities for which I have census data from the early eighties (representing about 3,000 people), church membership was differentially distributed across civilized and native towns and by gender. More men than women (32 percent versus 22 percent) considered themselves church members (defined by the payment of annual tithes) in the native town of Gbenelu, while the opposite was true in the civilized towns of Hoffman Station, Wuduke, Jeploke, and Waa Hodo Wodo. Since church affiliation is viewed as at least one aspect of being civilized and therefore of high status, native men are more likely formally to join a church as a result of their greater access to cash, facility with English, and generally more extensive knowledge of Western ways. This conclusion is borne out by the fact that many of these native male church members were among the elite of their communities, sitting on the council of elders or serving as the heads of their local kin groups. Among the native church members were the paramount chief, clan chief, and town chiefs of the Cape Palmas Glebo; church membership emphasized their standing as the representatives of their people to the civilized, Christian government of Liberia. Although officially members of the congregation, these men rarely attended church services except on special occasions such as funerals or national holidays. Those native women who were church members, although fewer in number, were more likely to attend weekly services and participate in prayer groups and other organized church activities.

In the civilized community, it was not necessary to be a regular church-goer or even a token member of a Christian denomination in order to claim civilized status if other criteria of education, "training," and professional employment were evident. In fact, people made a point of insisting that "civilization is different from Christianity" and pointed to devout but unquestionably native congregants as examples. Indeed, St. James Episcopal church in Hoffman Station, which could be viewed as the center of the civilized Glebo community in Cape Palmas, officially recognized and regulated these status differences among its members, but, significantly, only for women. The church set its annual tithe for men at five dollars, for civilized women, three dollars, and for "lappa women," two dollars, reflecting the presumed differential access to cash of each of these groups.

In addition to the basic membership in a congregation, churches also sponsored a number of men's, women's, and youth groups, prayer bands, junior and senior choirs, altar guilds, and so on. In any one congregation, the membership of these groups tended to overlap; thus I knew several individuals who belonged simultaneously to the Gospel Chorus, Girls Friendly Society, St. James Youth, Regional Episcopal Youth League, and Episcopal Church Women. In keeping with the Glebo definition of maturity as relative to the next ascending generation, the youth organizations included people in their thirties and forties who also belonged to the "adult" auxiliaries. These groups performed services related to the care and upkeep of the church and its graveyard, as well as raising money for their own activities by offering programs, dances, and plays. Although, like the church itself, these voluntary organizations were theoretically open to all church members, in practice they drew their members only from the civilized population.

These auxiliary organizations, especially those exclusively for women, also played an important role in codifying and elaborating the status differences between native and civilized Christians. Civilized women, through their church-based organizations, often played a prominent role in organizing the wake and funeral services for native Christian women, particularly where there was no local civilized branch of the bereaved family to take over these duties. Civilized women took seriously their expertise in "dressing the room" where the body was laid out, hanging white lace curtains (often lent from their personal collections) at the windows, and arranging furniture for the proper flow of visitors. This was in keeping with the cultural emphasis on aspects of "housekeeping" and home decoration which, like clothing style, were the most visible manifestation of civilized status. Just as they devoted great care to the clothing worn by their families, civilized women determined the clothes in which a corpse was buried, searching through the deceased's wardrobe to find items "fine enough" for all eternity. They also organized and conducted massive baking parties to prepare the biscuits served, along with hot tea and coffee, at about midnight during the wake, in order to keep the mourners awake and singing hymns until dawn. Indeed, those domains of knowledge which defined civilized women's contribution to the rituals surrounding death all echoed the domestic practices which defined not only themselves but their entire households as civilized.

Native women also have responsibilities to the dead, including crying and sitting "on the mat" receiving visitors for days or even weeks at a time. The arrangements for the "war dance," or secondary burial for men and women over the age of about fifty, an event which may take place up to two years or more after the death, are also in the hands of natives. Indeed, given the close ties to both native and civilized "sides" which most Glebo maintained during this period, a truly proper burial, with the full panoply of Christian and indigenous ritual practices, required the close cooperation and pooled expertise and resources of both civilized and native men and women. Even the most devout native Christians, however, deferred to the superior knowledge of civilized kin and friends in planning and carrying out what was mutually recognized as the Christian portion of the death rites.

While the civilized claim to Christian practice is not challenged, it must be remembered that there is great mutual respect across the status division. When the *blo nyene*, the elected "women's chief" and leader of the town's native women, died in 1983, the Episcopal Church Women of St. James attended her funeral in their uniforms of white dresses with blue collars, as they would for one of their own members. Although the deceased was acknowledged to have been at best a nominal Christian, her position in the indigenous hierarchy demanded respect. Regardless of the fact that the civilized women were not subject to the indigenous authority of the *blo nyene*, they explained their participation as a sign of respect for a "big big person" and "our mother," just as she is conceptualized in native discourse.

While the civilized/native distinction permeates the experience of Christianity for Glebo women, it does not explicitly devalue indigenous ritual and belief, leaving open the possibility for both native and civilized people to participate in both Christian and indigenous Glebo practices. It does, however, tend to solidify and overdetermine the distinction between civilized and native *women* to a greater degree than for men. The reason for this, as I have argued elsewhere, lies in the role of women's domestic practices in reproducing and reinterpreting the status hierarchy (see Moran 1990, 1992). The institutional arrangements of the Episcopal church in terms of tithing and auxiliary organizations, therefore, do not create the status distinction, but powerfully sanctify it with the authority of the church. As a symbol of the civilized world and by extension, of the nation of Liberia, the church serves as a constant reminder that not all Christians, or even Christian women, have equal access to knowledge, status, and prestige.

In the rural context, therefore, the dilemma of how a woman could be civilized without being somehow too modern was neatly solved; she could be civilized as long as she was economically and spiritually dependent upon men or male-controlled institutions. Her modernity was thus controlled and circumscribed. When this economic control was loosened, as with financially independent market women, the status was simply withdrawn. A woman who "used to be civilized" could still be a Christian and church member, of course, but she would not wear a dress to Sunday service. The few well-educated professional women in Cape Palmas who were employed as teachers, nurses, or clerks provided rare examples of civilized women who could afford to be without husbands. Competing with men for scarce jobs and operating in the public domain of professional work, they frequently had to defend their respectability and turned, in most instances, to very public participation in the churches to establish this. It was, not surprisingly, these women who were under the most pressure to live morally exemplary lives and who were frequently targets for gossip and speculation. Most women who wished to be considered civilized, however, had neither the education nor the personal connections for highly coveted white-collar employment. Unless they could formalize a relationship with a well-employed man, they were reduced to patching together a precarious subsistence by relying on kin, friends, and the fathers of their children.

In the more anonymous urban context, with its different and various opportunity structures, the constraints of the locally constituted community lose their power and the outward symbols of civilization (especially clothing) are increasingly commodified. Here, the gender dimension of civilized status becomes a highly visible field of contestation and struggle, not only in the daily negotiation of the status of a particular individual, but also in the abstract, in media such as newspapers. Commentary on popular films, radio programs, and print media comes to replace or at least augment word-of-mouth gossip. Obviously, people not only read newspaper features, but talk about them as well. Bastian has noted the textual interpenetration of oral and print narratives in the eastern Nigerian city where she worked: "Stories that appeared in the tabloids one week might very well make their way back to me as choice Onitsha gossip the next—with names and situations altered to suite the local taste" (1993: 131). Gupta's insight, that newspapers become a form through which "daily life is narrativized and collectivities imagined" (1995: 385), directs us to take very seriously the images that appear in their pages. When, as we shall see, narratives about civilization contain embedded narratives of "the nation," they are all the more crucial.

Monrovia newspapers in the 1980s carried, in addition to the usual feature stories and photographs, line drawings that seemed to speak directly to the lives of struggling urban residents at the time. Widely accessible to people of even minimal literacy, the dialogue was written in the Liberian English of working class urban neighborhoods rather than the more standard English of the newspapers' other articles and editorials. These cartoons were not comics in the sense of being always intentionally humorous or installments of an ongoing narrative. Neither were they exactly analogous to editorial or political cartoons, since they date from the period of military rule when overt political commentary was illegal and press harassment and restrictions on journalists were increasing.

Rather than directly portraying or satirizing government officials, they depicted and commented upon the personal and domestic problems common to both rural and urban dwellers: schoolgirl pregnancy, marital infidelity, and economic competition.

In 1982–83 a series of cartoons by the artists "Art Jimmy" and "Black Baby" appeared, focusing on the duplicity and cupidity of urban women. Although they depicted the lives of working-class people, the cartoons were also of interest to Monrovia's intellectual and academic elite, eliciting extensive comment and discussion among my colleagues at the University of Liberia, particularly among women who found them offensive. I was present when a young female university administrator confronted the newspaper's publisher, complaining that the cartoons were sexist. The publisher defended his artist by saying, "But Black Baby's not making them up, he hears them on the bus!" The publisher and the cartoonist believed, apparently, that they were representing the authentic voices of working-class Monrovians (since wealthier people ride in taxis or private cars, not on buses) and providing a forum for their concerns. My Cape Palmas informants were less critical of the Black Baby cartoons than the urban feminists. Many of the situations depicted, especially the fears of daughters "spoiling themselves" through early pregnancy, and the competition between unofficial cowives for their husband's meager income, were familiar aspects of life in the rural backwater as well as the cosmopolitan capital. They recognized and identified with the dilemmas represented in the drawings. Most simply sighed and said "that's right" in reaction to the cartoons, although occasionally someone would respond "that's Liberia"; a telling commentary on the perceived failings of national character.

I have selected eight examples to illustrate the most common themes in the Black Baby series (see Figures 7–14). What is immediately interesting is the transformation of civilized status, which in the rural context had a clearly moral, positive aspect, to something much more ambiguous and even sinister. As they are drawn in these cartoons, the women are marked with the outward signs of civilization, wealth, and modernity: recognizably Western clothing, hairstyles, and jewelry. They are metropolitan sophisticates rather than the upstanding, educated, indigenous elites delimited by the term in Cape Palmas. They are usually portrayed as predators and aggressors, except when cast as the suffering wives of men lured astray. Like the ambiguities attached to civilized status in the rural areas, however, these cartoons are not monolithic. They acknowledge both the possibilities and the attractions of civilized life, while criticizing both men and women (although mostly women) for neglecting family and job responsibilities, wasting money, and not thinking of the future. Rather than a hegemonic male vision in the production and representation of negative female imagery, they offer competing visions of civilized womanhood and female citizenship.

Figures 7, 8, and 9 illustrate the images common from other studies of urban African women, casting them as sexually and economically predatory. Yet these three cartoons also comment on the depressed and uncertain nature of the urban economy, as with the young man who can only afford $50.00 toward his girlfriend's rent (Figure 7), the mini-skirted woman who notes that "money business hard these days" (Figure 8) and the recently unemployed man who finds his young girlfriend losing interest (Figure 9). In Figure 10, we see the confrontation between a man and his wife, whose lappa suit marks her as probably native; the

Figure 7. *Daily Observer*, May 18, 1983.

traditional woman who puts her priorities appropriately on home and family. He addresses her as "Madam," the polite title for an married woman of relatively high status; prominent market women are usually addressed in this manner. The husband, who has apparently been missing for some time leaving his family "dying" for lack of financial support, excuses his behavior by pointing out that "those street girls are not easy," a reference to the common understanding of men as physically unable to resist displays of female sexuality. All four of these cartoons attribute to women an unfair advantage in the shrinking economy by virtue of their sexuality and their ability to lure men away from home and paycheck. In Schuster's account of newspapers from Lusaka in the early

Figure 8. *Daily Observer,* November 2, 1982.

1970s, such women were portrayed as betraying not only individual men, but the entire country, by drawing resources and attention from the common goal of national economic development. Here we see the tendency toward naturalization of both gender and nationalism as categorical identities referred to above. This naturalizing discourse casts women as the enemies of national development, less because of their actions than because of their very being. The patriotic Liberian citizen, concerned primarily with the overall good of the country, can therefore rarely be a woman. Furthermore, this discourse extends a moral judgment on all who would use material resources for their own selfish and unproductive purposes. In a period of increasing restrictions on the free press and a country-wide ban on "political activities," such comments may be a veiled reference to the military government then controlling access to government jobs, patronage, and wealth. Cloaking this political commentary as a critique of civilized womanhood serves multiple purposes for the cartoonist and his readers.

But the images contained in the cartoons are neither stable nor consistent from day to day or week to week. The contested and fluid nature of these constructs are obvious in Figures 11 and 12. One actually

Figure 9. *Daily Observer*, February 28, 1983.

acknowledges and comments on the scapegoating, noting that men "never blame themselves one day, but always blaming us." In Figure 12, a fatherly patriarch holds out the prospect of redemption and extols the potential of educated, civilized women's contributions to national life: "The time has come when women must no longer be armchair citizens, sitting back and criticizing or gossiping. Try to be a good women so your man and society will be proud of you." Here, an explicit reference is made to the local image of the civilized woman, the upstanding pillar of society, whose position depends on, reflects and represents not only the status of her man but also that of the nation as a whole. Recall that for the civilized Glebo of Cape Palmas, it is the domestic labor of women which reproduces the conditions necessary for civilized life; an ordered home, clean, pressed clothing, well-trained children (Moran 1992). Being only an "armchair citizen" is like being an "armchair housewife"; a contradiction in terms which threatens not only the family ("your man") but society in general. Ironically, the women in this drawing wear almost

Figure 10. *Daily Observer*, March 22, 1983.

Figure 11. *Daily Observer*, September 21, 1982.

smirking expressions; although they mouth a respectful thanks and promise to be "change[d] women," there is an air of defiance in their stance. The messages of these two examples and many others in the collection are clearly open to multiple readings, which may explain the popularity of the cartoons among such a wide range of Monrovians.

The claims of patrilineal kin groups, represented by either the husband or the father, over sexual access to and the fertility of young women is a theme throughout the collection which illustrates my second point about the intersection between gender and nationalism; the almost obsessive concern with reproduction. There is a sense of nostalgia expressed here for a traditional past in which sexuality was controlled rather than deployed and women "knew their place." Rather than "the moral values of the village," however, the concern seems to be with the danger of unwanted pregnancy in disrupting a young woman's education, her future prospects for civilized status, and her potential contribution to the nation.

Figure 12. *Daily Observer*, March 10, 1983.

This is a girl who told her father that she was about to graduate and needed some money.

Black Baby

I say Sarah! Is this the kind of graduation you think I want for you to have? What a big shame you have brought to us.

Father I never knew. He fooled me.

Figure 13. *Daily Observer*, September 22, 1982.

Norah, are you going back on campus this year?

But yes! You think I finish school? Please go with your foolish question. Do you think I am coming to allow any boy to spoil me for this "83". My parents spend a lot on me so I don't want to make them shame

She is not easy to tell

Black Baby

Figure 14. *Daily Observer*, January 18, 1983.

Schoolgirls who became pregnant were not allowed to return to regular public or parochial schools during this time but could continue their education only in private night schools. Since parents in Liberia tend to send their children to school when they are deemed "big" rather than at a set chronological age, and the educational career of any child may be delayed or disrupted by fluctuations in household income, it was not uncommon to find fifteen- and sixteen-year-olds in the fifth or sixth grade. Young women who are forced by motherhood to leave school at this point are usually ideologically committed to a civilized identity but lack the skills and education to maintain it themselves. This was precisely the subset of civilized Glebo I worked most closely with in Cape Palmas. These were the women who were so fearful of having to "tie lappa and make market" to support themselves and their children. From the point of view of the parents, not only has the investment in a girl's tuition, uniforms, shoes, books, and supplies been wasted, but she is now likely to be a financial dependent rather than a contributor to the household. Unless she can extract a reliable stipend from the father of her child, she has few other options for remaining civilized. Knowing the likelihood of this situation, parents were understandably reluctant to invest in the education of daughters.

The cartoons present two models of schoolgirl behavior, a positive one to be emulated and a negative one to serve as a warning. In Figure 13, the young woman's appropriation of her own sexuality results not only in her father's anger but in the loss of her status as a student ("You think this is the kind of graduation I want for you to have?"). In Figure 14, the female student rejects a young man's approach, but grounds her refusal in the name of her parents' investment in her education ("You think I am coming to allow any boy to spoil me for this 83. My parents spend a lot on me"). Like the evil temptresses pictured in Figures 7, 8, and 9, pregnant schoolgirls misappropriate and waste the resources of both their families and the nation at large.

But what of those women who, in the rush to modernity, insist on flouting the rules of respectability? The possibility of simply stripping women of civilized status, so effective in the rural community, appears to be useless in the urban context of increasing commodification of human bodies and social relations. How can a woman be categorized as one who "used to be civilized" when she refuses to participate in her own demotion, like my foster mother's relative, by giving up dresses for the market women's lappas? And why should she, when, as the cartoon in Figure 8 notes, she can always "freak those men's minds at least to get something from them"? Money, acquired from men in return for sex, can buy the external signs of civilization, and the opinions or gossip of others cannot dissolve these commodified relations. Again in Figure 8, the woman attributes her power to define her own status to her ability to "dress that kind of way," in other words, to the deployment of commodified sexuality within a Western aesthetic of beauty. The cartoonist has lavished considerable effort on the details of her costume, jewelry, and hairstyle. Replacing the local gossip networks, the popular press condemns such misappropriation by underscoring the ambiguous meaning of civilization as morally superior.

Other sources indicate similar battles over the meaning of civilization during this time. A poem, published in 1983 in the same newspaper as the cartoons and reprinted several times by popular demand, expresses this combination of ambivalence, attraction, and repulsion felt toward the uncontrolled civilized woman. Describing a woman wearing a short, tight red dress with matching shoes, makeup, and expensive jewelry (in effect, the woman in Figure 8), the poem comments:

> She's civilized, so she says
> But her body she turns into a commodity
> Whose price is determined by negotiation
> Shattering all traces of dignity.

The last stanza of the poem concludes:

> And she's very proud of her role
> Despising others she considers old-fashioned
> But if civilization is measured by this yardstick
> I want none of it. (Hne 1983)

In this image of the civilized woman as a prostitute, the consequences of loosened sexual control are equated with commodification and the proliferation of images inspired by the Western media. Clothing, which once served to enforce the standards of female behavior by limiting Western dresses to economically dependent and sexually controlled women, can no longer contain the forces of rampant commodification. The "miscarriage of society, the destroyer of people's dreams," as the poet describes this independent woman, can represent only the most amoral and alienating effects of modernity, not the "idealism, enthusiasm, and passion which it [civilization] really evokes for many" Liberians (Tonkin 1981: 233). The title of the poem, "The Spoilt Child," implies that something has gone terribly wrong with the social reproduction of Liberian citizens, for how can a commodified female body produce authentic human beings to carry forth the national agenda? The title also conjures up the images of selfishness, waste, and promotion of individual gain over communal responsibility given visible form by the cartoons (see also Ferguson 1997, 1999).

The sample of cartoons discussed above show clearly how naturalization, commodification, and an overdetermined emphasis on biological and social reproduction were implicated in the ideological construction of both gender and national citizenship in Liberia. In the early 1980s the contradictions between the precoup official nationalism, grounded in nineteenth-century ideas of civilization, and the role of the state as a means of resource allocation were becoming increasingly exposed. While the newspapers personified such contradictions in the image of the cartoon civilized woman, it was a man, Samuel K. Doe, who enacted them in real life. One way of explaining the ongoing salience of the civilized/native dichotomy in Liberia is with reference to its ability to occlude relations of political domination. David Brown, noting the tension in precoup Liberian political discourse between the myth of pure settler descent and the need for political collaboration with the indigenous elite, argues that the cultural elaboration of civilized status is a form of mystification. According to this view, allowing some natives to become civilized and giving them a stake in maintaining this status was a way of obscuring the fact that one ethnic group, the settlers, constituted a privileged class (1982: 299–301). In other words, the overlap of meanings between "civilized" and "settler" was left deliberately vague; again, this could only be accomplished in the absence of a *racial* definition of these terms. The precarious balance implied in a term like "civilized native" could only be maintained on the basis of individual, not national, identity.

Based on this analysis, Brown predicted that the military coup of 1980, in which soldiers of indigenous background overthrew the settler oligarchy, would require, in his words, "a radical redefinition of the legitimations of the state" (302). He was aware, however, that because the coup occurred so suddenly and unexpectedly, "the circumstances in which the Americo-Liberian elite was overthrown in 1980 prevented the mobilization of competing ideologies . . . so that the implications of the conceptual ambiguities in the ideology of the ruling class were never followed through" (302). The official nationalism of the precoup period held out the promise of inclusion to all who achieved civilized status, but in reality blocked the upward mobility of civilized natives like the Cape Palmas Glebo.

An expanding economy in the post-World War II years, fueled by world demand for Liberia's two major export products (iron ore and natural latex), had raised the expectations of a growing class of educated citizens. The global economic downturn in the early 1970s, particularly the energy crisis and its impact on heavy industry, had a tremendous effect on Liberia as a supplier of primary products. The death of President Tubman in 1971 created an opening for a number of progressive reform groups to challenge the single-party state and, by extension, settler hegemony. The result was an "outburst . . . of many political and social groupings in all sectors of the society" (Sawyer 1992: 287; see also Dunn and Tarr 1988: 67–85).

The military coup of 1980, although initially framed as the overthrow of the settler elite, in fact never really challenged the established hierarchies but merely replaced one group with another. The inherent contradictions embedded in how claims to civilized status were made, validated, and enforced were, by 1983, becoming publicly exposed in a manner that was hard to ignore. Indeed, the contest over the meaning of civilization intensified in tandem with the increasing awareness of the instability of state institutions and the new deployment of "tribal" ethnicity as a political tool (to be discussed in greater detail in Chapter 5).

What the young soldiers took by force in April of 1980 was not the civilized nation of Liberia but the *state*, that collection of apparatus, institutions, and technologies of power which, in the postcolonial African context, is the major route to resource acquisition and the accumulation of wealth and so the primary prize in any political struggle. Samuel Doe, who emerged from the small group of coup plotters to become chairman of the People's Redemption Council and later president of Liberia, had only a tangential and uncertain claim to be civilized himself. A member of the most obscure and remote ethnic group in the country and with about a tenth-grade education, Doe at first tried to present himself as civilized but only opened himself to ridicule. After receiving an honorary degree from the University of South Korea, he insisted on being addressed as "Dr. Doe" and later "earned" a bachelor's degree from the University of Liberia by importing faculty to the Executive Mansion for private courses. Twenty-six years old at the time of the coup, he quickly gave up the camouflage uniform of a noncommissioned soldier for three-piece suits and wireframed glasses in an effort to look older and more statesmanlike. While Doe, who at least had gotten relatively far in school before entering the army, attempted to solidify his claim to civilization, his wife, well known as a former Monrovia market woman, was constrained by a different set of rules. As we have seen, civilized women may temporarily fall to native status, but the process does not work in reverse. No unschooled market woman would dare to try and pass herself off as civilized, even when suddenly elevated to the role of First Lady. Mrs. Doe was careful never to appear in public wearing a Western dress.

By 1982, people were already commenting that Doe had become "fat" since taking office, but his other aspirations were not so easily accomplished. The Liberian scholar Zamba Liberty wrote in 1986 that Doe "desperately yearns to be considered a 'civilized' man. . . . [but] He cannot grasp its finer points and nuances nor the intricacies of its symbols" (Liberty 1986: 45). Liberty's remarks appeared in *Liberian Studies Journal* in a lengthy commentary entitled "Letter to an American Friend," but concern that Doe was "too native" for high public office was not limited to the intellectual elite. Although indigenous identity was celebrated in the initial euphoria of the coup in popular chants like "Native woman born [gave birth to] soldier, Congo woman born rogue," by 1983 soldiers were no longer highly regarded. It is clear that the experience of wrestling with and attempting to redefine the nuances and symbols of civilization permeated Liberian life in the 1980s, from those overheard on the bus by Black Baby to the highest office in the land. Ordinary Liberians, both rural and urban, could identify with the civilized aspirations of the cartoon characters and with Doe himself, but they also recognized the moral contradictions. For Doe to cast himself as the "redeemer" of the native people while manifesting all the greed and selfishness laid at the feet of the settlers opened him to the same critique as that leveled against the "Spoilt Child" of the poem. As we shall see in the following chapter, these ambiguities contained serious implications for violence and terror, particularly with regard to the role of civilized *men* as local representatives of the national political structure.

What was going on in the pages of Monrovia newspapers, therefore, was not only a contest about male control of media images or even the depressingly familiar scapegoating of urban women. What was at stake was how the civilized nation of Liberia would constitute itself and its citizens. This takes us far beyond the simple contrast between urban sophistication and the "morality of the village." The contradiction between the negative representation of civilized womanhood in the newspaper cartoons and the positive values placed on this term by the Glebo of Cape Palmas (and by other small communities throughout the country) is a displacement of the contradiction between civilization and the official nationalism of precoup Liberia. Just as the journalists and cartoonists who controlled the production and dissemination of media images seemed unable to project a unified, hegemonic representation of "civilized" womanhood, the government of Samuel Doe was unable either to dispense with or to productively modify the concept of civilization, even so as to include the top leadership. Like the cartoon civilized women, or the "Spoilt Child," Doe was directing resources away from their proper role of reproducing households, kin groups, and the nation. His pose of civilization was no more convincing than that of the poet's streetwalker, but like her he had the raw material power to ignore those who laughed at his pretensions. Yet he was also trapped by the official nationalism that linked the entity "Liberia" to civilization. Doe could not say of civilization, "I want none of it," without laying bare his own instrumental manipulation of the state for personal gain.

* * *

By 1986, Samuel Doe was finding that his claims to civilized status could not protect him from other ambitious young soldiers like himself. Faced with pressure from counter coups and organized civilian opposition, Doe fell back on ethnicity, promoting members of his own group, the Krahn, to high ranking government positions and surrounding himself with ethnically homogeneous military units. Eventually, he began taking revenge not only on those who were his rivals but on unrelated members of their ethnic groups as well, making utterly transparent the exclusive ethnic identity of those who controlled the state apparatus. and therefore, the opportunities for accumulating wealth. In effect, Doe was moving away from the official nationalism of civilized Liberia to its supposed opposite, native "tribalism." Doe began deliberately to manufacture and promote essentialized "tribal" rivalries in a desperate effort to maintain power. Predictably, his actions led to the emergence of a number of ethnically defined resistance groups with no political ideology beyond opposition to Doe himself, led by men whose sole objective was to replace him as head of state. Although even the most cursory analysis shows that such politicized ethnicity in Liberia is a product of the last fifteen years, the Western media, as discussed above, continue to describe such tragedies as the result of "ancient tribal hatreds" and explain the ensuing violence in these terms. Not surprisingly, having noted that the essentializing of gender and of other identities tends to occur together, the increasing militarization of Liberian political life has had implications for the ideological construction of gender, with new forms of violent masculinity taking privileged positions (Moran 1995; Enloe 1995).

Samuel Doe eventually lost both his struggle to become civilized and his life in 1990, as rebel factions closed in on Monrovia and a multinational West African force intervened. The newspaper images which both amused and annoyed Monrovia residents in the early 1980s represent only a moment in this crisis of redefining the Liberian nation. The cartoon representation of civilized women, whose relationship to both national identity and civilization was historically more tenuous and ambiguous than that of men, provides a striking metaphor for this moment in Liberian history.

Chapter 4
The Promise and Terror of Elections

In Chapter 1, I argued that a number of longstanding indigenous institutions might be characterized as democratic, if we broaden the definition of that term to include multiple means of direct participation in decisionmaking for people in a range of unequal social positions. In the Western world, however, it is undeniable that the institution most associated with democracy is the competitive election. While many commentators insist on viewing elections as recent importations into Africa, Liberians of all backgrounds have had a comparatively long history with this means of granting political legitimacy. The central government introduced the practice of confirming the appointment of local chiefs by popular election early in the twentieth century, requiring voters to line up physically behind their candidates in the presence of the district commissioner (Holsoe, personal communication; Gay 1972). This "staging" of elections (see also Ferme 1999) as legitimizing rituals was practiced on both local and national levels, as the national franchise was gradually extended to all Liberians over the age of eighteen during the period from the 1940s to the 1970s (Liebenow 1987: 63). Yet as Ferme has noted for Sierra Leone, elections, even in a one-party state where the outcome was not seriously in doubt, were charged with ambiguity and the fear of violence. The combination of indigenous political institutions focused on consensus with the competitive nature of "modern" elections produced "tension and ambiguity, and these together—not as dialectical stages alternating with peace and clarity—produced outcomes that were remarkably democratic in spirit, even under single-party rule" (1999: 161).

Pre-civil war Liberians, both rural and urban, encountered the election format in a variety of contexts beyond national and local governance. Church organizations, schools, market women's associations, and numerous other voluntary organizations chose their leadership through elections. One might say that the election, originally imported from America with the settlers and an integral aspect of civilized practice, has been "domesticated" in Liberia until it is an ubiquitous and well understood form. When I asked my Liberian informants in the United States how they first became involved with "politics," they interpreted my question in such a way that they often began with stories about elections, many of which deviated from the formal ideal. Indeed, the most significant thing about their experience with elections was the political awakening which ensued when the outcome was *not* fair or democratic. Elections are therefore understood as holding both great promise and great disappointment; the principles by which they are supposed to work are well understood but practical experience is too often disillusioning. Again, we see a contrast with the tendency of the popular press and of some political scientists to attribute to lack of "voter education" the frequency of election fraud in Africa.

The following is from an interview with a man from a rural, Grebo-speaking background in Maryland County who attended school through the local Catholic mission and went on to a career as a labor organizer in Monrovia:

I can remember one of my first experiences was the election for mayor in Plebo. That was in 1973. OK, they had this election in Plebo and they tell us our constitution says that there are multi-parties and people have the right to organize and different things. But then, during the election, the only party that was there was the True Whig Party. . . . there was a teacher from our government school who was running for Mayor. And then we had this lady who was the wife of the Immigration boss. . . . And I had already made up my mind to vote for [the] teacher, who spoke and went on a regular campaign. Well, when we got there, we stood around the field and after a while they came out and said, "well, the lady won." And, and nobody voted! So, when this happened. How can this happen? We just learned this in school! . . . Then as time went on I realized that what they did was, the True Whig Party went to caucus. And, you know, like a convention here, a party convention and they select who will represent the party. And, since the True Whig Party was the only party, the members of the True Whig Party in Plebo when they chose her to be their candidate, obviously, she became the mayor. So then I started noticing, well, the differences of what we had in the book and what was really the practice.

Recounting these events twenty years later, the voice of this man, preserved on my tape recorder, still shakes with disillusionment and dismay. He displays none of the cynicism about voting and elections often attributed to rural Africans, nor does he find the institution "foreign" or threatening to a more "consensus" model of granting legitimacy. The historical experience of national elections for many Liberians cannot have been much different.

However, another story presents electoral politics as much more open to contestation and unexpected results, the "ambiguity" cited by Ferme:

My first experience in the political thing was when I ran for student council president. Prior to that, it was like one or two persons running, but I started this party business. I started my own party. . . . The Student Progressive Alliance, and my opponents established their own party. And, you know, the election was going to be great! I was very open, you know, in my dealings and . . . officially, they didn't declare me the winner, but unofficially, I won because my position was too controversial and they didn't want . . . the school to go through the whole thing. For instance, there was a tendency in our school for the teachers to ask students to pay certain money for certain projects. By the time the students pay the money, at the end of the year, you know, you get a report card, you're happy, you just leave. So I raised the issue of what happened to the money and it affected a lot of teachers. . . . I mean it was obvious that I won the election because the amount of people that came. I went to the extreme of asking people to wear tee-shirts as a defiance. With the senior class, you know, you wear a [longsleeved dress] shirt and tie and all that stuff. Well, I went against that and we didn't wear a tie. And I could tell, you know, the whole school, most of the people were wearing tee-shirts! And [when] they declared that I was not the winner, well, I called for a student boycott of the government. So we had I guess about three weeks where the guy who was elected president could not get anybody to appoint to his government, you know, nobody would do it! . . . There was a big joint faculty-student meeting to resolve the whole thing. And they had just brought some priests and nuns from Nigeria so they were watching this thing going on. And they're saying, "How can this happen? Your students are too political!" So they had this big meeting in the church . . . we talked and everything came back together again.

Both of these examples demonstrate the tension inherent in a competitive political process with clear winners and losers, which also requires the participants to live and work together in the aftermath ("we talked and everything came back together again"). Ferme reports a similar "counterpressure to conform and compete, to renounce political ambitions in favor of consensus and yet to struggle to the very end" in Sierra Leone (1999: 184). The long history of Western institutions, including elections, in Liberia as discussed in Chapters 2 and 3 demonstrates that these tensions have not been easily resolved. What has emerged is a kind of "indigenous critique" (Taussig 1980) of electoral competition and, in particular, of the appropriation of individual voice embedded in the concept of "representation," that act of giving up one's right to speak to another who is empowered to represent one's interests. I argue that there is an inherent symbolic violence to this act of representing another which is expressed in the spread of rumor and panic about ritual killers, accompanying elections in many African countries as well as in Liberia. In Chapter 1, we saw how the egalitarian construction of occult power as available to anyone, of any social status, served as both a check on the abuse of power and a rationale for extreme violence during times of war. This "democracy of violence" is balanced by a recognition of "the violence of democracy," the understanding that choosing your own representatives requires a certain symbolic and sometimes, actual, loss of the self.

The desire for fair and democratic elections expressed by my informants above is no less real in that it exists within a context which views such processes as inherently dangerous. In fact one might say that under such circumstances, people who embrace and practice democracy are far more courageous than those who simply view voting as a "civic duty."

Indeed, in some parts of the country one stands the risk of losing one's life as well as one's ideals during national election "season." Episodes of panic periodically emerge at these times, as stories circulate of "heart-men" running behind random victims to extract body parts for election sorcery. Accusations of ritual murder have resulted in prosecutions, confessions, and executions, particularly in the Cape Palmas region of the southeast. So why should a practice that inspires anxiety and even terror in so many people come to be equated with "politics" (as by my informants, cited above) and with popular empowerment or "democracy" by international donors?

Ironically, the paradox of representational democracy is that, for most citizens, participation is virtually limited to the act of giving up one's autonomous voice by vesting it in a chosen representative. This transfer takes place through the magic of the ballot box, and may be conferred upon someone who is not well known to and may not share the interests of the voter. It is clear that the inherent *strangeness* of this process, conferring one's right to speak on another as the ultimate expression of one's right to speak, goes generally unacknowledged in the West, where people are "socialized" in the words of Wonkeryor et al. to see this as natural and normal (2000: 20). What ordinary voters in Liberia have realized remains obscure to most voters in the liberal democracies of the West; it is *not* the people's act of voting that actually confers power on an elected official. To contest an election, in the U.S. or Liberia or anywhere else, requires that a candidate be powerful *beforehand*, whether this power results from occult forces or from having made a "killing" in the stock market or in business. In the case below, I examine these questions in detail.

In the decade of the 1990s, students of contemporary African affairs have been divided into two camps, what Stephen Ellis (1996: 2) calls the "unhelpful dichotomy" of "Afro-pessimists" and "Afro-optimists." Exemplary of the pessimists, as discussed earlier, is the journalist Robert Kaplan, who takes recent conflicts in West Africa as a model of an apocalyptic global future. Representing the optimists, analysts such as Jennifer Widner (1995) pointed to a "wave of democratization" following the transition in South Africa and note the successful multiparty elections in Malawi, Mozambique, Zambia, and Benin. While for Kaplan "The argument over democracy in these places is less and less relevant to the larger issue of governability" (1994: 75), what seems to unite scholars on both sides of the debate is the assumption that "democracy" itself is self-evidently both good and desirable. Indeed, in most of this literature, "democracy" is used synonymously with "state institutions," and its success or failure is measured by such factors as transparent multiparty elections, lack of "statist" or planned economies, a "free" press, and the presence of a vaguely defined "civil society" (variously operationalized as the presence of numerous "voluntary" associations, nationalist senti-ment, or just a clear lack of tolerance for official corruption). A state is judged to be both democratic and "effective" when it has all or most of the above qualities at the same time as it delivers services such as edu-cation and health care, controls violence within its borders, and places at least some restrictions on the unfettered greed of elites (Widner 1995). As Americans have seen with the presidential election of 2000, it appears to be rigid adherence to the *procedure* of holding elections which confers legitimacy, not whether anyone considers the outcome to represent the will of the people.

Nowhere in this literature is there a questioning of one of the central features of republican democracy as it has evolved in the West: the pro-cess of vesting elected officials with the power to represent the interests and desires of their constituents. The fact that Liberians have a long his-tory with the act of going to the ballot box and with words like "democ-racy" does not mean they necessarily share with Western analysts the meaning of those terms, nor that these meanings are either stable or universal.

On July 19, 1997, Liberia successfully carried out its first presidential and legislative election in twelve years. The process was judged by a num-ber of highly regarded international observers, including the Carter Cen-ter and the private membership organization Friends of Liberia to be "free, fair, and transparent." Coming after almost eight years of bloody civil war, 200,000 deaths, the displacement of the majority of the popu-lation either internally or to neighboring countries, twelve or thirteen failed peace agreements, and the hurried demobilization and supposed disarming of approximately 60,000 fighters from at least seven armed factions, the election was reported to be almost miraculously orderly and free of "any systematic attempt at intimidation" (*Friends of Liberia Newsletter* 1997: 1–2). With thirteen registered parties on the ballot, the almost 700,000 war-weary citizens who exercised their right to vote had a greater range of choice than at any time in the 150–year history of the republic, which had been dominated for close to one hundred years by a single political party.

But to quote from the August 1, 1997 *Christian Science Monitor,* "to the dismay of many in the international community, this orderly democratic exercise yielded an overwhelming majority for Charles Taylor, an avowed warlord responsible for countless deaths, mutilations, and brutalities during Liberia's seven-year civil war." Receiving more than 70 percent of the vote, Taylor swept away all the other candidates, including his closest rival, Ellen Johnson-Sirleaf, a Harvard-trained economist, former World Bank and United Nations official, and the woman many foreign observers hoped might become Africa's first elected female head of state. That Taylor, who had brought Liberia to ruin, perpetuated the war, and defied the international community to make himself president by force should have it handed to him by popular mandate struck many observers as ironic if not tragic.

In explaining Taylor's victory, many have noted that, at various times during the war, he controlled about 80 percent of the country and had access to almost limitless resources through the sale of timber and diamonds from his occupied territories (Reno 1993; Harris 1999; Ellis 1999). Alone among the field of candidates, he owned his own radio and television stations and his own newspaper and had access to transportation to all parts of the country. As the man who had started the war and ousted the widely despised former president Samuel K. Doe, Taylor had the greatest "name recognition" and was perceived as fully capable of returning to the battlefield if the election did not go his way (Lyons 1998; Harris 1999). All this, combined with his campaign strategy of distributing free rice and tee-shirts (with his picture on them) to people who had little other access to food or clothing, makes Taylor's election victory seem self-explanatory.

There are still a few things, however, about the Liberian election that do require explanation. One is the continuing amazement on the part of the external observers over the "failure" of democratic institutions to weed out bad characters like Taylor. Another enigma is the campaign slogan, chanted by Taylor's supporters in the streets of Monrovia, "He killed my Ma, he killed my Pa; still, I will vote for him." How are we to make sense, *Liberian* sense, of this statement? What can it tell us about the historically and culturally constructed meaning of representational democracy in Liberia, and how does it reveal the internal contradictions and inconsistencies of that system as it has evolved in the West?

The juxtaposition of violence and voting, which strikes Western observers as incongruent, makes perfect sense in Liberia and elsewhere in Africa, where wealth and power are often attributed to "medicines" made from human body parts obtained through ritual murder. As Peter Geschiere writes in *The Modernity of Witchcraft* (1997), "The political implications of witchcraft in Africa conjure up unexpected parallels with feelings of power and powerlessness that mark popular conceptions of politics in Western democracies—the idea that one should have a grip on power and the realization that one rarely can. Witchcraft offers hidden means to grab power, but at the same time it reflects sharp feelings of impotence; it serves especially to hide the sources of power" (1997: 8–9). This recognition of the essential ambiguity of witchcraft, its lack of a moral valence as either entirely good or evil, and its ability to mobilize critiques of abusive political and economic power has characterized the emerging literature on modernity in Africa (see Comaroff and Comaroff 1993, especially Bastian 129–66, Auslander, 167–92, and Austen, 89–110).

To my mind, however, the most astonishing thing about the 1997 elections was not Taylor's victory but the *absence* of any reports of ritual murder before and during the election. Based on my experience in Liberia in the 1980s and on accounts I had collected in Cape Palmas, I was certain that fears of "heartmen" would surface as the crowded field of candidates jockeyed for support. In what follows, I hope to account for the mystery of why the election of 1997 did not generate charges of ritual murder by contextualizing and historicizing the election of Charles Taylor in light of elections which had come before.

In the spring and summer of 1983, the Republic of Liberia was beginning the process of transition from military to civilian rule. Following the overthrow of the settler dominated government by a military coup in 1980, the ruling "People's Redemption Council" set up a committee of academics and former politicians to redraft the nation's constitution in preparation for the projected return to democracy in 1985. The original Liberian constitution of 1847 had resulted from earlier commonwealth agreements among the scattered American repatriate settlements along the coast, grafted on to a governmental structure devised by a Harvard law professor and based on the U.S. constitution (Huberich 1947; Dunn and Tarr 1988: 23–26). Although for many years the document was believed to be entirely "American" in origin, the Liberian scholar Carl Patrick Burrowes has demonstrated how it was adapted and rewritten by the handful of literate African American settlers who made up the first constitutional convention (Burrowes 1989a, b). The 1847 constitution consolidated great power in the executive branch, making most other positions, including county superintendents, subject to presidential appointment. This provision reflected early nineteenth-century concerns with holding together the geographically separated settler communities as well as realistic understandings of the small scale of the nation at that time. In practice, however, it meant that local populations were never able to elect their own county-level officials and that the president had his "eyes and ears," serving at his pleasure, at all levels of government administration.

The period of the Tolbert administration (1971–80) was, as discussed in Chapter 3, one of widespread critique and agitation for government reform. The Movement for Justice in Africa (MOJA), begun as an anti-apartheid consciousness-raising group by students and faculty at the

University of Liberia, extended their analysis of colonialism and post-colonialism in Africa to the True Whig Party. Young activists agitated to abolish national holidays celebrating settler victories over the indigenous people and questioned the national motto ("The Love of Liberty Brought Us Here"). One of the leaders of MOJA, Amos Sawyer, directly challenged the TWP by running as an independent candidate for mayor of Monrovia; the election was cancelled when it became clear that he had the popular support actually to win. Another more radical group, the Progressive Alliance of Liberia (PAL), originated from an organization of young Liberians studying abroad in the United States. Back home, they called for the immediate resignation of the Tolbert government and were instrumental in organizing protests against a proposed increase in the price of rice. Tolbert overreacted by ordering police and military violence against the protesters, setting off the "Rice Riots" of 1979. The reluctance of the largely indigenous rank and file troops to fire on the protesters exposed Tolbert's vulnerability vis-à-vis his own army, later confirmed by the April 1980 coup (Dunn and Tarr 1988: 76–78).

Following the coup, the nineteenth-century constitution was held to be inadequate and in need of reform, particularly since the original language did not recognize the citizenship rights of Liberia's indigenous population, who constitute 95–97 percent of the country's population. Also, the separation of powers between executive, legislative, and judicial branches had long been ignored by Liberia's presidents. The process of drafting and approving the new constitution was seen by civilian leaders of the mass political movements whose activities had preceded the coup as the first step on the road to the new and more progressive government for which they had been struggling throughout the nineteen seventies; a Second Republic that would avoid the mistakes and abuses of the first. They hoped that the young military men who instigated the coup would honor their pledge to return to the barracks and that Liberia would prove the exception to the pattern of repeated coups experienced by other African states.

Funded by grants from the United States, Britain, and other countries interested in promoting democracy in Africa, the constitutional commission worked under a grant of immunity from the nationwide ban on political activities in place since the coup. The draft document, when completed, was widely circulated in print, on free cassette tapes translated into Liberia's indigenous languages, and on radio and television. Posters depicting Liberians from all walks of life earnestly debating the fine points of constitutional law were everywhere, even in rural areas (see Figure 15). Observing this process from my field site in the southeast, it was clear that people were sincerely interested in the process of constitutional reform. Both printed and cassette versions of the constitution were

KNOW WHAT THE DRAFT CONSTITUTION SAYS ABOUT:
- THE PEOPLE'S RIGHTS
- THE USE OF EMERGENCY POWERS
- WHO IS A LIBERIAN CITIZEN?

READ YOUR DRAFT CONSTITUTION TODAY!

SEND SUGGESTIONS TO: CONSTITUTIONAL ADVISORY ASSEMBLY GBARNGA

GET A FREE COPY NOW!

IN RURAL AREAS: SUPERINTENDENTS' OFFICE

IN MONROVIA: CONTACT THE NATIONAL CONSTITUTION COMMISSION O.A.U. VILLAGE, VIRGINIA (TEL. 224855, 224370)

Figure 15. Poster advertising the 1983 Constitutional Convention.

eagerly sought from the superintendent's office, although the "Grebo" language version turned out to be in an obscure interior dialect not easily understood by coastal Glebo. Although some complained that people were only picking up a "free cassette" in order to record popular music over the constitution (Michael Jackson's Thriller album was especially desirable at that time), others appreciated the lengths the government was seen to go to in inviting comment. Attempts were made to solicit the participation of all the nation's citizens, leading up to county electoral colleges which would select delegates to a national assembly in the centrally located city of Gbarnga. There, the assembly would discuss, revise, and amend the draft constitution in an open display of participatory democracy. In short, in 1983 the entire nation appeared to be seriously engaged in an exercise in democratic transition certain to warm the hearts of the American and European donors who were paying for all those "free cassettes."

Anthropologists are frequently confronted with the disjuncture between national processes and local interpretations of those processes. The loosening of autocratic military rule in favor of broadened representational democracy would appear to be a positive development, one that would receive wide public support among Liberians. The military leaders had justified their violent coup as the means of transferring real political power, held for almost one hundred and forty years by a settler minority, to the indigenous majority, and they were welcomed, in the initial months, as the "Redeemers" they styled themselves to be. Yet the announcement of impending county-level elections for delegates to the National Assembly touched off a wave of terror which swept the country. A summary of radio reports monitored in Paris for July of 1983 concluded, "Since a draft constitution was presented to the ruling military council here in March, the cases of missing people found dead, mainly children under eleven who had been mutilated, have headlined local newspapers. The situation is so serious now that no one feels safe any more in the entire country, especially at night, a prominent businessman who shares the views of many observers here said. It is not yet known who is responsible for the killings, but as in many African countries, ritual killings are common in Liberia, reportedly done by political aspirants especially during approaching elections" (Paris AFP in English, July 26, 1983).

It was clear that the impending return to civilian rule and "politics" inspired both hope for a better future and fears of what that future might cost. Michael Taussig, in *The Devil and Commodity Fetishism in South America*, suggests that in approaching the relationship between the locality and the state rather than ask the standard anthropological question Why do people in a foreign culture respond in the way they do . . . we must ask about the reality associated with our society. . . . By turning the questions this way we allow the anthropologists' informants the privilege of explicating and publicizing their own criticisms of the forces that are affecting their society—forces which emanate from ours. By this one step we free ourselves of the attitude that defines curious folk wisdom as only fabulation or superstition. At the same time we become sensitive to the superstitions and ideological character of our own culture's central myths and categories, categories that grant meaning as much to our intellectual products as to our everyday life. (1980: 6)

Taussig insists that the devil contracts and baptized bills of peasant communities in Latin America are not vestiges or holdovers of an earlier culture but rather "precise formulations that entail a systemic critique of the encroachment of the capitalist mode of production" (134–35). The growing literature on the "modern" uses of witchcraft in Africa likewise argues that the isolating and fragmenting aspects of modernity and globalization are given form in stories of stolen body parts, bloodsucking, and ill-gotten wealth which saps the broader community of its health and vitality (Austen 1993; Apter 1993: Auslander 1993; Bastian 1993; Ciekawy and Geschiere 1998; Geschiere and Nyamnjoh 1998; Ciekawy 1998; White 2000; Shaw 2002). Furthermore, some writers note that rumors of witchcraft and magic are central to the democratic opening celebrated by the Afro-optimists mentioned above (Meyer 1998; Geschiere and Nyamnjoh 1998). I see the Liberian association of ritual murder with elections as a systemic critique of the tendency of representational democracy to fragment local constituencies and interests, just as ritual murderers fragment the human body in their quest for power. Also known as "heartmen" in reference to one of the human organs they seek to acquire, ritual murderers do not desire whole bodies as constituents but partial bodies, literally, "parts," with which to secure elective office.

As indicated in the above radio report, however, Cape Palmas was not the only region in Liberia concerned with ritual killers that summer of 1983. While on a trip to Monrovia during this period, I found taxidrivers unwilling to deliver me to any areas off the main roads after dark. They expressly warned me about "heartmen" and one even told me he was considering carrying a gun for protection. Well before that summer, when I first arrived in Liberia in the fall of 1982, I had been cautioned by new friends in Monrovia about my intentions to conduct research in Cape Palmas. Maryland County was a hotbed of witchcraft and ritual killers, I was warned: "those people down there are strong-oh." Fresh in their minds was the notorious case of Moses Tweh, found dead on the beach in Harper on July 4, 1977, with his eyes, ears, nose, tongue, and genitals missing. Ten people were accused of carrying out the crime, including men from two of the most powerful settler families in the county, Allan Yancy and James Anderson. Anderson at the time represented Maryland County in the House of Representatives and Yancy was the county superintendent, the equivalent of a state governor. They, along with five others, were convicted and publicly hanged in 1979. The tensions and traumas of that event were still quite fresh in 1982.

A two-day journey overland from the capital, Cape Palmas and the county seat of Harper City are relatively isolated from national events. Even the coup of 1980 resulted in only minor disturbances and little change in the distribution of local political and economic power. The first signs of concern about the transition from military rule back to "democracy" and, especially, elections came in a series of church sermons and rumors circulating in both native and civilized communities.

In early June 1983, a woman minister in the African Methodist Episcopal Church in Harper announced that she had a vision. The vision revealed that there was "wickedness" in Maryland County: high public officials, including clergy, were guilty of "adultery and ritualistic killing." The woman reported her vision to the county superintendent, the highest local representative of the military government, and called for all Cape Palmas churches to observe a day of fast and prayer on the following Wednesday. The prophecy was taken seriously, since it was widely reported that this woman had also foreseen the 1980 coup and had tried to warn the former president to repent before it was too late (see Ellis 1999 on the role of prophets and churches in Liberian politics). On the next Wednesday, the very day the populace was supposed to be fasting and praying, a body was discovered in the shallow water of the Hoffman River, by the dirt bridge connecting the city of Harper with the indigenous Glebo community. On first hearing the news, one friend of mine nodded sagely and commented that this was "the policy" for those seeking government jobs. "They make you get in the water," she observed. Others agreed that "they are getting ready for running for the House and Senate in '85; they have to start making juju now to get power then." When I asked why anyone would want a political office enough to commit murder, I was told, "for the salary." A witness returning from the scene where the body was found noted that it was definitely "witch business" because certain "parts" were missing, specifically the lips and the tongue. But another commentator added that the victim, a member of a nonlocal ethnic group and therefore a "stranger" with no resident kin, was a cripple and known to be unwell. "Maybe he was sick and went there to toilet and fell in and just drowned," she reasoned. She attributed the missing parts to the action of fish.

That Sunday, Cape Palmas churches were filled with calls to repent.

Rumors circulated and people became reluctant to leave the immediate vicinity of their houses after dark, even taking baths by flashlight at the back door rather than venturing to the "bath shed," a circle of tin roofing material located in the yards of most households. At the same time, plans were going forward for the local electoral college which would select Maryland's delegates to the National Constitutional Assembly. A group of forty-two men were chosen by the county superintendent and his citizen's council, with attempts to represent both Harper, the interior city of Plebo, and the rural districts of the county. I attended the county convention on June 21, 1983, at Harper City Hall, at which "technical advisors" from Monrovia explained that the military government's ban on "political activities" was suspended only for the duration and specific location of the convention. The delegates chose four of their number on a series of secret ballots to represent the people of Maryland County. They were warned by the technical advisors that election to the assembly should not be considered a "stepping stone" to future political office. There was some grumbling among the county delegates that there were too many "former this and former thats" among the nominees and the final slate elected; indeed, all had been prominent in the precoup regime. Amos Sawyer, then dean of the University of Liberia and chair of the national commission which produced the draft constitution, has written that "Most of those selected to the assembly by the caucuses had either had close ties with the TWP [True Whig Party, for the previous hundred years the party in power] or were committed to TWP-style political practices. . . . In every Liberian community, there appears to be a standard list of individuals who are perennially available as 'leaders.' . . . If Liberia were declared a Marxist state, this group of 'leaders' would present themselves as members of the central committee and presidium. And if the tide were to change and Liberia became a fascist theocracy, the same clique will constitute the 'council of mullahs'" (1987a: 22).

In the case of Maryland County, the "leaders" selected included the principal of the public high school, the county planning officer, a former superintendent of schools and then president of the Maryland Farmers Cooperative Union, and the county attorney general. Some officials noted regretfully that there were no women and no young people among those selected.

It is hard to convey the experience of living through a "moral panic," but by the first week of July, dread and danger were palpable in Cape Palmas. Rumors were circulating wildly, centering on Hoffman Station, the "mission town" or "civilized town" of the local Glebo community. Significantly, Hoffman Station is historically associated with the "civilized natives," educated, professionally employed Glebo, many of whom had been closed out of the highest political offices under the TWP regime.

Also, Hoffman Station was the home of one of the newly elected delegates to the national assembly, specifically the high school principal. Reports of mysterious knocks on doors at night and of people being chased home in the dark by unseen pursuers were everywhere. Children who normally played throughout the community by moonlight or infrequent electrical current were locked up in houses at sunset by nervous parents. People talked in low voices about *bokyos*, the local term for "heartmen." A car was said to be parked by the newly elected delegate's house every night with its motor "running and running," ready to chase down victims. Such images of "technologically enhanced" witches equipped with cars and even airplanes are common elsewhere in Africa (Bastian 1993; Geschiere 1997; Shaw 1997, 2002). Reports were heard on the radio of near riots in the northern Liberian counties, and head of state Samuel K. Doe issued stern but contradictory warnings. There were no ritual killings, he insisted, only rumors, and those guilty of rumor mongering would be punished. On the other hand, the government insisted that ritual killers who *were* discovered would also be dealt with harshly. The minister of defense, a Glebo man from Cape Palmas, suggested that those found guilty of ritual murder should be executed by firing squad.

In Hoffman Station, tension was brought into the open when a case of false witness against a local man was brought to the Nyomowe Glebo paramount chief's court. A routine accusation of insult or slander would normally have been dealt with quickly and quietly, but this case concerned a native Glebo man who was accused of "naming the names" of several important civilized men as ritual killers. The case had actually been brought first to the county superintendent because the men who claimed they were falsely accused were civilized. The superintendent, however, sent it back to the paramount chief on the grounds that this was "native business." During the trial, which was attended by almost the entire community packed into the chief's parlor or hanging in through the windows, numerous witnesses testified that the accused had named prominent local men as *bokyos*, asserting that they were the ones "running behind people" at night. The accused man denied spreading rumors even when confronted with the parade of witnesses against him. He insisted that his allegations were true and that others were "covering up" for these powerful but dangerous men. One of the men he named was the high school principal who had just been elected to the national constitutional assembly. The accuser was sent to jail pending a full investigation, and suspicion remained focused around the two men he had named, the high school principal and newly elected delegate and his neighbor, a businessman who owned several drug stores and other small shops. These men complained plaintively that their children were being teased in school as the offspring of *bokyos*.

At my teaching job at the local technical college, I was questioned sharply by faculty and staff about my continued residence in Hoffman Station; likewise, the Harper market women with whom I was conducting interviews expressed concern for me in such a dangerous place. People seemed genuinely concerned for my safety, although opinion was divided almost evenly on whether the "parts" of white people were useless, or *especially* potent in making medicine to secure elective office. Disconcertingly, I was present at several hotly contested debates on the subject of whether I was the safest person in Cape Palmas or the most vulnerable. Street demonstrations by Pentecostal prayer bands became a regular feature in downtown Harper, calling on the citizens of Maryland County to repent and give up sin. Hoffman Station was becoming known as "*Bokyo* Town," and the list of names mentioned as suspects had grown to include the male heads of the most prominent civilized families. A Fanti man claimed to have been chased by a car in downtown Harper and escaped only by leaping into the river. In my neighborhood, a quarrel over a game of checkers nearly escalated into a riot when insults such as "rogue" and "*bokyo*" were loudly exchanged, turning out the whole community armed with clubs and machetes. Interestingly, people seemed to derive comfort from this reaction. "*Bokyos* and thieves are afraid of Hoffman Station, because the people can turn out fast!" I was also assured that such evildoers were afraid to operate in the native towns of the interior, because "those people would kill them quick" by setting a trap with a small child as bait.

A public meeting was called in Hoffman Station, at which local military officials warned against false accusations and promised that a company of soldiers would be sent to guard the town. The people found this ridiculous and said so; if the accusations were false, why did they need soldiers for protection? The general feeling seemed to be that the soldiers and officials were colluding to "let the killing go on." It must be remembered that all these events took place in the absence of any evidence that killing *was* going on. All the same, a church sermon in early August warned, "From now to '85 [the projected return to civilian rule] will not be easy. It is hard to get a man making money to give it up. But don't worry about all the positions to be filled in '85. Let God worry about filling them."

By late August, with the high school principal out of town at the national assembly, the fear seemed to have lessened. Not even the discovery of another drowning victim, also said to be missing his lips and tongue, generated much interest. It was clear that this episode was merely preliminary to the real opening of the political field in 1985. Tragically, since it could be supposed from this account that *reports* of ritual murder and its occurrence are quite different things, a few years later in 1986, two little boys, ages six and seven, were found dead and mutilated in

Harper. Local students led extensive demonstrations calling for the government to respond and accusing the local chairman of the governing National Democratic Party (created by Samuel Doe as a vehicle for his transformation from military to civilian leader). Cars and offices belonging to the NDP were burned and up to twenty-five people were arrested. Once again, the people of Cape Palmas demonstrated their willingness to use violence to call the national government to account. In an eerie parallel with the 1979 executions, six men including the county NDP chairman, a former mayor of Harper, the Maryland county attorney, a bank guard, an embalmer, and a butcher confessed, were convicted and publicly hanged for the crime (*New York Times,* May 4, 1987). But returning to the point about local practices as "systemic critique" of encroaching ideological systems, how may the events of 1983 be viewed in this light?

Representational democracy, as it has evolved in the West, makes certain assumptions about the ability of one individual to stand for or represent others. Constituents and their elected representatives are assumed to have interchangeable interests, in some fundamental sense. The representative inserts his/her body between the constituents and the state; through their representatives the desires and demands of the people are enacted on the national stage. Yet the concept of representation contains a paradox; how can one represent many, ignoring the diversity of their interests and glossing over the differences with an electoral mandate? The representative is not just a mediator but an usurper, one who claims the right to speak for the masses while remaining captured in a particularly gendered, class- and ethnic-defined body. In Chapter 1, we saw the culturally coded unwillingness of women to allow male representatives to make their case for them to the national government; the women protesting the national hut tax stopped to see the paramount chief as a courtesy for passing through his territory, not to ask him to intervene on their behalf. I would like to suggest that something similar may be at work here.

For close to one hundred and twenty years, indigenous Liberians had little or no representation in the formal political structure of the republic. The senators and representatives sent to Liberia's legislature were mostly of repatriate origin and members of the True Whig Party. Before the Tubman period Unification Policy, hinterland ethnic groups were allowed, for a fee, to send "observers" who might be consulted on issues related to their home regions but could not speak in congressional sessions (Liebenow 1987: 63–64). National elections in the one-party state occurred regularly, but as described by my informants in the opening pages of this chapter, the only candidates were carefully chosen TWP stalwarts. Some presidents claimed electoral mandates that greatly exceeded the known population of the country. How to explain the continued electoral success of a small minority who always seemed to win, no matter how anyone might vote?

The disjuncture between democratic ideals and political practice did not go unnoticed by ordinary Liberians, as demonstrated by the accounts of local and school elections above. Although knowledge and understanding of such mechanisms as described above was widespread, Liberians of all ethnic and class backgrounds also widely believed that at least one source of True Whig Party power lay in the practice of human sacrifice and ritual murder. Such sacrifices were believed to be carried out in the Masonic temples to which most Americo-Liberian men and all of the most important national and local officials belonged. Longstanding indigenous systems of sorcery include the metaphorical consumption of human victims; to "eat witch" is to practice deadly magical acts against others.

With the partial opening of the political field in Liberia in the 1950s and '60s, when the indigenous population was enfranchised and new congressional districts created, educated people of indigenous back ground could make claims for representation on the basis of Liberian citizenship. The association of ritual murder and electoral politics seems to date from this time (see Ellis 1999: 252–56). In Harper, local tensions reached a peak with the 1979 executions. For local sentiment to be so strong that the ruling elite allowed the execution of their own kinsmen to placate it tells us much about the delicate process by which the settler minority retained their power. In many Glebo homes, both civilized and native, a locally produced calendar from 1979 was still prominently displayed in 1982–83. This calendar featured closeup photographs of the condemned ritual murderers, both before and after their execution. In showing it to me, my friends emphasized two themes. The first was the fearsome reputation of Cape Palmas as the home of powerful witches; everyone in Liberia knows it, and fears the people from there. The second theme was that the conviction and punishment of such powerful members of the Americo-Liberian community represented a victory for justice, but came at the terrible cost of their murdered children. It was not at all clear that the supposed benefits of democracy and elections were worth this cost. The sense of having exposed the hypocrisy behind the electoral process and having forced Monrovia to acknowledge it was clear in newspaper accounts of the hangings, which reported that members of the crowd held up signs reading "President Tolbert Is a Man of the People, Maryland Thanks You," "Hail President Tolbert, He Is Fearless and Just," and "Moses Tweh (the victim of the killers) Is a Hero in Maryland, He Has Saved Us from These Witches" (*Express Special*, Monrovia, February 17, 1979). The paper also reported the great tension produced by the heightened security force sent from Monrovia to "protect" the accused from mob violence and the fears that the men would be "freed by a high commando unit" or pardoned at the last minute. The carrying out of the sentence was received with jubilation, drumming, and the dancing of the Glebo war dance, or *doklor*.

It was in this context that the military government's ban on political activities was viewed by many as a welcome hiatus. It is also significant that when the news of the 1980 coup reached Cape Palmas, the major target of the celebrating crowds was the Masonic Temple in the "up Cape" section of Harper. The temple, presumed to be the site of many past human sacrifices and thus the source of TWP power, was looted and burned. Located right across the street from the temple, the Maryland residence of the late W. V. S. Tubman, who had done most to consolidate the overwhelming power of the party through the cult of himself, was left untouched.

With the constitutional assembly of 1983, the fears and tensions about how power is produced through ritual murder were reopened, centering, not surprisingly, on the new group of indigenous professionals and businessmen poised to take advantage of the return to civilian rule. With ethnicity no longer the primary barrier to advancement, an even worse *bokyo* was on the loose, not a distant elite looking for the occasional sacrifice for his Masonic temple, but one who preyed on his own community. This analysis reverses one offered by Smith (2001) in his account of riots sparked by accusations of ritual murder in the Nigerian city of Owerri in 1996. Smith notes that historically witchcraft accusations have tended to be *between* kin and close associates; the Owerri case is striking for the lack of relations between the victims and the accused, who were all young "millionaires" who refused to take on the role of generous patrons. "Indeed, the impersonal, anonymous, and random nature of the evil acts these men allegedly perpetrated was popularly perceived to be one of the most troubling aspects of this 'new' brand of satanic practice" (2001a: 595; see also Smith 2001b). Liberians, it seems, had been dealing with reports of anonymous, random killers for many years during the TWP ascendency. Interestingly, the two men who were most frequently mentioned as Hoffman Station *bokyos* both lived in a section of the community known as "millionaire quarter." Taking the concept of "running for office" to its logical end, these candidates were "running behind" terrified townspeople, winning the right to speak for others by literally appropriating their lips and tongues. The individual voices, so central to indigenous ideas of democratic inclusion, are here appropriated through violence and mutilation. Rather than winning the hearts of potential constituents thorough promises, as we expect of politicians, these "heartmen" quite literally built their power through the extraction of hearts from human bodies.

Birgit Meyer has suggested that "talking about those in power in terms of the occult stems by no means from a failure to understand modern, allegedly secular politics. . . . I propose taking popular criticisms seriously as appropriate political statements rather than dismissing them as products of "false consciousness" far removed from political realities— the way more conventional political science discourse steeped in secularization theory would have it" (1998: 18). In this vein, I argue that Liberians view the secret of electoral success as located outside the electoral process. Ritual murder is recognized as both a horrendous *and* a pragmatic response to the structures of exclusion confronted by political aspirants in the 1970s and '80s and today. As in many postcolonial states, government office, or at least a civil service job, was the most reliable source of income in an economy in which the major extractive industries, iron mining and rubber and timber production, were controlled by foreign investors and the domestic secondary sector was all but nonexistent. The fragmented body became the means by which higher office, and the salary and opportunities which accompany it, were obtained, but the horror of this enterprise marked the whole arena of elections as evil and unnatural; the "systemic critique" of the concept of representation mentioned above.

It is particularly revealing that the targets of heartmen accusations during the 1983 constitutional process were civilized Glebo men; in some ways, this mirrors the demonizing of urban civilized women discussed in the previous chapter. Once again, the ambiguities of civilized status, the potential for both great gain and great harm, were emphasized. Like the parasitic civilized woman who deflects resources from the goal of national development, the local civilized "big men," poised to inherit the mantle of national leadership from the now-discredited Americo-Liberians, were failing to act in the interests of the common good. The heartmen not only steal the hearts of their victims, but the heart of the nation as well, mortgaging the dream of progressive political change and faith in democratic institutions, so poignantly expressed in the stories which opened this chapter, in favor of private and particularistic interests. At a one of the public meetings in Hoffman Station in 1983, the high school principal defended his reputation vigorously by listing his accomplishments and contributions to the church and the community. He did not need "medicine," he asserted to win public office because "I am fit for it!" and he challenged anyone who saw him "running behind someone" to "kill me on the spot!" Like the rural civilized women, he asserted the positive moral valence of his position with reference to the primary civilizing institutions of the church and the school.

In 1985, Liberia held the multiparty elections for which it had been preparing during my fieldwork. In spite of spite of serious harassment and violence from soldiers at the polls, huge numbers of Liberian men and women turned out to vote. Once again, their hopes were dashed. The military head of state, Samuel Doe, who had manipulated his own age in order to be constitutionally eligible to run for the presidency, announced that he had won the election with 50.1 percent of the vote. Exit polls revealed that, on the contrary, a civilian politician named Jackson Doe (no relation to Samuel) was the actual winner. Foreign news photographers published pictures of soldiers burning confiscated ballot boxes, but the Reagan administration state department certified the election as "free and fair," signaling its continued support for Doe as a Cold War ally.

Electoral "victory" did not render Doe immune to political challenge, however. Accusations of ritual murder continued against top government officials throughout the eighties. In 1989 General Gray Allison, Doe's Minister of Defense and the man who had suggested the firing squad for heartmen in 1983, was arrested and charged with ritual murder along with his wife and nine others, after a decapitated body with its heart removed was found on railroad tracks behind his house (*New York Times*, August 1989). The object of his occult practice, according to the indictment, was to gain "strong medicine" to use against his commander-in-chief.

From 1989 to 1997, over 200,000 Liberians were killed, 600,000 have lived as refugees in other countries, and 800,000 have been internally displaced (out of a prewar population of 2.5 million). As many as seven warring factions controlled various parts of the country, financing their operations by selling off natural resources like timber and diamonds, pressing children as young as seven and eight into their "armies," and using starving local populations as "bait" to attract donors of relief aid. Horrendous massacres of civilians have been recorded, and human rights organizations have documented the use of rape, torture, mutilation, and ritual cannibalism to instill terror in the civilian population. The old "heartman" scares of the 1970s and '80s faded to insignificance in comparison. Miraculously, in 1997, a working ceasefire with provisions for encampment and disarmament of the armed factions finally took hold. Elections were scheduled first for May 1997, then postponed to July when it became clear that not enough time had been allotted to secure weapons, return refugees, organize political parties, and set up an administration capable of registering voters and carrying out an election. Although many argued that the process was too rushed, both international agencies like the United Nations and the multinational African peacekeeping force which had been embroiled in Liberia for many years were anxious to have a resolution. Despite serious lack of equipment and organization and the bad timing of being held in the middle of rainy season, the

Liberian election of 1997 was apparently successful. Former U.S. President Jimmy Carter, whose Carter Center participated in the peace negotiations and who personally monitored the elections, reported the following: "We [he and his wife Rosalynn] were out early and witnessed by far the longest lines and most patient people we have ever seen. Many had slept at the polling sites and had been lined up as early as 2 a.m., and it seemed that almost all the registered voters were there when the polls opened at 7 a.m." Although the landslide winner, Charles Taylor, was the military adventurer who set off the civil war in 1989, the Carter Center and other observers concluded that the election was "a uniformly excellent process" (*Friends of Liberia Newsletter* 1997: 2).

Since I had a number of friends who participated as election observers for a variety of organizations, I asked them all to collect evidence of ritual murder accusations for me. Based on my earlier experience and given the large number of contesting parties, I assumed that the ambivalence with representational democracy would surface again, either in rumor or in practice, as it did in the '70s and '80s. I also monitored an e-mail network and Internet sites on Liberia. I was quite surprised to find no mention of heartmen in the foreign press reports. My friends in Liberia likewise found no references to heartmen in the local press nor among the people with whom they spoke. Rather, the press and the Nigerian commander of the multinational African force exhorted the population to refrain from partisan, rather than ritual, violence and threatened that anyone who reacted violently to the election results would be severely dealt with.

Other observers of ritual murder accusations in Africa have documented this form of popular critique and its relationship to political openings labeled "democratization." Geschiere and Nyamnjoh, in their analysis of Cameroon, argue that democratization and the advent of multiple political parties produce a new awareness of "to what extent the new opportunities for accumulation in the city can be legitimized within the rural setting" (1998: 71). Political reform intended to extend the franchise, they argue, gives village connections new importance for urbanites and opens the possibilities for rural people to demand their share of national resources. "In practice, democratization seems to engender fierce and often violent struggles over who 'really' belongs and who is a stranger" (71). Meyer likewise argues that rumors of ritual murder in Ghana "suggest that power may stem not from 'the people,' as the language of democracy claims, but from secret rites in a hidden room where it is generated in exchange for life and for the sake of personal profit" (1998: 25). In attempting to explain why such rumors did not appear during the 1997 Liberian election, it is important to understand how the long years of civilian atrocities had changed the context in which murder and dismemberment were understood. The power that accrued to heartmen came at least partly from the very horror of their deeds. Human body parts were needed for the medicines to achieve high office, but the aspirant had also to immerse himself in the process of obtaining them to prove his own heart was "strong enough" to operate such powerful forces. The very randomness and impersonality of "running behind" unlucky victims was part of the electoral candidates' potency. How was this to compare with the equally random and even more horrific (in terms of scale) massacre of over 600 civilian refugees in a Monrovia church in 1990, or of another two to three hundred refugees at the Carter Camp on the Firestone Plantation in 1993? Liberians exercised their right to vote in 1997 by choosing Charles Taylor, the most notorious heartman of all, in a deliberate attempt to stop those atrocities and in the full knowledge that "he killed my Pa, he killed my Ma; still I will vote for him." Since the object of Taylor's conduct of the war was to gain the presidency, he had already proved himself so powerful, so full of "witch business" that he could seem to bend international institutions like the United Nations and ECOWAS to his will.

Taylor deliberately manipulated his grisly reputation, referring to himself as "the most mischievous man in Liberia" in the full knowledge that "mischief" is a synonym for witchcraft in Liberian English. Furthermore, he demonstrated a profound understanding of the magical properties of an electoral mandate; one of his first acts after winning the election was to abrogate the provision of the Abuja II peace accords which provided that the Liberian military would be reorganized by international forces from ECOWAS. Arguing that, as the democratically elected president he was also commander-in-chief of the nation's armed forces, Taylor declared that to turn over this authority to outsiders would be to violate the constitution. Catching the international community in the contradictions of their own rhetoric of democracy, he was able to reconstitute his rebel army, the National Patriotic Front, as the Armed Forces of Liberia, bolstering his electoral victory without giving up the real source of his power. The United Nations and ECOWAS, committed to the goal of respecting the "will of the people" expressed through the ballot box, simply stood aside and allowed Taylor to institute his own security forces as the national army.

*   *   *

Just days after the election of 1997, while votes were still being counted, I spoke by phone with one of my foster brothers in Monrovia. He told me that Taylor had most certainly won, even though the final results had not yet been announced. When I expressed dismay, he said, "But why?

He's a nice man." Worried that he was afraid our conversation was being monitored, I did not press him for an explanation at that point, but found it hard to reconcile his statement with the experience of disrupted education, exile in refugee camps in Ivory Coast, loss of family members, and general impoverishment which I knew he had suffered during the war. A year later, he called me in a panic, desperate for money for a plane ticket to Ivory Coast. Taylor was using his reconstituted "national army" to move against his one of his former rivals, Roosevelt Johnson, and anyone associated with Johnson and his base in the ethnic Krahn region of the southeast was being picked up and "disappearing" from Monrovia. My brother had no connection to Johnson and was not Krahn, but it was not unusual for Grebo-speakers to be mistaken for Krahn, since the languages are similar and he had been told by someone that "his name was on a list." Desperate to get to the relative safety of Cape Palmas, he was afraid to travel overland for fear of government road blocks and planned to fly to Ivory Coast and reenter southeastern Liberia from there. After I assured him that I would wire him the money immediately, he reminded me of our conversation about the election. "You know, we were just hoping," he said, "that Taylor had been fighting for so long to be president, you know, that if we just gave it to him, he would be a good person. But we were wrong; elections can't make you a good person."

It is clear that indigenous Liberians clearly distinguish between *democracy* as a system in which all, even unequal, voices are heard, and *elections*, as a flawed and possibly illegitimate means of appropriating the voices of others. They are quite willing to fight for their right to self-determination, and to make demands on the central government knowing full well that to do so may unleash the violence of state power. They are also keenly aware that some individuals act violently to secure access to that power in ways that threaten individual lives and the nation as a whole. Charles Taylor took the logic of the heartman to such an extreme of bloodletting that to contest his supremacy in the 1997 election by claiming a few more victims was perceived as futile. It is of interest that since the most recent settlement in Liberia, which included Taylor's exile to Nigeria, there are increasing reports of heartman activity throughout the country. The current transitional government led by a Glebo civilian businessman, Guyde Bryant, has, like previous governments, condemned both the rumors and the actual events of ritual murder, but these are widely seen as almost inevitable in the runup to elections in 2005. Bryant, who has never been accused of ritual murder or of violence of any kind, does not present anything like the formidable threat posed by Taylor. As a result, Liberians no longer have a heartman for a president, but must live in fear of heartmen in their own communities; the enduring contradiction between "intimacy and inequality" identified by Geschiere (1997).

Chapter 5
The Lock on the Outhouse Door: Discourses of Development

What do people expect, in practical terms, of living in a democratic state? While political theorists may focus on elections, transparency, and good governance, for most poor, rural people in nonindustrialized countries, "democracy" is measured in more mundane amenities like clean running water or reliable electrical current. The close conceptual linkage between democracy and "development," which has become the catchall term for any form of economic diversification and the provision of what the West considers to be "basic services," grounds most neoliberal economic theory and a great deal of foreign policy. Only with democratization, it is assumed, can the incentives of the market be freed to work for the benefit of all. It is an article of faith that nondemocratic political structures, especially patrimonial or statist forms, have inhibited the growth of African economies and produced stagnation, misery, and despair (for examples see Bayart, Ellis, and Hibou 1999; Mamdani 1996). In this sense, the democratization of Africa is viewed as much more than free elections and civil rights; it is essential to lifting the poorest continent out of abject poverty and realizing the enormous potential of its material and human resources.

Charles Taylor, although the recipient of an impressive electoral mandate, failed to restore electricity to Monrovia during the seven years he held office. For this he was criticized far more roundly and regularly in the press than for his numerous and well-documented human rights violations. It is clear that what Richards has called the "structural violence of underdevelopment" and the sense of isolation and exclusion from modernity, civilization, and the routes of access to upward mobility, are powerful motivating factors for joining armed rebel movements, especially for young people (1996a, b; see also Utas 2003). The failed promises of what Diouf has called "the bankruptcy of the nationalist project of development" (2003: 4) were becoming apparent, as we have seen in

Chapter 3, in urban Liberia in the early 1980s and in rural areas as well. A baseline economic survey of Maryland County in 1982, prepared by the United Nations Development Program and based on interviews conducted in 32 rural villages throughout the county (with a total of 1,323 persons) found Maryland to be one of the least "developed" areas of Liberia. Depopulation due to out-migration had reached "alarming proportions," the agricultural labor force was aging and not replacing itself, many households could not provide themselves with food throughout the year, cash crop production (of cocoa, coffee, rubber, and sugar cane) had reached a "point of collapse" due to inadequate transportation and marketing, 75 percent of the population had no access to safe drinking water, and "more than half of the households do not use a latrine" (Bindels 1983: 1). During the boom years of the 1960s and '70s, low-skilled wage labor was available on the Firestone rubber plantations or the iron mines of the west, further draining the population of the rural southeast. By the early 1980s, however, most employment possibilities in these sectors had been reduced due to global recession, and both the government and external agencies like the UN were desperate to bring some modicum of "development" to the rural areas, if only to stem the constant swelling of cities like Monrovia.

In this context, the residents of Maryland County generally experienced development in two forms, or sets of defining practices. One was the "demonstration project," in which a government ministry or external agency would provide the materials and expertise to introduce some new feature to the community, hoping that it would be "adopted" by the people once its benefits were clear. Such projects varied from genetically engineered rice and poultry to latrines, low-fuel stoves, and pump-driven wells. The other form in which "development" was manifest was in a process of extraction by which poor people were solicited for funds, ostensibly to be used for their own benefit; to build a clinic, school, or road, for example. Both of these development practices invoked explicit values of democratic participation, local decisionmaking, and self-sufficiency. Both forms also contained at least the risk of some form of violence.

In the course of fieldwork in Maryland County, I often traveled into the interior, sometimes with my foster father, and briefly visited a number of small Grebo communities that were at least accessible by the unpaved road that traveled, eventually, all the way to Monrovia. In almost every small rural town, there was a standard pattern to my welcome: a visit to the chief and some of his elders, the consumption of kola nut and palm wine or raw local rum ("cane juice"), no matter how early in the morning, followed by an invitation to inspect "our development project." Inevitably, this would turn out to be a latrine, sometimes perched above a water source, constructed (if it was a truly "modern" development project) out of cement blocks. Each demonstration latrine that I observed also had a stout door securely locked with a large padlock. Why the lock? I often asked. Wasn't the latrine for the use of all the people? Oh no, this was to be used only by the chief, and important visitors (like me); to have such an amenity available for visiting dignitaries was a symbol of the integration of the village into the Liberian state, a link to the promise of national development for all. But for now, the lock remained on the door, the majority of people had to be content to use the bush to relieve themselves. The outhouse, used or unused, was clearly a source a of pride, however, and a hopeful promise of more "development" to come. Often the newest and most substantial structure in the village, it was, like the chief's government-issued Liberian flag, a tangible symbol of the presence of the state in a remote place.

The failure of such projects actually to change local behavior was not unnoticed by development planners. The UNDP baseline survey cited above complains bitterly that, in spite of concerted efforts toward health education, even local school teachers, often the lone representatives of "civilization" in rural communities, could not be prevailed upon to adopt Western sanitary standards. "What is astonishing is that quite a good number of educators, teachers, are not convinced of the argument for the building of a latrine, or prefer the risk of an infection above the tedious work of digging the pit, and tolerating the smell of an open latrine. . . . Most of the latrines built are frightening and outright dangerous for use by the visitor" (Bindels 1983: 36–37). The curious equation of privatizing and controlling human elimination with modernity has been noted in numerous times and places (Frykman and Lofgren 1987; Appadurai 2002: 38–39). What is most fascinating about the lock on the outhouse door is the jarring combination of development with exclusion; the opposite of democratic equality of access. While expatriate theorists may see an obvious connection between development and democracy, and while these terms are constantly and inevitably linked in political rhetoric, it is not clear that the local experience in any way confirms this alliance. On the contrary, the staging of "development events," both in rural areas and in regional centers like Harper, makes visible the new and increasing forms of economic differentiation which challenge indigenous ideals of equality. In particular, these projects and performances depend on the ability of local and national elites to demonstrate their control over resources, both material and symbolic, and to emphasize relations of dependency and patronage.

In the pre-civil war decades of the 1970s and '80s, the prevailing ideology in development practice included an emphasis on local participation. Communities were encouraged to form development committees and to "define their own priorities." Such invitations could often backfire, however, as when local desires did not conform to external definitions of development. In one coastal Glebo town, the UNDP Self-Help Village Development Project initiated discussions with the community to determine their list of development priorities. The expatriate planners worked hard to make sure that discussions would include the input of women and young people, although they seemed to think that this was a genuine innovation, not recognizing that institutionalized means of providing for the voices of subordinate groups already existed. The request to the UN staff which emerged from this democratic process, however, presented a dilemma: the community had determined that their most pressing need was new band instruments for their town brass band.

Glebo brass bands have their origin in the migratory labor experience of southeastern men on European ships along the West African coast during the eighteenth and nineteenth centuries (see Brooks 1972; Frost 1999). Several generations of men from this region worked on contract for European employers, bringing home their wages in the form of consumer goods and incorporating aspects of naval military ritual into local practice. Brooks cites one account by a French traveler on the upper Cavalla River in 1895 of a band of young men, dressed as British sailors, "who preceded the chief and executed formations to the blowing of a whistle" (1972: 68). Brass band performance, utilizing trumpets, French horns, tubas, and trombones, had by the twentieth century become an essential element of many Glebo ceremonies, particularly funerals. The music played on these instruments, consisting of repeated phrases, echoes the drum rhythms performed on more traditional instruments for the "war dances" honoring the dead. Men who can play these instruments have high status and are well paid for their work; many Glebo join burial insurance societies, paying a small amount each week or month into a fund that will be used to provide several days of music at their funeral. Most of the instruments I saw in the field certainly looked well worn (although lovingly taken care of), and musicians often complained that their instruments needed repair or replacement. It is therefore not surprising that one community determined that new band instruments constituted their highest development priority.

From the point of view of the expatriate development workers, this was a request that was impossible to meet. "It's not economic" one explained, arguing that UN funds could only be spent on items that would contribute to infrastructure or produce some recognizable form of material value. From the perspective of the community, however, band performances did have an economic benefit. Funerals, particularly lavish ones, bring many visitors into town, even if they have migrated to distant regions in search of employment, to enjoy the music and dancing. The returnees might make purchases from local vendors and will most certainly give gifts of cash to their rural relatives. The band members benefit as individuals from the supplement to their income, and since most bands consist of at least ten men, this can have a significant impact on a community of year-round residents numbering under three hundred. The populace as a whole benefits from their enjoyment of the music, at funerals as well as national holidays like Independence Day, when chiefs or visiting dignitaries sponsor band performances, as well as from the prestige accruing to a village whose band is well equipped and proficient. In sum, the request for band instruments was a far more "democratic" development request than a locked latrine used only by important visitors.

The development workers made several attempts to convince the community to alter their request, but eventually moved on to another town which was simply told that they would receive a new well and pump. This was accepted, although with a certain amount of cynicism. "It will break," one informant predicted, "and they won't be able to get the parts to fix it." The pretense of democratic participation in decisionmaking was simply stripped away in the interest of efficiency. Like the lock on the outhouse door, the unwillingness to *really* engage with local priorities reveals the disjuncture between democracy and development and highlights exclusion and stratification rather than participation for all. I do not mean to disparage the hard work and sincere commitment of the many development workers, both foreign and Liberian, who have struggled to provide rural populations with safe water, to reduce infant and child mortality, and to enhance rural incomes. The UNDP report was correct in documenting the grinding poverty and constant struggle to eke out a living faced by both rural and urban Marylanders in the 1980s. I am arguing, however, that the experience of being subject to "development" during this time was more similar to the process of forcible state incorporation than to democratic inclusion in a national project, no matter how many times those terms were conflated.

While rural villagers encountered development primarily as receivers of demonstration projects, another form of development work characterized the more urbanized coastal areas and civilized communities of Cape Palmas. A category of events known as rallies, or public competitive fund raising programs similar to the American telethon, were the primary venue in which discourses of development were manifest. A subset of these events, the "queen rally," married the popular form of the Western beauty contest to a fundraiser. While the specific history of queen rallies is unknown, Lawrence Breitborde's informants in the mid-1970s reported that they had been practiced since at least the midtwentieth century (1977: 234). Widely employed by churches, schools, and other private organizations for the support of their own activities, most rallies are explicitly nationalist events because the money they raise is earmarked for local and national "development," usually infrastructure like roads, buildings, libraries, public works projects, and so on. One of the largest public marketplaces in Monrovia is called the "Rally Time" market because the funds which built it were raised in this manner. Nationwide rallies during the sixties and seventies included "voluntary" contributions from all civil servants, conveniently withheld from their paychecks. Of course, in theory, taxpaying citizens should have public infrastructure provided for them by the state without being solicited for additional donations. "Development rallies" are therefore an odd commentary on the failure of the central government to fulfill its part of the bargain for local allegiance.

This observation is not meant to imply that centralized tax collection is either the best or most efficient means of allocating resources to such projects. Liberian citizens, like those of many postcolonial states, however, found themselves both taxed *and* exhorted by their national governments to provide for their own local development needs without expecting the state to "do everything for them." As we shall see in the following examples, the tension between the ideal of "development" as a collaborative, integrative project incorporating the locality and the nation and the actual unwillingness of the state to direct resources to rural areas or to engage seriously with local priorities emerges quite definitively in the queen rallies I observed in Harper in the 1980s.

Queen rallies are a form of public entertainment as well as serving the practical purpose of resource accumulation. In the standard format, the contestants, or "queens," often represent specific local constituencies and are introduced and displayed briefly to the audience before being seated at a long table. On the table in front of each contestant is a bowl to hold donations; the audience members pass in a line along the table, placing their donations in each bowl, with the largest amount going to their favorite. The queen who generates the highest total is the winner and is crowned and paraded through the streets by her supporters.

On the superficial level, the queen rally does resemble a beauty contest; the language of the introduction emphasizes the beauty of the queens and the fineness of their clothes. They usually walk back and forth before the audience so everyone can get a good look at them before taking their seats behind the table. Such promenades also take place between "rounds" of giving, on the premise that the beauty of a particular woman may cause some to change their minds and switch allegiance at the last moment. Yet, in another sense, the Liberian version inverts the standard form of the international beauty pageant, in which women move and perform before a seated audience and (usually) male judges. In this instance, it is the sponsoring constituencies which are "on stage," demonstrating their wealth, prestige, and organizational skills. The women are essentially passive tokens; they *represent* the competing groups without actually competing themselves.

In fact, a close analysis makes clear that a woman's age or physical appearance usually has little or nothing to do with her following. Breitborde, in his linguistic analysis of a series of queen rallies from Monrovia, reports that one church youth group entered a woman in her fifties as their queen (1977: 236). The exception would perhaps be small rallies held by competing high school classes, which may turn on differences in the locally defined attractiveness or popularity of the queens themselves. So widespread is this form of fundraising, by the way, that I have seen mixed-sex groups of young children playing queen rally; setting up a row of little girls, placing stones, representing coins, in tin cans, crowning the winner with a bit of tin foil, and parading her around the neighborhood in a wheelbarrow.

In the following analysis, I will argue that queen rallies have come to be linked inextricably with notions of progress and development. The format of the beauty contest operates internationally and cross-culturally within a discourse of evolutionary change that includes a hierarchical understanding of the relationship between center and periphery. This implicit evolutionary model assumes that economic and infrastructural alterations in the countryside will inevitably result in lifestyle changes, bringing rural populations into contact with national and global cultural practices. For a small locality, far from the national capital, the act of sponsoring beauty pageants signals the acceptance of a number of "foreign" but recognizably advanced, civilized, or modern ideas, including putting women on public display, which may contradict local sentiments. It is an enactment of the aspirations of local elites, usually men, and may therefore provide a site of contest for differing notions of nationalism and national identity. Displacing these highly charged contests onto something which is both, as Lavenda (1988) notes, "deadly serious" and simultaneously utterly trivial, means that none of the real competitors has to take a dangerous stand in opposition to state power. Using women's bodies as camouflage, local elites and their national allies can literally experiment with different combinations of class and ethnic blocks, exposing lines of cleavage in the community and deliberately pitting them against each other. But in the end, the winners and losers are only powerless young women, obviously no threat to anyone.

Since Liberian queen rallies were not defined as "political" events (and continued throughout the early 1980s ban on "political activities" issued by the military government), they usually allowed any semiorganized collectivity to enter and compete on an equal basis. In the contrast between successive years, discussed below, we see the implications of limiting participation to groups representing only one kind of social identity, specifically, ethnicity. It is here that some of the earliest warning signs of the coming Liberian civil war were to be found.

The following analysis will consider two queen rallies from consecutive years, 1982 and 1983, which took place in the Maryland County capital of Harper. Both rallies were held as part of the celebration of former president Tubman's birthday, a national holiday. As noted above, the southeastern counties of Liberia are the poorest and least integrated into the national economy of all Liberia's regions. Although only a few hundred miles from Monrovia, lack of all-weather roads makes the overland trip between the national capital and Harper a grueling two days.

Like the other Liberian coastal towns which began as settler enclaves, Harper became over time a multiethnic service center for the surrounding county. The dominant economic and political class consisted of descendants of the American settlers and a few highly educated professionals of indigenous Glebo origin who were recognized as civilized. Most import-export trade and local retailing were controlled by a few hundred Lebanese citizens, some of whom had lived in Harper for most of their lives. Barred from citizenship by the Liberian constitution (which limits naturalization to those of at least one-eighth African descent), they could play no official political role but held considerable economic power. The majority of Harper's population was drawn from the southeastern Liberian ethnic groups, with a small number of Muslim traders from the north, and another group of resident aliens, the Fanti people of Ghana, who specialized in offshore fishing. The population in 1982–83 was estimated at between ten and twelve thousand people, not including the surrounding Glebo towns and villages (Moran 1990: 74).

W. V. S. Tubman, the national hero whose birthday was being celebrated, was born in Harper and was the first non-Monrovian to become president of the Republic of Liberia. The descendant of freed slaves from Georgia, Tubman ruled Liberia from 1944 until his death in office in 1971 as president and head of the single political party, the True Whig Party. His home town benefited from his generosity, receiving a great deal of infrastructure and impressive public buildings. Much of this was eroded under the administration of his successor, William Tolbert, when power was transferred back into the hands of the Monrovia-based settler families. Since Tubman had presided over a period of unprecedented growth in the Liberian economy and was associated with popular reforms such as the enfranchisement of the indigenous population, his birthday, November 29, continued to be celebrated as a national holiday after his death. The military coup of 1980, while ostensibly directed against the entrenched power of the True Whig Party, never challenged the mystique and affection surrounding Tubman's memory. Although, since the coup, political authority in Harper and elsewhere had been transferred to young army officers of local indigenous origin, Tubman's birthday remained a national holiday and was celebrated in Harper with an especially elaborate three-day program of events.

In 1982, still in the first months of fieldwork, I first heard the upcoming "Birthday Queen Rally" being discussed by the city market women. The "chief" of the market women, herself an important city official and member of the military mayor's advisory board, was exhorting the other marketeers to "support our queen." Another market seller, a member of one of the Islamic ethnic groups who are resident aliens in the southeast, told me that she was "looking for a little girl" to be a queen and trying to raise money among her compatriots "for the clothes." From these conversations, I came to understand that a queen rally was an annual and highly anticipated part of "the Birthday" celebrations and that it required a great deal of preparation. It was also clear that women were important organizers and actors in the behind-the-scenes management of major queen rallies.

The rally was held in the evening at Harper City Hall, an elaborate product of the Tubman era. My estimate of the size of the crowd was something over 700 people, packed into a large ballroom on the second floor. A local brass band played at the rear of the room and a "cultural troupe" performed an idealized version of local indigenous dances. A master of ceremonies introduced the three queens who had been formally entered in the contest: a very young girl (perhaps twelve years old) representing the Lebanese business community, a young woman in a blue evening gown representing Harper city, and a queen for "Marylanders Outside of Maryland." This woman, a member of a local Glebo family who was now stationed with the national police in a distant, northwestern county of Liberia, was herself a "Marylander outside of Maryland" who had come to visit her family for the holiday. Her support came from a group of government officials, including a few cabinet ministers, who were originally from the Harper area and had also come "home" to celebrate. They included the Minister of Youth and Sports, the Minister of Rural Development, both members of local indigenous groups, as well as military officers, university students, and others who had "come for the Birthday." The Minister of Justice, a member of the illustrious Tubman family, was also in attendance. It is important to note that the "Marylanders Outside of Maryland" did not constitute a permanent organized group, but had formed from the random "homecomers" specifically for the purposes of the queen rally.

The master of ceremonies called on three other nonlocal resident constituencies, the Fullah and Mandingo (both Islamic groups who are traders) and the Fanti, to put forth queens. Finding no organized response, the M.C. simply asked for volunteers. Three women representing these "stranger" groups were prevailed upon to enter the contest. The audience was repeatedly reminded that they were chosen at the last moment and so had not come "prepared to sit" (that is, elaborately dressed). An additional queen was entered by a soccer team made up of more expatriate Marylanders, mostly university students living in Monrovia. This brought the number of queens in the rally to seven, representing the Lebanese, Harper city, the Marylanders Outside of Maryland, the Fullah, the Mandingo, the Fanti, and the soccer team. The chief of the market women arranged bolts of beautiful and expensive cloth, symbolizing wealth and royalty, over the backs of the chairs on which the queens were seated and on the floor in front of the table. The M.C. announced that there would be three fifteen-minute "rounds" during which contributions to the bowls in front of each queen could be made. The band struck up, and the rally began.

The contributors who approached the queens in the first round were primarily the important visitors from Monrovia, local officials, and business people, including the Lebanese shopowners and prominent market women. The hundreds of people crowding the back of the hall looked on with interest, but did not offer cash. At the end of the first round, proceeds were counted and the Lebanese queen was ahead with over one hundred dollars, followed by the expatriate Marylanders and the Harper City queen. The partisans of each queen were exhorted to "bring money" for the second round. The band played as contributors literally danced across the platform before the queens. As the competition heightened, the market women dropped out and the contributors became exclusively men.

In the second round, the expatriate Maryland contingent made a stronger showing. With support from the three cabinet ministers, the policewoman moved into first place, passing the Lebanese queen. The Harper City queen lagged far behind, in spite of backing from local Harper officials, the county superintendent, and the market women. The third and final round was shaping up as a battle between the local Lebanese business community and the national government officials from Monrovia.

Indeed, during the last round, both the crowd and the participants seemed gripped by a frenzy of excitement. Young men of the Lebanese community pulled packets of bills from their pockets, waved them dramatically in the air, and slammed them on the table before their queen. The Monrovia contingent followed suit with the crowd whooping encouragement. Since U.S. currency was used in Liberia at the time and there were few large denominations in circulation, substantial contributions were made in thick wads of one-, five-, and ten-dollar bills. The sheer abundance of currency on the table seemed to whip up the crowd as they stamped and cheered with each new contribution. The Maryland County superintendent made a valiant effort to generate support for the Harper queen, but attention was riveted elsewhere.

The Minister of Youth and Sports announced that the expatriate Marylanders intended to "carry the queen" and challenged the crowd by offering to double any amount given to the Harper queen in the next ten minutes. He was wildly cheered, but no one took him up on his offer. The last round ended and the M.C. and the queens began counting the money. The room was tense as people speculated about who had won.

The Minister of Youth and Sports was to announce the winner, but first he delivered a lecture, criticizing the local people for not participating, just sitting back and letting the "Monrovia people" do everything for them. They must take their development on their own shoulders, he insisted. Tubman was dead, he reminded them, and they couldn't look to him for help any more. They should take the Lebanese community, the Minister continued, as an example; they were, after all, "strangers," yet they had done their part for the development of Maryland County. With that, he announced that the expatriate Marylanders had won, beating the Lebanese by just ten dollars (which no one, especially the Lebanese, really believed). The total amount raised was $2,910.10; the expatriate Maryland queen bringing in $1,089.00, the Lebanese queen $1,079.00, the Harper queen $400.00, and the soccer team queen, the Fanti, Fullah, and Mandingo queens $100 or less apiece.

The winning queen was crowned with a gold paper crown. She commented that she would take the crown back with her to Nimba County and tell all the Marylanders there what had happened. She added that she hoped that next year the crown would stay in Maryland. The County superintendent reminded the visiting ministers that the lack of participation was not due to "deficiencies in spirit, but in means." In his travels around the country, he had noted that recent declines in the national economy seemed to have hit the southeast more severely than anywhere else, and he emphasized the necessity of help from Monrovia. He then collected the evening's proceeds, announced that it would be put to use on some as yet undisclosed development project, and the queen rally was over. Note that simply by invoking the theme of "development," the superintendent was able both to link the event which had just transpired to the nationalist project *and* to avoid specifying the use to which the money would be put.

Exactly one year later, many of the same participants were gathered in the same hall for the 1983 Tubman Birthday Queen Rally. There were, however, notable exceptions and significant changes from the previous year. The Lebanese community, convinced that they had been the victims of a deliberate miscount, declined to put forward a queen. The queen rally was now in combination with a fashion show, sponsored by the "Women of Harper." Glebo informants referred to these women as "the married women in town," meaning respectable, civilized, middle class and wealthy women, primarily of settler background, although the "barely civilized" young wife of the superintendent was prominently listed. This year, an admission fee was charged at the door, perhaps to discourage the large crowd of nonparticipants from the year before.

There had been much anticipation that Samuel K. Doe, the military head of state, would appear at the queen rally; he was in Harper for the holiday and had participated in a development rally just that morning, in which he had personally pledged $12,000. Apparently, one rally a day was enough for the head of state, but the deputy vice head of state, the speaker for the military government, and several other military and civilian cabinet members were in attendance. The most significant change was in the constituencies represented by the queens. They were now identified with officially recognized Liberian "tribes"—Kru, Grebo, Bassa, Krahn (the group to which the head of state belonged), Fanti, and a "Muslim queen" for the Fullah and Mandingo combined. The master of ceremonies explained that the queens represented "some of the tribes in Liberia and two from outside," meaning the Fanti and the "Muslims." The attire of the queens ranged from evening gowns and bouffant wigs to a modified version of the white paint and minimal clothing of a Sande bush school initiate. The latter was apparently an effort to incorporate a "tribal" understanding of feminine beauty, but was strangely misplaced since the Sande secret society does not exist in the southeast.

After the first round, in which all the queens averaged about sixty dollars, the Fanti queen was leading. In between rounds, the fashion show, with clothing modeled by prominent Harper women, drew more attention than the queens. In fact, it was the fashion show which most relentlessly followed the Western model of a beauty contest, since the women modeled a number of revealing outfits, including shorts and bathing suits, which were considered quite daring in a provincial community like Harper. In the second round there was a pronounced lack of enthusiasm, demonstrated by the fact that the queens only averaged about ten or eleven dollars each from the round. A local official appealed to the crowd, pleading that the Grebo queen (representing the local population) *must* "carry the crown"; they must not lose to "foreigners." Those in the crowd murmured that if they had not been charged admission at the door, there would be more for the queens.

The third round was a bit more spirited and larger amounts of cash began to appear on the table. It was clear that many had been "holding back" for the last round. In the end, the Grebo queen won the round but not the rally; the Fanti "carried the queen" with a little over three hundred dollars. After the queen was crowned, one of the cabinet ministers made a speech warning, ironically, against "tribalism and sectionalism." The event ended with the Fanti literally carrying their queen in triumph through the streets of Harper for most of the night. I learned later that they had coordinated their efforts, pooling money from many small contributions and holding it back until the last round in a concerted effort to win.

What accounts for the differences between these two consecutive queen rallies? In neither case was the sponsoring locality successful in winning the competition, but is winning, after all, the objective of holding a queen rally? The goal of the rally, from the perspective of the organizers, is to raise money: money that is destined to link the locality to the national project of development. In the 1982 rally, the three primary competing groups represented essentially *class interests*. The expatriate Marylanders were the new national elite; people with roots and loyalties in the rural, indigenous sector, but who had only recently gained access to all the resources of the state. The local elite, those who lined up in support of the Harper queen, had fewer resources to command. Their salaries, positions, and lifestyle, as well as their ability to carry out their jobs, were dependent upon a continuing flow of cash and services from Monrovia. Even the market women, while less directly dependent on government salaries, must respond to the constraints of the local economy. If the contributions made by visiting national elites, both in such structured events as rallies and on a more informal basis in the form of gifts, remittances to local kin, and purchases made on trips "home" are considered part of the local economy, it was in the interest of local elites at the 1982 rally to promote competition between the expatriates and the Lebanese, even at the expense of their own pride. The Lebanese were in a vulnerable position as resident aliens, who could not transform their considerable economic power into overt political clout. Once the limit to competitive giving had been reached and someone had to win, local elites had more to lose by offending the Monrovia officials than the Lebanese business community. The Lebanese perception that they had been cheated was probably correct.

During the intervening year between November of 1982 and 1983, the Liberian economy continued to slide downward. Harper city infrastructure deteriorated even further, with electrical power only a distant memory and the provision of purified water at public taps sporadic at best. Popular support for the military government, still relatively high in 1982, was on the wane a year later. An attempted coup, just a few weeks before the Birthday celebration, had shaken the country and produced some amazement that the head of state would risk leaving the capital for a trip to Maryland County. To ensure his security, large numbers of soldiers and military equipment had accompanied him to Harper, giving the town the appearance of a siege. Unnerved by the coup attempt, the soldiers were edgy and continually harassed the local population, destroying the holiday mood for everyone.

Another factor was the "feminization" of the queen rally from 1982 to 1983. In 1982, although there were other rallies associated with particular projects held during the Tubman Birthday holiday, the City Hall queen rally was the major fundraising event for local development. Although the women represented various constituencies, the 1982 rally was clearly and obviously the primary arena for male prestige competition (excluding the organized sports) of the holiday events. In 1983, in connection with the head of state's visit, a major development rally was held during the day (possibly for security reasons, to avoid traveling after dark), which combined speeches by local leaders and an address by Doe. Individual pledges were announced by local business leaders and officials and Marylanders in government and the military in amounts ranging from ten to two thousand dollars. With Doe's personal pledge of twelve thousand, something over thirty thousand dollars, at least in pledges, had been raised for Maryland development that morning, with ample opportunity for all to demonstrate their wealth and generosity. There was not much cash or inclination for a second rally that night.

In addition, the fashion show and sponsoring group organizing the 1983 queen rally stamped it as a "woman's event." There were many more women in attendance than had been at the morning development rally and, having less access to cash than men, they had less to give. The class identity of the women organizers had also changed from 1982 to 1983. The market women, always resolutely native, had been specifically recruited by the military mayor of Harper to organize the event in 1982. In 1983, it was civilized women who were asked to take charge. While civilized women, as the consorts of powerful men, have considerably higher status than the native market women, they also, ironically, have less right to allocate cash, even in relatively wealthy households (see Moran 1990). While the role of the market women had been tacitly acknowledged in 1982, their relative invisibility in the actual performance marked the queen rally as a prestigious "civic" event. In contrast, the explicit visibility of women as organizers and sponsors (and as fashion models) in the 1983 queen rally emphasized its lack of prestige in the overall Birthday celebration.

The organization of the queens by ethnic group was probably designed to extract a large sum from the head of state in support of "his" Krahn queen. Without his presence, there was not enough ethnic competition to generate anything like the excitement of the previous year. The restriction on competing groups to represent themselves only as "tribes" eliminated the possibility of last-minute entries, like the soccer team queen, which had lent excitement the year before. This strategy also enforced a homogenized, inclusive ethnicity which had little relevance to the actual sociopolitical realities of southeastern Liberia, as in the conflation of ethnic groups to produce a "Muslim queen" and the loading together of many competing local identities onto the queen representing the "Grebo." The cabinet members who were present seemed much less willing to identify themselves with these so-called ethnic groups than they had along class lines the year before. The only appeal which seemed to move the crowd was a defensive one against "foreigners" (the Fanti). In the end, no one seemed very upset when the Fanti "carried the queen."

In practical terms, the admission fee charged for the 1983 queen rally may have made up for the low donations collected during the rally itself. I do not wish to speculate about what actually happened to the proceeds from rallies like these; certainly, Maryland County and Harper city infrastructure seemed to see little of it. It is important to view such events as not just reflective of local politics, however, but as structured in crucial ways by national events and the relationships national leaders have with those still in their communities of origin. Deeply held Liberian values concerning loyalty to a patrilineally defined "home," the generosity expected of the wealthy, and the ties of personal obligation were all enacted in the queen rallies and constrained individual choices about giving and not giving. Furthermore, the 1982 rally came at a time when new elites of indigenous background, both national and local, could still see themselves as having finally come into their own after generations of subordination to the settler minority. Education, technical knowledge, and connections to the new leadership really did seem to be what mattered most in the newly opened field of opportunities created by the 1980 coup.

Under settler hegemony, simply being of "tribal" origin was the important distinguishing factor; membership in a particular ethnic group was not considered important in terms of socioeconomic mobility. Fearful of ambitious young soldiers like himself, Samuel Doe began the systematic purge of all but members of his own Krahn region from the ranks of the elite military forces and strategic government posts. While the original post-coup cabinet had been truly multiethnic, even including prominent Americo-Liberians like Justice Minister Tubman, by 1983 a Krahn power block was emerging which owed its existence and its allegiance to Doe alone. Only two years later, in 1985, Doe would retaliate against the already dead leader of an unsuccessful coup by massacring about 400 random members of his home community. This brutality prompted the formation of ethnically defined resistance groups, with no political ideology beyond opposition to Doe and led by men like Charles Taylor, whose sole ambition was to gain control of the apparatus of the state. These resurgent ethnic identities continue to define armed factions in Liberia into the present.

* * *

With the benefit of hindsight, it is tempting to view the switch from class to "tribal" identification for the Harper queens as an ominous portent of what was to come. While the local officials who organized the rallies may have been merely trying to extract the largest possible donations, as I have suggested, they were also certainly aware of the prevailing trends in Monrovia. Although the national officials delivered their cliched warnings about "tribalism," they were themselves complicit, along with the local elites, in the manufacture of ethnicity as an overriding category of identification. The queen rallies may thus be read as a public discourse about political and economic power, national ideology, and personal identity as these are negotiated between the central government and the locality, often by individuals with ties in both places. In the local context, such divisions could be highlighted in a setting that was safely defined as apolitical, slightly frivolous, and "women's business." In this sense, the queen rallies provided a forum for expression and competition that was simply unavailable elsewhere. Translated into national policy, however, these newly fabricated tribal identities could not be contained by mapping them onto the bodies of young women. A few years later, they would explode into real violence and ethnic massacres.

In spite of these dispiriting encounters with the practices of development, Liberians remain committed to the concept, as they do to the concept of democracy. Development rallies, with or without queens, continued to be held throughout the dark days of the civil war and are practiced by expatriate organizations in the United States. An announcement from the Rhode Island chapter of the Tappita District Development Association invited all "sons, daughters, friends of the District, and all development-loving people" to a fundraiser rally to benefit a new school building (Friends of Liberia News Network, November 26, 2002), just one example among many. Regional self-help groups have transformed themselves into relief and reconstruction programs, as the extent of infrastructural damage caused by the war becomes clear. Liberians, rural and urban, continue to value the complex of associations development entails, but they know from experience that it is not "democratic" in its effects.

Chapter 6
The Crisis of Youth and the Promise of the Future

For most of the sixteen months that I lived in Liberia in the early 1980s, I lived in an extended household of "civilized Glebo" in the community of Hoffman Station, outside Harper city, Maryland County. The male head of the household, the *kai bua* or "house father," was an ordained Episcopal priest and pastor of St. James Church, the original "Glebo church" of Cape Palmas. His wife, from a prominent family in the town of Waa (Fishtown), his mother-in-law, four sons, nephew, granddaughter, and several foster children or "servants," along with the resident anthropologist, completed the household. At the time, the four sons, survivors of a total of eleven children born to the couple, were aged twenty-three, fourteen, twelve, and six. The oldest, a high school graduate, was employed as a clerk in the circuit court in Harper; although he had fathered two children by different women, he lived in his parents' home and cultivated the identity of young bachelor about town. Due to the closeness of our ages, he and I often talked about "youth" issues, sometimes went dancing together at the local disco, and carried on a bantering, teasing relationship consistent with our fictive roles as brother and sister. When the mother of his infant son began calling me by the kin term for "husband's older sister," it was greeted by the family and neighbors with both hilarity and some ambivalence. The young man's parents certainly hoped that he would settle down, even marry the young woman, but also felt she was using me to deliver a rather a broad hint that she presumptuously thought herself already a member of the family. This young man died by drowning, under mysterious circumstances, during the early years of the civil war.

The youngest brother, at age six, was a sweet child just beginning school. With paper and markers, I made him a set of alphabet flash cards and worked with him in the evenings, taking great satisfaction as he progressed to fluent reading during the course of the year. He often napped with me on a mat on the veranda during the heat of the day or slept part of the night in my room, curled up like a small warm puppy against my back. As I write, he is a young man in his twenties, struggling to complete his university education in the chaos of contemporary Liberia. But it was the middle brothers, the fourteen- and twelve-year-olds, their fifteen-year-old patrilateral cousin, who lived with us, and two matrilateral cousins, also in their early teens and living nearby, that I probably spent more time with than anyone else in Liberia.

Outside school hours, these five boys were my constant companions, language teachers, interpreters, interlocutors, and guides to the surrounding area. When the family spent several weeks in Monrovia during the school vacation, the neighbors commented that I must be very lonely without the "children." Although I employed several adult women as census assistants, it was mostly through the eyes and ears of these boys that I tested my hesitant understanding of witchcraft trials, funeral ceremonies, church sermons, and other events conducted in the Glebo language. I was drawn into their squabbles with each other, with other established peer groups of boys and girls, and most especially with the primary disciplinary force in their lives, their mother. I slipped them money for snacks, treated them to swimming excursions at the "tourist" hotel in Harper (where you had to buy expensive soft drinks in exchange for using the beach), and bought them new sneakers for the start of the school year. They borrowed my bicycle, my boots, my clothes, my typewriter, and my medical supplies. When I brought them a soccer ball from one of my trips to Monrovia, they immediately formed a team, named after me, Siede's Invaders (Siede is my Glebo name), and their mother almost killed me, despairing of ever getting them to stop playing and do their chores. It was the twelve-year-old who accompanied me to the Cape Palmas airfield the day I left for the last time and waited with me almost six hours for the plane. His small figure waving from the runway was the last thing I saw, clouded with tears, as the plane lifted off.

Obviously, my relationship with these boys, now men, had a significant impact on me, both emotionally and intellectually, and on the scholarship on Liberia that I have produced. It is with some degree of shock, then, that I realize it was boys like these, of rural backgrounds, incomplete educations, and precisely these ages, that carried out the worst violence and atrocities during the endless war of the 1990s and early twenty-first century (see Fleischman and Whitman 1994; Utas 2003; Murphy 2003, among others).

The "problem of youth" has emerged as a central issue in African studies in the last decade, as the demographic impact of high birth rates and low life expectancy produces an increasingly younger population for the continent as a whole. This interest builds on the longstanding recognition that age features as a significant category of meaning, power, and stratification in many African societies and in the "classical" Africanist literature concerned with the succession of organized age grades and sets and their role in the political construction of "stateless societies" (among others, see Eisenstadt 1954, 1956; Gulliver 1958; Wilson 1951; and more recently Bernardi 1985; Simonse and Kurimoto 1998). These earlier studies were concerned primarily with rural populations, where tensions between older and younger men over access to material and symbolic resources, including land, animals, and the labor of women and other men, were regulated by orderly systems of age sets. In many cases, the age grade system which defined and structured the male life cycle also doubled as a military organization, organized for the defense of the community or for territorial expansion against others. Southeastern Liberian communities, where Poro and Sande societies are not present, are characterized by such an age/military system, weaving together ideas of gender, seniority, the regulation of violence, and the distribution of political authority. These durable institutions are experienced by rural southeastern men and women as the organizational structure of their lives.

A more recent literature is concerned with generational conflict in Africa outside the regulation of indigenous institutions, especially as these are manifest in anxieties about urban crime and violent conflict. BBC World News writer Elizabeth Blunt has noted "The picture of the child soldier, clutching a gun almost as big as himself, has become the enduring image of West Africa's civil conflicts" (BBC World News, June 1, 2004; see also Utas 2003: 7–8). Utas argues that this image is part of larger set of "implicit ideas of development and evolution," part of a differentiating discourse of African inferiority and primitiveness (2003: 8). As we have seen, the New Barbarism hypothesis rests heavily on demographic and Malthusian explanations that demonize the young as products of unregulated sexuality (or improperly regulated sexuality, as with polygyny) and out of control population growth, high on drugs and utterly without morals or scruples of any kind. Mamadou Diouf notes that the fact that young people constitute a demographic majority in Africa, along with the perceived failure of nationalist projects of development and progressive change, "seems to have resulted in the construction of African youth as a threat, and to have provoked, within society as a whole, a panic that is simultaneously moral and civic" (2003: 3; see also Cruise O'Brian 1996).

In Liberia as well as in neighboring Sierra Leone, it is undeniable that children under the age of eighteen made up between ten and forty percent of the fighting forces (Utas 2003: 14–15). Some of their stories, of atrocities committed and experienced, of the pure joy of looting, killing, and instilling terror in others, are hard to reconcile with my memories of the playful, intelligent boys with whom I spent so much time at home, or with my thoughtful young students at Tubman College of Technology. Utas, in his research with young ex-combatants conducted during the brief lull in hostilities between 1997 and 2000, speaks of the range of individual motives and personal responses of the fighters, from clear-headed political analysis to vague ambitions to simply owning a new pair of shoes. While much of the literature on child soldiers regards them as either hapless victims or, as noted above, inherently violent subhumans, several scholars have attempted to address issues of coercion and agency, socioeconomic context, and postmodern fragmentation through a focus on youth. For example, Richards argues that the young fighters in Sierra Leone were motivated by ideals of democracy and a highly informed critique of the corrupt politics of the ruling party (1996). Abdullah and other Sierra Leonian scholars, however, have contested this characterization (1997, 1998), arguing that the marginalized urban youth who were drawn into the fighting were a "lumpen" product of blighted expectations and prewar criminal enterprises (1997). Diawara contributes the idea of "homeboy cosmopolitanism," a globalized repertoire of styles, music, and rebellious attitude toward authority in any form (1998).

What all these approaches have in common is a fairly unitary understanding of exactly what it is that youth is rebelling against: the entrenched gerontocratic rule of elders, whether the "traditional" version or modern, national elites who control access to education and jobs. In any case, the relationship between elders and youth is understood as inherently unequal and undemocratic, and here once again, the ethnographic literature on northwestern Liberia is marshaled as evidence. Murphy has analyzed the structural relations between military commanders and the young people under their command as "military patrimonialism" (2003). In this essay, he emphasizes the vulnerable state of children separated from their families during the war and the exploitative relations of dominance by which military strongmen turned them into patrimonial "staff" (in the Weberian sense) through a "cruel mixture of brutality, personal benevolence, and reciprocity" (2003: 65). While viewing child soldiers through the lens of patron-client relations does return some element of agency to the children themselves, Murphy notes that it is crucial to locate these "choices" on the part of young people in the "ideology of dependency in this cultural region of West Africa" (2003: 75). This ideology, enacted locally in the practices of individuals attempting to attach themselves to more powerful actors while at the same time seeking to attract lower-status dependents themselves, is represented as fundamental to indigenous cultures of the region. In actuality, Murphy uses d'Azevedo's ethnography of the Gola and his own work on Mende and Kpelle as the basis for his analysis (2003: 75–76). Once again, the more stratified, Mande-influenced societies of the northwest are represented as "Liberian" or "regional" indigenous culture in general.

As a corrective to the overemphasis on northwestern ethnography in understanding how concepts of relative age have shaped recent events in Liberia, I offer below a detailed description of age-based organizations in the southeast. I argue that, rather than functioning as a strict "gerontocracy," such institutions serve as a system of checks and balances which ensures the participation and voice of people in various social locations. I then turn to a discussion of intergenerational relations among political activists and government officials in the 1970s and '80s, drawn from interviews with Liberian expatriates in the United States. How have young men with explicitly nationalist ideologies understood the process of orderly (or disorderly) transmission of power and authority between elders and juniors? Finally, I return to the dilemma raised by a number of commentators: can this generation of child soldiers, hardened by the violence of the last twenty years, build and sustain new democratic state institutions in Liberia? Since this is the generation that includes those "sweet boys" of my early fieldwork, I have more than an intellectual interest in the answer to this question.

In 1844, Bishop John Payne, whose views on Glebo democracy have been cited above, also described the agebased institutions he saw operating in Cape Palmas. His observations provide evidence of men's age *grades*, or a system of age-determined roles that are "specific, defining, and limiting" (Gulliver 1968: 157), but also of age *groups*, or corporate bodies "based on criterion of coequality; . . . a permanent collection of people who recognize a degree of unity, a unity that is acknowledged by nonmembers" (159). Since the nineteenth century, other authors have confirmed and expanded on Payne's account, including his description of the women of Cavalla as "divided into two or three classes, according to their ages, who dance together and have certain regulations and privileges as a community" (1845: 115), to argue that both men and women were organized in this fashion (for examples, see Johnson 1957: 53–54; Kurtz 1985: 110–11; Martin 1968: 21).

Inspired by these sketchy but enticing reports, I searched for evidence of women's age grades and corporate age groups when I worked with the Cape Palmas Glebo in 1982–83. I was both disappointed and disconcerted to find my Glebo informants contradicting themselves; either women's age divisions were presented as a mirror image of the men's system or they were denied even to exist. Perhaps significantly, it was the women I spoke with who were more likely to state categorically that they did not participate in organizations comparable to those of the men. An incident from my field notes is emblematic of numerous conversations:

an older man was leading me through the well documented men's system of named grades. When I asked about women, he repeated himself; women of such an age are "juniors," the next level is the "warriors," and so on. But I was becoming suspicious, since I had never heard women referred to collectively as warriors, only individually, as when faced with a particularly dangerous or painful childbirth. Questioning more closely, I apparently exhausted my informant's patience, for he sighed and said, "Mostly, we just call them 'women.'" I am therefore forced to conclude that neither Glebo men nor Glebo women consider the categories that punctuate the lives of men as salient for women.

But a more interesting question arises from this case: how does age, which is clearly an important ranking mechanism for Glebo men, intersect with gender in determining an individual's prestige, or standing in the community? How are the interests of men at different times in their lives balanced and contested within a political/military system that also has structured, institutionally defined roles for women? Can these institutions be understood as a complex bureaucracy which distributes and ensures the rights of different categories of persons? How and when is violence seen as a legitimate recourse for asserting and defending these rights? Such a perspective sheds new light on the idea of a continental "youth rebellion" against "gerontocratic rule" in Africa.

As mentioned above, the southeast has been, comparatively speaking, neglected in comparison with the northwest, and the full ethnographic complexity of the region is little understood. Complicating the lack of intensive ethnographic work is the variation in dialect and local cultural practices over very short distances; within ten miles to the interior of my field site on the coast, a different dialect is spoken. Differences in dialect may be used as markers of "tribal" or *dako* identity. A *dako* consists of a cluster of towns, sharing a common origin myth and formerly allied with each other in time of war. There is, however, no indigenous *dako*-level administrative structure and the component towns are free to handle their own external and internal affairs.

Cutting across *dako* identities and linguistic differences are the named patrilineal clans, or *pane* (Sabo, *tua*; Kru, *panton*). Not all towns have a local branch of each *pano* (singular), but persons sharing a common clan name do have the right to hospitality in each other's towns, even in times of war. The interlocking *pano* identities seem to be the only regional integrative structure in the southeast and, like the *dako*, have no centralized system of authority (McEvoy 1977).

Characteristically, the age-grading of men in the southeast is *dako*-specific and highly variable from place to place, both in the number of ranked levels and the names used to describe them (Kurtz 1985: 100–104; McEvoy 1971: 598–616), although Kurtz notes that every southeastern *dako* has one level which is designated "soldiers" or "warriors" (1985: 109). Keeping this diversity in mind, it is possible that formal age grades and groups for women do (or did) exist somewhere in the southeast. I have argued, however, that Payne and later McEvoy mistook elements of the parallel men's and women's political hierarchies for organized women's groups based on age (Moran 2001). While age is an important marker of status for women as well as for men, it does not determine their political participation to the same extent or in exactly the same way.

Glebo men's age grades and groups have both political and ritual functions. Little boys, from toddlers through about age twelve, belong to the grade (which at this level is little more than an age category, following Eisenstadt 1956: 22) called *kyinibo* or *pede nyinibo* ("those who fail to look after their own excrement"). McEvoy reports that the lowest level in the Sabo system translates similarly as "those who defecate around the house" (1971: 180). Along with girls of the same age, they constitute the category of *wodo yudu* or "town children." Young boys have fewer domestic responsibilities than their female contemporaries, unless they are unlucky enough to live in a household with a shortage of girl children to do the work of fetching water and firewood. Such tasks are not gender specific, in that any young person may be pressed into service by an elder, but girls are more likely to have regular duties at an early age (Moran 1990: 26).

The next grade, the *kinibo*, consists of adolescents and young men who are not yet married. In former times, the *kinibo* seems to have operated as a kind of police force, carrying out the judgments of those above them in the hierarchy (Johnson 1957: 53). With marriage and the building of a house, a man passes into the *sidibo* or *gbo*, the "warriors" or "soldiers." McEvoy writes that entrance into this grade is marked by initiation into the men's secret society among the Sabo and that the *gbo* are internally divided into four subgrades (1971: 181). I found no evidence of a similar internal structure among the Glebo of the early 1980s, but as a young woman ethnographer there were areas of men's knowledge that were necessarily closed to me. The *sidibo* or *gbo* in both the Sabo and Glebo cases are a clear example of a corporate age *group*; they have an internal system of officers, share ownership of drums and other ritual equipment, and have their own building, the *tiba kae*, for meetings.

Martin, who has extensively surveyed the nineteenth-century missionary reports on the Glebo, suggests that internal politics in the coastal towns were characterized by an ongoing power struggle between the *sidibo* and the council of elders, the *gbudubo* or *takae* (1968: 19–20). This council, for the Glebo at least, is not an age grade in the sense that cohorts or even individuals are automatically promoted at a certain age or life stage. Rather, the *takae* is made up of the oldest living male member of each resident *pano* or clan in a town. Some very elderly men, therefore, remain *sidibo* or warriors all their lives, due to the longevity of a slightly older kinsman (Moran 1990: 30).

I once saw this illustrated in the behavior of a very elderly, toothless gentleman who was said to have "retired" from his responsibility to dance at a man's funeral ceremony due to his advanced age. Although disabled with swollen legs, he disappeared partway through the dancing and returned in an improvised *sidibo* costume of leaves and vines over a bare chest and black waist cloth. He said that when he heard the drums, "his heart could not be still," and he felt compelled to join the dancers. It was explained to me that he had held one of the leadership or "war priest" positions among the *sidibo*, and although he had stepped aside in favor of a younger man, he could still claim some of the prerogatives of that office. Those observing were approving of his actions; his physical condition and chronological age were unrelated to his status as a warrior.

The *takae* is the primary administrative body of a Glebo town, serving as advisors to the *wodo baa* or "town's namesake," a largely ceremonial post which is held by a particular clan in each town. Members of the *takae* are widely feared for their presumed supernatural power and ability to kill through sorcery (having survived to such exalted age, they must necessarily be spiritually very powerful) and for their legitimate authority to impose fines for infraction of town laws or ritual taboos. In theory, no adult is supposed to leave town for an extended period without seeking the permission of the *takae*, or a fine of one or two cows may be levied (27, 37). I have seen sophisticated Monrovia-based professionals make a visit to the *wodo baa* and *takae* their first order of business on trips home because "you don't fool with those people."

The men's age grades are clearly visible in public displays such as funeral dances, for which the different grades wear distinctive costumes and dance together. Women's funeral dances, although also called "war dances," do not distinguish age classes by differences in dress, although there is a tendency to cluster the youngest and least experienced dancers at the end of the line. Less obvious, however, is the women's parallel political structure which operates in conjunction with that of the men. A women's *takae*, consisting of an elder female member of each resident clan (either a natal daughter or an inmarrying wife) meets in joint session with the men's *takae* and on their own for specifically women's issues. As a check on the power of the men's side of the structure, an elected female officer, the *blo nyene*, is said by both men and women to have veto power over decisions made by the *wodo baa* and his councilors (Moran 1990: 33). Evidence exists of similar parallel structures, representing women but without emphasizing relative age as a criterion for participation or leadership, in other southeastern groups (Kurtz 1985: 110–11;

McEvoy 1971: 176–77, 611–14; Schroder and Seibel 1974: 76, 100–101). It is this parallel political structure which I believe McEvoy has mistaken for women's age grades among the Sabo. The age grades he describes for Sabo women include a generalized category of girls aged five to fifteen, the *nesauwulu*, or "those who take the water road," characterized as "apparently unorganized" (1971: 173). Following Gulliver's use of the term, such an "unorganized" collectivity would not be a "grade" at all, but rather an age *category*, a "generalized role disposition into which specific roles may be built" (1968: 157, following Eisenstadt 1956: 22). Like the Glebo *kyinibo* for boys or *wodo yudu* for both sexes, the *nesauwulu* appears to be a recognized category of young adolescents, not an organized grade with clearly defined roles.

Next for the Sabo women is a grade which McEvoy sees as also an age *group*, the *wainyo*, or Wire Company. This is a dancing society for young unmarried and married women up to the age of about forty (McEvoy 1971: 174) It is said to have been started in 1961 among Sabo migrant workers at the Firestone rubber plantation at Cavalla and spread quickly to the home villages. Performances are sponsored by a "big man," who calls the group to dance at his house and offers them food and drinks. The group has several male officers and raises money internally to buy cloth of the same pattern for each member to wear as a dancing costume (176). The Glebo also have such dancing companies, known as *glorro*, but these appear to be voluntary associations and are not based on universal ascription. It is not clear from McEvoy's account if membership in the Sabo *wainyo* is compulsory for all women of a certain age. Based on its recent origins and similarity with the Glebo *glorro* and other Kru, Krahn, and Grebo women's performance clubs documented in the literature (Banton 1957; Buelow 1980–81; Schroder and Seibel 1974), I find it highly questionable to characterize the *wainyo* as an age grade and certainly not as an age group.

The next level in the Sabo system is the *denyino* or "town women," whom McEvoy defines as those past the age of childbearing but still economically active. Although he claims they are also an age group, McEvoy admits they have no organized dance company or officers. All the women of a Sabo town are represented by the *nyinokei* or women's chief, a position apparently analogous to the Glebo *blo nyene*. McEvoy says only that the *nyinokei* may "argue" with the men's council of elders, and there is no mention of a veto power, as among the Glebo (McEvoy 1971: 176). The women's *takae* or *gbudubo* in Glebo towns is also referred to as the "town women" (*wodo nyeno*), but unlike McEvoy's report for the Sabo, this decisionmaking council does *not* include all women over the age of childbearing; it is made up of one female representative of each resident *pano* in town.

Given the noticeable differences between the Sabo and Glebo, this may well be a case of very different structures, but it is also possible that McEvoy misunderstood the actual composition and purpose of the "town women." At public events, middle-aged women generally sit together as a solid block and are sometimes referred to collectively as "town women," although only a select few are actually members of the *takae* (Moran 1990: 31). Likewise, Bishop Payne's famous discussion of Glebo women's age grades is followed by a description of the essentially political functions of such officers as the *blo nyene* and her female *takae* (1845: 115, 334). McEvoy notes that the Sabo *nyinokei*, like the Glebo *blo nyene*, is selected by all the adult women of the town, based on her speaking ability and recognized qualities of leadership rather than on a hereditary basis or by virtue of her advanced age. Further, she may be "backed up by a 'second chief'" (1971: 176) and McEvoy mentions parenthetically that "this structure then parallels the town political organization" (176).

Schröder and Seibel document the presence of similar female elders and "women's presidents" among the Krahn (1974: 99–103), yet do not include these positions on their ten-page list of "Leaders and Officers of the Kran Tribes" (71–82). These authors, in fact, conclude that "in the affairs of the village and the tribe women had practically no voice" (66). Kurtz likewise provides a listing of the "political roles" of all the Grebo towns surveyed, yet admits that he has omitted the "highly significant" roles of the *deyo* (a ritual specialist; this position is held by both men and women), the high priest's wife, and the leader of the elder women, admitting that he does not understand how to fit these offices into the hierarchy of roles he has outlined for men (157).

Such "dual sex" political structures, as they have been designated by Kamene Okonjo (1976: 45), are characteristic of many African political systems, including the Glebo and, based on the evidence, other southeastern groups as well. It is clear that the participation of men and women of all ages was institutionally structured into "town political organization" of southeastern communities. The tenacity of these structures, in spite of repeated attempts to suppress them, is visible in the history of mass demonstrations by African women against both colonial and postcolonial states which have refused to acknowledge women's claims as independent political actors (for only a few examples, see Rosen 1983; Van Allen 1972, 1976). McEvoy, Kurtz, Schröder and Seibel, and even Bishop Payne before them appear to have interpreted this parallel administrative structure as evidence of all-inclusive age-based groups. The irony here is that, while men's age grades and groups are assumed to be important precisely *because* of their political functions, the act of naming women's organizations "age grades" relegates them to the category of mere social or economic bodies, thus obscuring and denying the real political authority of women.

Likewise, the insistence that political authority for men was distributed only on the basis of age obscures the other sources of power and legitimacy for men, as well as evidence that the power of elders over youth was never uncontested. The fact that younger men held a monopoly over the use of military force which was balanced by the spiritual power of the elders speaks to the ability of both parties to enforce their interests through violence of one kind or another. Both kinds of force were seen as legitimate expressions of power, depending on the context, as was the power of women to withhold their labor through strikes and boycotts. The age-structured hierarchies of the southeast look, from this perspective, more like a bureaucracy designed to ensure collective rights of unequal groups than a patrimonial or patronage system dominated by gerontocratic elders.

How much of this organization was destroyed by the long years of civil conflict and disruption? Richard Nisbett, visiting the southeast in 1997, 1998, 2000, and 2001 reported that

The elders were reverting to established social institutions and hierarchies. . . . For example, in a major (economic) village in the Pynstown district, the village elders gathered all the ex-combatants together at a huge village meeting and demanded an apology from each combatant for abandoning the "old ways," for bringing shame and retribution (from one or another warring faction) on the clans. If the young males would apologize publicly, they would be welcomed back, never called "combatant" again, and forgiven and reintegrated. Otherwise, they were ostracized and forbidden to return to their natal areas. (personal communication, 2002)

Utas reports similar reintegration ceremonies of confession and forgiveness in neighboring Sinoe County (2003: 238). What Martin referred to as the "ongoing power struggle" between the nineteenth-century *sidibo* and the elders is clearly still operating, as are the checks and balances, the ability to back up threats with violence, and the possibilities for schism and reintegration.

The struggle between generations in rural areas takes place not only in the formal hierarchies of community politics but in the daily interactions of family members within households. Teenaged boys and girls rebelled against their parents and superiors quite regularly during my fieldwork, and protested injustice when they felt victimized by the illegitimate claims of others. Such rebels were disciplined with everything from physical beatings to being "put out of the house" and denied food for up to two weeks. The young people responded by mobilizing their friends to share food, to "beg" elders for forgiveness and relief, and to thwart the attempts of elders to control their behavior (see Utas for similar patterns of sharing and mutual support among young ex-combatants during the Taylor presidency, 2003: 64–70). They also took every opportunity to proclaim publicly their innocence or victimization at the hands of exploitative superiors. Adults and elders who were known to be abusive and unfair were sanctioned with gossip and loss of participation in networks that exchanged the labor of young people through relationships of fosterage (see Moran 1992). The young people I knew did not strike me as feeling helpless or powerless; they recognized their dependence on elders, but within a system of reciprocal rights and responsibilities that they were not afraid to invoke.

The integration of an explicitly military experience into the lives of all men through the age grade system and, since the category of the warrior transcends gender, into the lives of women as well, helps to account for the widespread participation of very young boys and girls in the civil conflict. Utas has argued that "Liberian society has for a long time actually been thoroughly militarized" (2003: 85). The integration of military training into the Poro organization of the northwest and the structural tension between opportunistic "war chiefs" and Poro elders echoes the power struggle Martin identifies in the southeast. Throughout the region, then, warfare was a means of opposition and rebellion and route of upward mobility for younger men, although within limits imposed by the threat of sorcery and a general lack of tolerance for abusive leaders on the part of the populace (see Utas on the archetypal Mende warrior, Sunjata, 2003: 139–43).

This militarization was intensified in national life following the coup of 1980. During this period, national holidays were celebrated with displays of military-style drilling by school children, and the image of a soldier appeared on currency and in public monuments. As I have discussed elsewhere, however, this "modern" or national form of militarization was by no means unitary or monolithic (Moran 1995). Like the contradictory messages encoded in the cartoons of urban civilized women, the militarized Liberian man took several forms, from indigenous warrior to Rambo-style commando. What is evident is that leaders such as Charles Taylor and his rivals sought to invoke all these models to serve their own purposes.

The militarization of children and youth, therefore, was not a new phenomenon in Liberia, although the arming of nine-year-olds with AK-47s can hardly be called "traditional." Where the age grade systems of the southeast incorporated young boys into warfare, it was in the role of messengers or carriers, not as combatants. Turning young people into a brutal patrimonial "staff," as Murphy notes, could only be accomplished when the technology of killing became simple and lightweight enough to be operated by children. Likewise, the economic context of the conflict, in which territory could be controlled and resources exploited and sold without the legitimizing umbrella of the state, encouraged the use of children to spread terror and extract labor from the civilian population (Reno 1998; Murphy 2003: 69, 74–75). With state institutions such as schools, national security, and criminal justice completely suspended, armed bands used local populations to extract resources such as diamonds and timber for sale to international buyers. Child labor was used for these purposes as well as to instill terror in civilians. Inverting the expected hierarchy of elders and juniors was an aspect of the ideological control exercised by regional warlords, as was the dissolving of kinship relations when children were forced to kill members of their own families. In other instances, distributing guns to young followers ensured their loyalty and gratitude when this allowed young people to protect family members or avenge their deaths. The emergence of child soldiers in West and Central Africa in the late twentieth century, therefore, is as much a product of the Western arms industry and world market forces as of indigenous concepts of age, hierarchy, and violence.

Perhaps not surprisingly, similar themes of the struggle between generations arise in interviews I conducted in the United States with Liberian men who had been active both in government and in opposition politics in the 1970s and '80s. One, who had held a cabinet-level position in the Tolbert administration, told of how he had chosen to enter government service upon his return from the United States with a brand new Ph.D. in the early 1970s. The sense of Liberia as then embroiled in a "youth rebellion" was an aspect of his decision not to take a teaching post at the University of Liberia, which seemed to him on the brink of anarchy. Tolbert, who admired educated technocrats and wanted to differentiate himself from his predecessor Tubman, drew many of the "first set of Ph.D.s" into his administration, but could not accommodate their desire to make substantive changes in the one-party state. "They found out before long that their opportunities to bring about reforms and so forth were very, very, limited. In fact, some of them were thrown out after a short period of time." Tolbert could not transcend his own class and generation, nor could he resist the conservative tendencies of the group of men with whom he had grown up, gone to college, and entered government service. Speaking of his attempts to influence Tolbert toward more progressive policies, my informant explained, "In Liberian terms, I'm just a little boy, whereas those people are his colleagues. I mean, they are elderly people in my father's category and so forth." Tolbert felt "he couldn't break away from those people, say to them, 'Forget it. I'm moving with this new crowd, this new crowd that happens to be the ages of my children, because they see the light, they know better'" (see also Sawyer 1992: 286–93).

In the analysis of my informant, Tolbert was prevented from recognizing the "legitimate need for legitimate opposition to the government. . . .

I just felt that the government had a responsibility to the people . . . other groups had the right to organize and challenge the government. In fact, it seems to me that when they did that, they made the government work better." In other words, Tolbert could not be persuaded to recognize the kinds of balanced power relations between opposed groups represented by the age and gender-sensitive political structures of the indigenous southeast.

For other young men of this time period, political activism was located outside the halls of government in the streets, on university campuses, and in progressive organizations like the Movement for Justice in Africa (MOJA). Here too there were generational tensions, with young student radicals pushing their established leaders, who were also often their faculty, to take a more confrontational stance toward the government. One student leader, who was arrested for criticizing the military government shortly after the 1980 coup, recalled the terrifying and yet thrilling moment when he realized he was no longer a "small fish, you know, throw you back, I eat you later," but was seen as a direct threat to the government. "It had a kind of good feeling to it too, kind of an eerie good feeling. It was serious, they kept us at this place, the National Security Agency."

After abbreviated "trials" for treason, the student leaders were scheduled for execution but young people all over the city rallied to their defense. "The students were going to burn Monrovia until Doe definitely gave a pardon and said your people were free. And so we came outside and we just saw this huge crowd. People! We took off at the Post Stockade. My feet never touched the ground. I mean people had us in the air! From the Post Stockade to the university campus, we were just like from one person's hand to another, on top of the crowd."

His exhilaration, however, was tempered by a sense of betrayal by the older generation of activists. "All of a sudden, the things that opposition politicians in the country were supposed to be doing became, you know, the responsibility of the student movement, which you know, was a great responsibility and something that most of us should not have been placed in. We were too young, immature, and secondly, it was kind of dangerous! To expect that, somehow, we would be the conscience of society, when you know, we were just using the time to try to grow up. So it kind of forced us to grow many years before our time."

Perhaps significantly, this young man grew up in the southeast, in Sinoe County. His sense of being a young "warrior" cut adrift from the guidance of the elders, his expectation of benefiting from the creative tension of balanced opposition, may derive from that context. Yet he grew up in a coastal city and his father, although not literate, was a construction worker, not a subsistence farmer. His first real understanding of rural Liberian life came, ironically, when he was again arrested and sent to the maximum security prison camp at Bella Yella, far in the interior. There, the prisoners worked making farms for the army base and also volunteered their labor for the local farming community. "That exposed me to the real difficulty and the difficult life that people had. We weren't even talking about those things [in the student movement], we were talking about individual liberty, human rights, that was the level we were at." He began to understand the concentration of wealth, the appropriation of tax monies and other rural resources, and the systematic deprivation of vast areas of the country in a new way. "Those people had raised, many years before, several thousand dollars to build a road to come there and then the road never reached them. It was inaccessible by car, only by plane and then by foot. And, people had been raising money for years and years. And so it began to make sense, when they (the government) misappropriated this money, what the real implications are for these kind of people, who are paying taxes." Like the funds raised by development rallies in Cape Palmas, the resources extracted from rural populations never saw their intended purpose.

Educated, activist Liberians are divided in their interpretation of the meaning of generational conflict in their country. Some believe that Liberians are too used to "having the big man do everything for them." Others feel their fellow citizens are too compliant, too willing to obey orders, too trapped by the historical legacy of one-party rule, indigenous authoritarianism, and patronage politics. I have listened to these debates at numerous academic conferences and watched them unfold on Internet discussion boards. Others see the "youth rebellion" and extreme violence of the war as having successfully swept aside the practices of the past, leaving a clean slate on which to begin anew. The former student activist is of this opinion, feeling that it is time for the older generations to step aside. "We thank them, but they're limited by their own historical experience, their period, their socialization. I think we need to move beyond that limitation." His words echo the analysis of the Tolbert-era politician, although he is speaking of the generation of movement activists, not government officials. The struggle between elders and youth is clearly not unique to Africa, but an aspect of human life in all societies and all times. The trauma inflicted on young people who were denied education, security, and humane treatment during the war is not to be minimized, but the end of the war will not bring an end to generational conflict.

* * *

The experiences of these men and others attest to the strong democratic expectations present in urban as well as rural Liberian society. When the former cabinet minister spoke of his efforts to keep lines of communication open between the university-based opposition movements and the Tolbert administration, he described a "sense of responsibility to civil society out there." His speech on the occasion of his installation made reference to his desire to "meet the expectations of friends inside and outside of government." Afterward activists told him "we heard what you said," and he was followed and monitored by Tolbert's security operatives. Likewise, the student leader offers a vivid description of the crowd that carried him back to Monrovia after his release from prison and the widespread support the activists received from high school students, market women, and other urban residents. Later, when he was isolated at Bella Yella,

you know, when I was in jail, I think when I came out of jail I weighed fifty pounds more than when I went in. When I came out I was getting less food because when we were in jail, people were extremely nice. They would collect money in Monrovia and buy things and send them to Bella Yella. [Even in the rural southeast], they would come to my mother's house and they would say "you know, the thing your son is doing, we can't do that ourselves, but he did it, so here's our help."

Throughout all the interviews runs a theme of the just demands of the people for participation and voice, long denied but finding expression in numerous ways.

This optimism is in stark contrast with prevailing view of the Liberian population as apathetic, passive, and tolerant of autocracy. The young men's understanding of their historical role in relation to their elders was not to deny the value of age and experience but to insist on the creative tension which emerges from the conflict between generations. This dialectical understanding of the relationship between elders and juniors is an aspect of a deeply felt democratic tradition in Liberia, one which resonates through the indigenous communities as well as among educated urbanites. To limit the discussion to "big men" and "small boys" in patron-client relations is to fail to account for the generations who have dedicated their lives (and sometimes lost them) in the cause of progressive change.

Chapter 7
Conclusion:
A Wedding and a Funeral

I began this book with three broad goals: to "denaturalize" the violence taking place in Liberia and elsewhere and, in so doing, to challenge the "New Barbarism Hypothesis"; to argue that a democratic tradition exists in the political institutions of indigenous communities as well as in the cities of the nation-state; and to posit that violence and democracy are not opposite ends of a continuum but may be part of the same general understanding of political legitimacy. In the course of working through the events of my fieldwork and of the last twenty years, I have found myself questioning many other pairs of oppositions in Liberian studies, those between settler and native, civilized and country, rural and urban, and traditional and modern, to name a few of the most salient. Many Liberian intellectuals, although dedicated and committed scholars, seem willing to accept these dichotomies as both descriptions and explanations for events in their homeland. Many times over the years, at conferences and in the pages of scholarly journals, I have heard the "Liberian problem" endlessly reduced to an unchanging struggle between colonizing settlers and oppressed natives. Debates over the constitution circle relentlessly around questions of the lack of a democratic tradition embodied in the founding principles of the American Colonization Society, the centralized power of the executive branch, and whether or not rural people are "ready" to choose their own administrators at the county level (see Seyon 2000). Some analysts insist that Liberians both want and expect "strong leaders" who will rule with an iron hand and serve as both religious, secular, and economic patrons for the entire country (Kieh 1988). The proliferation of political parties in 1985 and 1997, widely seen as having divided the electorate and allowed such figures as Doe and Taylor to "win," attests to the idea that only the presidency is worth contesting. In January 2003, with Taylor in power and quite capable of eliminating his rivals, there were still 23 people who had declared their candidacy for president in elections that were never held.

The chapters above demonstrate that there is an indigenous democratic tradition in Liberia, too often ignored by those who assume an evolutionary model of political change. According to such models, rural people expect their leaders to be patrimonial autocrats; they respect authoritarianism, enforced through violence, and dissolve into chaos and anarchy when such control is absent. Their acts of resistance, whether these take the form of mass marches by women, accusations of witchcraft, or economic support for the mother of a jailed activist, are understood as spontaneous and individual rather than as shaped by *institutions* of balanced powers and rights.

It is clear that not all Liberians recognize the settler/indigenous encounter as the defining moment in Liberian history, nor as the prototype and exemplar of all subsequent relations between the locality and the state. The multiple interpretations of the Maryland Centenary Monument and dissenting versions of local history provide evidence that other historical discourses are possible. Such discourses recognize that the civilized/native divide is neither stable nor unitary. Indeed, for most rural communities, the human "face of the state" is not a member of the Monrovia elite with an American pedigree, but a "civilized native" with local ties and kinship obligations. Such people, as we have seen, can be benevolent patrons who dispense funds at development rallies and give gifts of latrines to their home communities, or they can be malevolent heartmen, literally tearing the life from children in their drive for power. As women, they can be gracious examples of civilized living, elegant "queens" who represent their communities, or parasitic prostitutes, commodified beyond recognition. What is clear is that ordinary Liberians recognize that these identities are shifting and complex; that being civilized can encompass *both* moral superiority and antisocial destructiveness, if not in the same individual at the same moment in time. Such ambiguities have found little space in most academic discussions of Liberia.

This situation has changed in recent years, as the ongoing violence has led to new interpretations and radical reimagining of the familiar contours of Liberian history. In early 2003 I attended a remarkable conference of Liberian and Liberianist scholars. Held in Bloomington, Indiana, its goal was to "begin a discussion designed to provide a deeper understanding of Liberian governance institutions and their potentials to contribute to peace and democratic governance in Liberia." For what was probably the first time, the definition of "Liberian governance structures" included not just the constitutions of 1847 and 1985, but *indigenous* governance structures as well. Two American anthropologists and an ethnomusicologist were invited to participate, along with a number of former Liberian government officials, including a former interim president.

At the meeting, the former government officials acknowledged the failures of the past and struggled to find new solutions to what had become a "zero-sum game." They recognized that political theory usually locates sovereign authority in the centralized state, but that many current models of decentralization serve only to relocate authority onto local agents who may become oppressive despots in their turn. What they wanted to know from the anthropologists was this: were there any "authentic" local institutions and practices which were truly democratic?

It was to this group that I first presented some of the ideas described in this book, arguing that there were, indeed, local practices and expectations of democracy in the southeast. Another anthropologist, specializing in the northwest, noted that during the period in which Samuel Doe "punished" Nimba County by cutting off all funding for schools, health workers, roads, and so forth, local people had created their own mechanisms to sustain these services. The ethnomusicologist reminded the group that, in Kpelle music, the soloist is not an all-powerful "center" but creates the finest of performances in a balance of part/counterpart sequences with a chorus; the goal is to weave a complex, multilayered performance that transcends any individual. From all over the country came examples that centralized, autocratic government was not the only form of politics with which Liberians are familiar.

Conference participants also reminded me that not everything that comes from "the bottom up" is necessarily good. There was concern that patterns of deference to centralized authority and respect for "big men" and elders were so entrenched in governance practices, both rural and urban, in the villages and in the civil service, that a true meritocracy could never be established. It was noted that local institutions were often not designed for protecting the rights of resident minorities, or those not connected by kinship or patronage to the dominant families. It is clear that, whatever form the new Liberian state takes, there will never be complete autonomy for local people and some services and rights guarantees will remain centralized at the national level.

But the discussions revealed an astonishing openness to include seriously the views of rural people in drafting governance structures. Amos Sawyer recounted his experience as chair of the post-coup constitutional commission, in which the input of rural residents was solicited for the construction of a draft document to be discussed and amended by the elected convention in Gbarnga. Two points came up again and again in discussions across the country. First, people wanted to elect their own county and district administrators. The 1847 constitution had given the power of appointment to the national president, and this ensured that his agents were in place at all levels of the governance structure. The second request that was made during the public hearings was that the vice president should not sit in on legislative sessions, as had been the practice.

It was felt that he served as a "spy for the president" and hindered free debate among the elected representatives. This indicates a fairly high degree of constitutional sophistication and a desire for the legislature to truly serve as a check on the power of the executive branch. Sawyer noted that the commission felt that the desire for direct election of county superintendents would be too costly; they proposed a compromise whereby the county council would submit a list of names from which the president could choose. Even this provision was taken out of the draft constitution by the Gbarnga convention, which was under a great deal of pressure from the Doe government. Sawyer stated that one of his greatest regrets was not listening more closely to the demands of the people for direct election of local officials. It was difficult, he noted, for educated Liberians to break out of "monocentric thinking" and take seriously the political concerns of rural people.

In addition to the desire that their county officials be directly accountable to them, rural constituents also wanted control over locally raised revenues and resources. After participating in decades of queen rallies and other fundraising efforts with no visible result, people were adamant that they wanted to make decisions about their own development needs. They called for some kind of revenue sharing between the central government and the localities, and a suggestion was made to eliminate some seats in the national legislature and put the money saved into a county-level decisionmaking body. They requested the right to impeach a superintendent if they had cause. None of these provisions were included in the new constitution which came into effect in 1985 and still governs Liberia today.

The Bloomington meeting took place in a curiously surreal atmosphere. Some of the best minds of their respective generations were earnestly debating how to restructure governance in Liberia without mentioning the man who stood in the way of all their hopes and plans: Charles Taylor. At that point, Taylor had been successfully holding off the Liberians United for Reconciliation and Democracy (LURD) rebel movement, based in Guinea, for three years. Although the country and Taylor himself were under a number of United Nations economic sanctions, it was clear that valuable commodities such as timber were still leaving the country and large shipments of weapons were arriving. A new rebel movement was just beginning to stir in the southeast, but had not yet proved itself a threat. Elections were scheduled for the fall of 2003, but the political opposition was fragmented into at least twenty-three competing parties, none of which seemed capable of defeating Taylor. The scholarly deliberations in Bloomington seemed only a hypothetical exercise.

Six months later, everything had changed. The southern rebel movement, Movement for Democracy and Elections in Liberia (MODEL), had emerged as a force to be reckoned with and diverted Taylor enough for LURD to launch an allout assault on Monrovia. When Taylor ventured to Nigeria for peace talks in June, an indictment against him for war crimes was unsealed by the United Nations court in Sierra Leone. He hurried back to Liberia, but it was the beginning of the end. The rebels, having little incentive to bargain with an international criminal, intensified their attack, cutting off Monrovia from the rest of the country. By August, Taylor resigned and left for exile in Nigeria, leaving his vice president in power for a few weeks until an interim government could be put in place.

U.S.-based governance groups, like the one I had attended in January, sprang into action. In early August, the Liberia Peace and Democracy Workshop was held at the University of Pennsylvania in Philadelphia, attended by twenty-six participants, almost all Liberians. The time to consult foreign experts was over; this group had received a copy of the peace agreement then under discussion in Accra, Ghana, and were determined to have a role in the process. The participants in Accra consisted of representatives of LURD, MODEL, and Taylor's government, while those in the United States were academics and former officials of past governments. Some of the ideas about decentralization and local administration that were discussed in Bloomington were included in the recommendations of the Philadelphia meeting, and of another held in September at Dover, Delaware. Soon after, several participants at these meetings traveled to Liberia to join or advise the interim government, which took power in October 2003.

How effective the new government will be in preparing the country for a peaceful transition to elections, scheduled for 2005, is still unclear. The immediate priorities include the disarmament and demobilization of something close to 60,000 fighters, some of them very young, and to bring security to parts of the country that have been under rebel control for a long time. It is encouraging, however, that some of the participants in the governance meeting who had engaged with the revolutionary ideas of truly meeting the political and development desires of rural populations are now involved with implementing the peace agreement. At a minimum, they have been exposed to the notion that local people have experience in running their own communities and expect to continue doing so. Additionally, the idea of rebuilding the nation-state from the bottom up, rather than the top down, has gained credence in the face of the spectacular failure of the centralized state.

During the past years, as I have wondered if anyone and anything in Liberia could survive, I received several reassuring documents from my foster family in Cape Palmas. One was the negatives from a roll of film taken at the funeral of my foster father in 1999. There are photographs of him lying in state in his coffin in the front room of the house, the walls still painted the same fluorescent green that I knew. The windows are hung with white lace curtains, used only at times of mourning and carefully stored away between deaths. Having a supply of such curtains, which could be loaned out to poorer relatives when needed, was an important marker of prestige among civilized Glebo women in the nineteen eighties. Scenes in the interior of St. James Episcopal Church during the funeral mass show it to have survived relatively unscathed. The elaborate cement tomb and headstone implied that the family was not completely destitute in spite of the years in refugee camps in Ivory Coast.

Another visual document arrived two years later, in 2001. It was a videotape of the wedding of the oldest surviving son, who had been a fourteen-year-old boy at the time of my fieldwork. A number of events were captured on the tape, including a "bachelor party" the evening before, the entire wedding ceremony and reception, and the departure of the bride and groom afterward. The ceremony took place in St. Mark's Episcopal Church in Harper, the local "cathedral" associated not with the civilized Glebo but with the Americo-Liberian Episcopal congregation. It was an elaborate event, with numerous attendants and the bride in a stunning white wedding dress. To judge only from these two sets of images, one would think that the war had left Cape Palmas untouched; that nothing had really changed in twenty years.

I did not realize until much later, since I had always turned off the tape at what seemed to be the end of the wedding, that there was a personal message for me attached to the end. One day while reviewing the tape, I was startled to hear a voice say "Hello Mary" and looked up to see the groom, my foster brother, standing in front of his house, apparently some days after the wedding. He then proceeded to give me a "virtual tour" of the neighborhood, including the graves of his father and older brother, the church, and the Episcopal elementary school he and his siblings had attended. The school was in ruins, without a roof and clearly unusable. He pleaded with me to find a donor to help reconstruct the school so the children of the community would be able to get an education.

Obviously, things have changed in Cape Palmas as they have all over Liberia. The expectation of my foster brothers when they were teenagers was that they would be able to finish their educations and get professional jobs in their own country; their reality was fragmented educational careers and a present in which 80 percent of the population is unemployed. They survive now by making "small business" with remittances I send them. The activists and intellectuals I interviewed in the U.S. likewise had every reason to expect brilliant careers in Liberia rather than a life of exile. Many are poised now to return, but the uncertainties are great.

The wedding and the funeral speak to the continuity in people's lives, despite great disruption. Life cycle events are celebrated, "traditional" practices, from the blowing of the *sidibo* war trumpets to the hanging of white lace curtains, are retained, and resources are mobilized to reflect well on the status of the family. The wedding and the funeral are a testament to the fact that community life goes on in Liberia, and that people look to the future and their fellow citizens with hope. The argument I have tried to make in this book, that violence is an integral aspect of the struggle for voice and autonomy we call "democratic process," that ordinary people in rural areas have a clear sense of their rights and are willing to defend them, and that there are structured relationships already existing in these communities that could be integrated into a new national governance system, is located in this hope as it has been communicated to me.

Some African states, such as Uganda, have been experimenting with forms of proportional representation not unlike the "dual sex" organization of men's and women's offices among the Glebo. The old goal of local participation in development planning could be realized with genuine attention to people's stated needs and desires, even if these seem "irrational." The "official history" of the schoolbooks could incorporate multiple versions of the colonizing encounter. Elections, when they are reintroduced, could begin with county level offices, with clear procedures to ensure accountability. Local revenues should be used on local projects, the benefits of which are available to all (no more locked latrines). Elections for national level offices, like the presidency, could be phased in gradually, so as not to generate the "heartman" panics of the past. Clearly, it will take some time before the act of voting is seen as not subject to manipulation by blood magic, but the *local* experience can certainly be given a different meaning and value if the candidates are to serve in the community rather than leave immediately for Monrovia. Men and women will continue to struggle with the implications of modernity and civilization, but in the full knowledge that these identities are situational and ambiguous rather than defining.

For those who venture outside the capital city, consider the strengths of indigenous institutions in *all* parts of the country, and can look beneath the formal deference and defiance of elders and youth, it is clear that Liberia has the resources it needs for rebuilding. In addition to the intelligence and commitment of people on the ground, the role of diaspora communities, which sustained and generated the telephone networks during the years of crisis, should not be underestimated. Organizations like Friends of Liberia, which circulates the news by e-mail, make possible the kind of research on which this book is partly grounded. Liberian activists both in West Africa and abroad see themselves as connected in a common struggle and, if not unified in their plans and goals for the country, at least are aware of the terrible cost of failure. In a globalized world, the new means of communication condition the shape of historical events. As one of my interview informants put it,

Just the fact that everything is so advanced now. If any government in Africa arrests someone today, before he wakes in the morning there's a fax on his table and he only arrested the guy two hours ago! With just our own cases, I mean, six of us over there in Liberia, you know, but when the people announced the death sentence, the [Catholic] Father came, the United Nations people, the White House, you know, the Congress. Why? Because some of us had traveled abroad and met people. I met a woman from Kansas, she had Nancy Kastlebaum and Bob Dole, you know, all the Kansas delegation were calling them because of this woman. We had met and talked, she liked my politics, we were writing one another in Liberia. When she heard I was in jail, she went berserk! So that kind of interaction among people will sustain that kind of momentum. And I think I can never be afraid of persecution now, because of the kind of friends I have around, they'd be asking for trouble! I have lawyer friends now, I didn't used to have lawyer friends! So that's the basis of our hope.

Michael Jackson ends his biography of his old friend and Sierra Leonian politician S. B. Marah, on a similar note of hope: "It was then that I was returned to the theme of natality and renewal with which I had begun, and that nothing in Sierra Leone had destroyed—the smile of the boy standing beside his father at Makeni, small S. B.'s panache, the young war widows in Kabala dancing in a tight circle with their babies asleep on their backs" (2004: 207). Although S. B. Marah's story is one of imprisonment, loss, suffering, betrayal, and the harsh use of power and sometimes violence to maintain his own position as a "big man," it is also a story of survival, of rebuilding, and of the trust that comes with long association. The Liberian experience since 1989 also produces such stories of great suffering and great triumph, of distrust in human relationships balanced against the belief that justice is worth fighting for. This story has only begun to be told.

References

Abdullah, Ibrahim
 1997 "Lumpen Youth Culture and Political Violence: Sierra Leoneans Debate the RUF and the Civil War." *African Development* 22: 171–216.
 1998 "Bush Path to Destruction: The Origin and Character of the Revolutionary United Front/Sierra Leone." *Journal of Modern African Studies* 36: 203–35.
Abu Lughod, Lila
 1990 "The Romance of Resistance: Tracing Transformations of Power Through Bedouin Women." *American Ethnologist* 17: 41–55.
Adebajo, Adekeye
 2002 *Liberia's Civil War: Nigeria, ECOMOG, and Regional Security in West Africa.* Boulder, Colo.: Lynne Rienner.
Adeleke, Tunde
 1998 *UnAfrican Americans: Nineteenth-Century Black Nationalists and the Civilizing Mission.* Lexington: University Press of Kentucky.
Ake, Claude
 2000 *The Feasibility of Democracy in Africa.* Dakar, Senegal: Council for the Development of Social Science Research in Africa.
Alonso, Ana Maria
 1988 "The Effects of Truth: Re-Presentations of the Past and the Imagining of Community." *Journal of Historical Sociology* 1: 33–57.
Anderson, Benedict
 1991 *Imagined Communities.* London: Verso.
Anthias, Floya and Nira Yuval-Davis, eds.
 1989 *Woman-Nation-State.* London: Macmillan.
Appadurai, Arjun
 1981 "The Past as a Scarce Resource." *Man* 16: 201–19.
 2002 "Deep Democracy: Urban Governmentality and the Horizon of Politics." *Public Culture* 14: 21–47.
Apter, Andrew
 1993 "Atinga Revisited: Yoruba Witchcraft and the Cocoa Economy, 1950–1951." In *Modernity and Its Malcontents: Ritual and Power in Postcolonial Africa,* ed. Jean Comaroff and John L. Comaroff, 111–28. Chicago: University of Chicago Press.

Ardener, Shirley
  1975   "Sexual Insult and Female Militancy." In *Perceiving Women*, ed. Ardener, 29–53. New York: Wiley.
Auslander, Mark
  1993   "Open the Wombs!:The Symbolic Politics of Modern Ngoni Witchfinding." In *Modernity and Its Malcontents: Ritual and Power in Postcolonial Africa*, ed. Jean Comaroff and John L. Comaroff, 167–92. Chicago: University of Chicago Press.
Austen, Ralph A.
  1993   "The Moral Economy of Witchcraft: An Essay in Comparative History." In *Modernity and Its Malcontents: Ritual and Power in Postcolonial Africa*, ed. Jean Comaroff and John L. Comaroff, 89–110. Chicago: University of Chicago Press.
Banton, Michael
  1957   *West African City: A Study of Tribal Life in Freetown.* London: Oxford University Press.
Bastian, Misty
  1993   "Bloodhounds Who Have No Friends: Witchcraft and Locality in the Nigerian Popular Press." In *Modernity and Its Malcontents*, ed. Jean Comaroff and John Comaroff, 129–66. Chicago: University of Chicago Press.
  1995   "Mami Wata and the Lure of Mrs. Money: Spirits and Dangerous Consumption in the Nigerian Popular Press." Paper presented at the Annual Meeting of the African Studies Association, Orlando, Florida.
Bayart, Jean-François
  1993   *The State in Africa: The Politics of the Belly.* London: Longman.
Bayart, Jean-François, Stephen Ellis, and Beatrice Hibou
  1999   *The Criminalization of the State in Africa.* Bloomington: Indiana University Press.
Bellman, Beryl
  1975   *Village of Curers and Assassins: On the Production of Fala Kpelle Cosmological Categories.* The Hague: Mouton.
  1984   *The Language of Secrecy: Symbols and Metaphors in Poro Ritual.* New Brunswick, N.J.: Rutgers University Press.
Bernardi, Bernardo
  1985   *Age Class Systems: Social Institutions and Polities Based on Age.* Trans. David I. Kertzer. Cambridge: Cambridge University Press.
Besteman, Catherine
  1996   "Representing Violence and 'Othering' Somalia." *Cultural Anthropology* 11: 120–33.
  1999   *Unraveling Somalia: Race, Violence, and the Legacy of Slavery.* Philadelphia: University of Pennsylvania Press.
Besteman, Catherine and Hugh Gusterson, eds.
  2005   *Why America's Top Pundits Are Wrong: Anthropologists Talk Back.* Berkeley: University of California Press.
Beyan, Amos J.
  1991   *The American Colonization Society and the Creation of the Liberian State: An Historical Perspective, 1822–1900.* Lanham, Md.: University Press of America.
Bindels, J. A.
  1983   Self Help Village Development Project in Eastern Liberia: Baseline

Survey, Maryland County. Harper, Maryland County, Liberia: United Nations Development Project.

Bledsoe, Caroline
1980 *Women and Marriage in Kpelle Society.* Stanford, Calif.: Stanford University Press.
1984 "The Political Uses of Sande Ideology and Symbolism." *American Ethnologist* 11: 455–72.
1990 "'No Success Without Struggle': Social Mobility and Hardship for Foster Children in Sierra Leone." *Man* 25: 70–88.

Blunt, Elizabeth
2004 "Child Recruitment Was War Crime." Electronic Document. http://news.bbc.co.uk/1/hi/world/africa/3767041.stm. Accessed June 1.

Bourdieu, Pierre
1979 *Outline of a Theory of Practice.* Cambridge: Cambridge University Press.

Bratton, Michael, and Nicolas van de Walle
1997 *Democratic Experiments in Africa: Regime Transitions in Comparative Perspective.* Cambridge: Cambridge University Press.

Breitborde, Lawrence
1977 "The Social Basis of Linguistic Variation in an Urban African Neighborhood." Ph.D. dissertation, Department of Anthropology, University of Rochester.

Brooks, George E.
1972 *The Kru Mariner in the Nineteenth Century.* Liberian Studies Monograph Series 1. Newark, Del.: Liberian Studies Association.
1993 *Landlords and Strangers: Ecology, Society, and Trade in Western Africa, 1000–1630.* Boulder, Colo.: Westview Press.

Brown, David
1982 "On the Category 'Civilized' in Liberia and Elsewhere." *Journal of Modern African Studies* 20(2): 287–303.

Buelow, George
1980–81 "Eve's Rib: Association Membership and Mental Health Among Kru Women." *Liberian Studies Journal* 9: 23–33.

Burrowes, Carl Patrick
1989a *The Americo-Liberian Ruling Class and Other Myths: A Critique of Political Science in the Liberian Context.* Occasional Paper 3. Institute of African and African-American Affairs. Philadelphia: Temple University.
1989b "Black Christian Republicans: Delegates to the 1847 Liberian Constitutional Convention." *Liberian Studies Journal* 14: 64–87.

Chabal, Patrick and Jean-Pascal Daloz
1999 *Africa Works: Disorder as Political Instrument.* Bloomington: Indiana University Press.

Ciekawy, Diane
1998 "Witchcraft in Statecraft: Five Technologies of Power in Coastal Kenya." *African Studies Review* 41: 119–41.

Ciekawy, Diane and Peter Geschiere
1998 "Containing Witchcraft: Conflicting Scenarios in Postcolonial Africa." *African Studies Review* 41: 1–14.

Clapham, Christopher
1985 *Third World Politics: An Introduction.* Madison: University of Wisconsin Press.

Comaroff, John L. and Jean Comaroff, eds.
   1993   *Modernity and Its Malcontents: Ritual and Power in Postcolonial Africa.* Chicago: University of Chicago Press.
   1997   "Postcolonial Politics and Discourses of Democracy in Southern Africa: An Anthropological Reflection on African Political Modernities." *Journal of Anthropological Research* 53: 123–46.
   1999a "Occult Economies and the Violence of Abstraction: Notes from the South African Post Colony." *American Ethnologist* 26: 279–303.
   1999b *Civil Society and the Political Imagination in Africa: Critical Perspectives.* Chicago: University of Chicago Press.
Cruise O'Brian, Donal B.
   1996   "A Lost Generation: Youth Identity and Stable Decay in West Africa." In *Postcolonial Identities in Africa,* ed. Richard Werbner and Terrence Ranger, 55–74. London: Zed Books.
Daniel, E. Valentine
   1996   *Charred Lullabies: Chapters in an Anthropology of Violence.* Princeton, N.J.: Princeton University Press.
Davis, Ronald W.
   1968   "Historical Outline of the Kru Coast, 1500 to the Present." Ph.D. dissertation, Indiana University.
   1976   *Ethnohistorical Studies on the Kru Coast.* Liberian Studies Monograph Series No. 5. Newark, Del.: Liberian Studies Association.
d'Azevedo, Warren
   1962a "Uses of the Past in Gola Discourse." *Journal of African History* 3: 11–34.
   1962b "Some Historical Problems in the Delineation of a Central West Atlantic Region." *Annals of the New York Academy of Sciences* 96: 512–38.
   1969–70 "A Tribal Reaction to Nationalism, Parts I-IV." *Liberian Studies Journal* 1(2): 1–22; 2(1): 43–63; 2(2): 99–115; 3(1): 1–19.
   1989   "Tribe and Chiefdom on the Windward Coast." *Liberian Studies Journal* 14: 90–116.
Diamond, Larry, Juan J. Linz and Seymour Martin Lipset, eds.
   1988   *Democracy in Developing Countries: Africa.* Boulder, Colo.: Lynne Rienner.
Diawara, Manthia
   1998   *In Search of Africa.* Cambridge, Mass.: Harvard University Press.
Diouf, Mamadou
   2003   "Engaging Postcolonial Cultures: African Youth and Public Space." *African Studies Review* 46: 1–12.
Dolo, Emmanuel
   1996   *Democracy Versus Dictatorship: The Quest for Freedom and Justice in Africa's Oldest Republic—Liberia.* Lanham, Md.: University Press of America.
Duitsman, John
   1982–83 "Liberian Languages." *Liberian Studies Journal* 10: 27–36.
Dunn, D. Elwood and Byron S. Tarr
   1988   *Liberia: A National Polity in Transition.* Metuchen, N. J.: Scarecrow Press.
Earp, Charles
   1941   "The Role of Education in the Maryland Colonization Movement." *Journal of Negro History* 26: 365–88.
Eisenstadt, Shmuel N.
   1954   "African Age Groups." *Africa* 24: 100–113.
   1956   *From Generation to Generation: Age Groups and Social Life.* New York: Free Press.

Ellis, Stephen
  1996   "Africa After the Cold War: New Patterns of Government and Politics."
         Development and Change 27: 1–28.
  1999   *The Mask of Anarchy: The Destruction of Liberia and the Religious Dimension
         of an African Civil War.* New York: New York University Press.
England, Harri
  1996   "Witchcraft, Modernity, and the Person: The Morality of Accumula-
         tion in Central Malawi." *Critique of Anthropology* 16: 257–81.
Enloe, Cynthia
  1988   *Does Khaki Become You? The Militarization of Women's Lives.* London: Pan-
         dora/HarperCollins.
  1993   *The Morning After: Sexual Politics at the End of the Cold War.* Berkeley:
         University of California Press.
  1995   "Feminism, Nationalism, and Militarism: Wariness Without Paralysis." In
         Feminism, Nationalism, Militarism, ed. Constance Sutton, 13–32. Arling-
         ton, Va.: American Anthropological Association/Association for Fem-
         inist Anthropology.
Fabian, Johannes
  1983   *Time and the Other: How Anthropology Makes Its Object.* New York: Colum-
         bia University Press.
  1991   *Time and the Work of Anthropology: Critical Essays, 1971–1991.* Chur,
         Switzerland: Harwood Academic.
Fairhead, James and Melissa Leach
  1998   *Reframing Deforestation: Global Analysis and Local Realities, Studies in West
         Africa.* London: Routledge.
Ferguson, James
  1997   "The Country and the City on the Copperbelt." In *Culture, Power, Place,*
         ed. Akil Gupta and James Ferguson, 137–54. Durham, N.C.: Duke
         University Press.
  1999   *Expectations of Modernity: Myths and Meanings of Urban Life on the Zam-
         bian Copperbelt.* Berkeley: University of California Press.
Ferguson, R. Brian and Neil L. Whitehead, eds.
  1992   *War in the Tribal Zone: Expanding States and Indigenous Warfare.* Santa Fe,
         N.M.: School of American Research.
Ferme, Mariane C.
  1999   "Staging *Politisi*: The Dialogics of Publicity and Secrecy in Sierra Leone."
         In *Civil Society and the Political Imagination in Africa,* ed. John L. Comar-
         off and Jean Comaroff. 160–91. Chicago: University of Chicago Press.
  2001   *The Underneath of Things: Violence, History, and the Everyday in Sierra Leone.*
         Berkeley: University of California Press.
Fleischman, Janet and Lois Whitman
  1994   *Easy Prey: Child Soldiers of Liberia.* New York: Human Rights Watch.
Foucault, Michel
  1979   *Discipline and Punish: The Birth of the Prison.* New York: Vintage.
  1983   *Power/Knowledge: Selected Interviews and other Writings, 1972–1977.* New
         York: Pantheon.
Fox, George T.
  1868   *A Memoir of the Rev. C. Colden Hoffman, Missionary to Cape Palmas, West
         Africa.* New York: A.D.F. Randolph.
Frankel, Merran
  1964   *Tribe and Class in Monrovia.* London: Oxford University Press.

Frost, Diane
  1999   *Work and Community Among West African Migrant Workers Since the Nine-teenth Century.* Liverpool: Liverpool University Press.
Frykman, Jonas and Orvar Lofgren
  1987   *Culture Builders: A Historical Anthropology of Middle Class Life.* New Brunswick, N.J.: Rutgers University Press.
Gay, John
  1972   *Red Dust on the Green Leaves.* Thompson, Conn.: InterCulture Associates.
Geertz, Clifford
  1973a "The Impact of the Concept of Culture on the Concept of Man," In *The Interpretation of Cultures.* 33–54. New York: Basic Books.
  1973b "Person, Time and Conduct in Bali." In *The Interpretation of Cultures.* 360–411. New York: Basic Books.
Gershoni, Yekutiel
  1985   *Black Colonialism: The Americo-Liberian Scramble for the Hinterland.* Boulder, Colo.: Westview Press.
Geschiere, Peter
  1982   *Village Communities and the State: Changing Relations Among the Maka of Southeastern Cameroon.* London: Kegan Paul.
  1997   *The Modernity of Witchcraft: Politics and the Occult in Postcolonial Africa.* Charlottesville: University Press of Virgina.
Geschiere, Peter and Francis Nyamnjoh
  1998   "Witchcraft as an Issue in the 'Politics of Belonging.'" *African Studies Review* 41: 69–91.
Giddens, Anthony
  1990   *The Consequences of Modernity.* Stanford, Calif.: Stanford University Press.
Gottlieb, Alma
  1998   "Do Infants Have Religion? The Spiritual Lives of Beng Babies." *American Anthropologist* 100: 122–35.
  2004   *The Afterlife Is Where We Come From: The Culture of Infancy in West Africa.* Chicago: University of Chicago Press.
Greenhouse, C. J. and Roshanak Kheshti, eds.
  1998   *Democracy and Ethnography: Constructing Identities in Multicultural Liberal States.* Albany: State University of New York Press.
Guinier, Lani
  1994   *The Tyranny of the Majority: Fundamental Fairness and Representative Democracy.* New York: Free Press.
Gulliver, Philip H.
  1958   "The Turkana Age Organization." *American Anthropologist* 60: 900–1022.
  1968   "Age Differentiation." In *International Encyclopedia of the Social Sciences,* 1: 157–62. New York: MacMillan.
Gupta, Akhil
  1995   "Blurred Boundaries: The Discourse of Corruption, the Culture of Politics and the Imagined State." *American Ethnologist* 22: 375–402.
Gupta, Akhil and James Ferguson, eds.
  1997   *Culture, Power, Place: Explorations in Critical Anthropology.* Durham, N.C.: Duke University Press.
Gutman, Matthew C.
  2002   *The Romance of Democracy: Compliant Defiance in Contemporary Mexico.* Berkeley: University of California Press.

Hair, P. E. H.
 1967   "Ethnolinguistic Continuity on the Guinea Coast." *Journal of African History* 8: 247–68.
Hall, Richard L.
 2003   *On Africa's Shore: A History of Maryland in Liberia, 1834–1857.* Annapolis: Maryland Historical Society.
Harley, George W.
 1941   *Notes on the Poro in Liberia.* Peabody Museum Papers 19, 2. Cambridge, Mass.: Peabody Museum.
 1950   *Masks as Agents of Social Control in Northeast Liberia.* Peabody Museum Papers 32, 2. Cambridge, Mass.: Peabody Museum.
Harris, David
 1999   "From 'Warlord' to 'Democratic' President: How Charles Taylor Won the 1997 Liberian Elections." *Journal of Modern African Studies* 37: 431–55.
Henries, A. Doris Banks
 1966   *Civics for Liberian Schools.* New York: Collier-Macmillan International.
Hne, J. Dio
 1983   "The Spoilt Child." *Daily Observer,* February 18.
Holphe, Stephen S.
 1979   *Class, Ethnicity, and Politics in Liberia: A Class Analysis of Power Struggles in the Tubman and Tolbert Administrations from 1944–1975.* Washington, D.C.: University Press of America.
Holsoe, Svend E.
 1974   "The Manipulation of Traditional Political Structures Among the Coastal Peoples in Western Liberia During the Nineteenth Century." *Ethnohistory* 21: 159–68.
 1979   *A Social Survey of Grand Geden County, Liberia.* Tenafly, N.J.: Institute for Liberian Studies.
Holsoe, Svend E., Bernard L. Herman, Max Belcher, and Roger P. Kingston
 1988   *A Land and Life Remembered: Americo-Liberian Folk Architecture.* Athens: University of Georgia Press.
Huberich, Charles Henry
 1947   *The Political and Legislative History of Liberia.* 2 vols. New York: Central Book Co.
Huntington, Samuel P.
 1993   "The Clash of Civilizations?" *Foreign Affairs* 72 (Summer).
 1996   *The Clash of Civilizations and the Remaking of World Order.* New York: Simon and Schuster.
Hyden, Goran
 2000   "The Governance Challenge in Africa." In *African Perspectives on Governance,* ed. G. Hyden, D. Olowu, and H. W. O. O. Ogendo, 5–32. Trenton, N.J.: Africa World Press.
Hyden, Goran and Michael Bratton, eds.
 1992   *Governance and Politics in Africa.* Boulder, Colo.: Lynne Rienner Publishers.
Ifeka-Moller, Christine
 1975   "Female Militancy and Colonial Revolt: The Women's War of 1929, Eastern Nigeria." In *Perceiving Women,* ed. Shirley Ardener. New York: Wiley.

Ingemann, Frances and John Duitsman
  1976   "A Survey of Grebo Dialects in Liberia." *Liberian Studies Journal* 7: 121–31.
Innes, Gordon
  1966   *An Introduction to Grebo.* London: School of Oriental and African Studies.
Jackson, Michael
  2004   *In Sierra Leone.* Durham, N.C.: Duke University Press.
Jackson, Michael and Ivan Karp, eds.
  1990   *Personhood and Agency: The Experience of Self and Other in African Cultures.* Washington, D.C.: Smithsonian Institution Press.
Jackson, Robert H.
  1977   *Plural Societies and New States.* Berkeley, Calif.: Insitute of International Studies.
Jackson, Robert H. and Carl G. Rosberg
  1982   *Personal Rule in Black Africa.* Berkeley: University of California Press.
Johnson, S. Jangaba
  1957   *Traditional History and Folklore of the Glebo Tribe.* Monrovia: Bureau of Folkways, Republic of Liberia.
Johnston, Sir Harry
  1906   *Liberia.* 2 vols. London: Hutchenson.
Joseph, Richard, ed.
  1999   *State, Conflict, and Democracy in Africa.* Boulder, Colo.: Lynne Rienner.
Kaplan, Robert
  1993   *Balkan Ghosts: A Journey Through History.* London: Macmillan.
  1994   "The Coming Anarchy: How Scarcity, Crime, Overpopulation and Disease are Rapidly Destroying the Social Fabric of our Planet." *Atlantic Monthly*, February, 44–76.
  2000   *The Coming Anarchy: Shattering the Dreams of the Post Cold War.* New York: Random House.
Karlstrom, Mikael
  1996   "Imagining Democracy: Poltical Culture and Democratisation in Buganda." *Africa* 66: 485–505.
Keim, Curtis
  1999   *Mistaking Africa: Curiosities and Inventions of the American Mind.* Boulder, Colo.: Westview Press.
Kieh, George Klay, Jr.
  1988   "Guru, Visionary, Superchief: An Analysis of the Impact of the Cult of the Presidency on the Development of Democracy in Liberia." *Liberia-Forum* 4/6: 8–19.
Kopytoff, Igor
  1987   "The Internal African Frontier: The Making of African Political Culture." In *The African Frontier: The Reproduction of Traditional African Societies*, ed. Igor Kopytoff, 3–84. Bloomington: Indiana University Press.
Kurtz, Ronald J.
  1985   *Ethnographic Survey of Southeastern Liberia: The Grebo-Speaking Peoples.* Liberian Studies Monograph 7. Philadelphia: Institute for Liberian Studies.
Lavenda, Robert H.
  1988   "Minnesota Queen Pageants: Play, Fun, and Dead Seriousness in a Festive Mode." *Journal of American Folklore* 101: 168–75.

Leach, Melissa
  1994   *Rainforest Relations: Gender and Resource Use among the Mende of Gola, Sierra Leone.* Washington, D.C.: Smithsonian Institution Press.
Lee, Dorothy
  1977   "Lineal and Nonlineal Codifications of Reality." In *Symbolic Anthropology: A Reader in the Study of Symbols and Meanings,* ed. J. L. Dolgin, D. S. Kemnitzer, and D. M. Schneider, 151–64. New York: Columbia Univeristy Press.
Liberty, Clarence E. Zamba
  1986   "Report from Musardu (Letter to an American Friend): Reflections on the Liberian Crisis." *Liberian Studies Journal* 11: 42–81.
  2002   *Growth of the Liberian State: An Analysis of its Histography.* Northridge, Calif.: New World African Press in association with the Liberian Studies Association.
Liebenow, J. Gus
  1987   *Liberia: The Quest for Democracy.* Bloomington: Indiana University Press.
Little, Kenneth
  1973   *African Women in Towns.* Cambridge: Cambridge University Press.
  1980   *The Sociology of Urban African Women's Image in African Literature.* Totowa, N.J.: Rowman and Littlefield.
Lyons, Terrence
  1998   "Peace and Elections in Liberia." *In Post Conflict Elections, Democratization, and International Assistance,* ed. Krishna Kumar, 177–94. Boulder, Colo.: Lynne Rienner Publishers.
Mamdani, Mahmood
  1996   *Citizen and Subject: Contemporary Africa and the Legacy of Late Colonialism.* Princeton, N.J.: Princeton University Press.
Martin, Jane Jackson
  1968   "The Dual Legacy: Government Authority and Mission Influence Among the Glebo of Eastern Liberia, 1834–1910." Ph.D. dissertation, Boston University.
  1969   "How to Build a Nation: Liberian Ideas About National Integration in the Later Nineteenth Century." *Liberian Studies Journal* 2: 15–42.
  1982   "Krumen 'Down the Coast:' Liberian Migrants on the West African Coast in the Nineteenth Century." Working Paper 64, Boston University African Studies Center.
Mayer, Tamar, ed.
  2000   *Gender Ironies of Nationalism: Sexing the Nation.* London: Routledge.
McEvoy, Frederick
  1971   "History, Tradition, and Kinship as Factors in Modern Sabo Labor Migration." Ph.D. dissertation, University of Oregon.
  1977   "Understanding Ethnic Realities Among the Grebo and Kru Peoples of West Africa." *Africa* 47: 62–79.
Meyer, Birgit
  1998   "The Power of Money: Politics, Occult Forces, and Pentecostalism in Ghana." *Africa Studies Review* 41: 15–37.
Monga, Celestin
  1996   *The Anthropology of Anger: Civil Society and Democracy in Africa.* Boulder, Colo.: Lynne Rienner.

Moran, Mary H.
  1989 "Collective Action and the 'Representation' of African Women: A Liberian Case Study." *Feminist Studies* 15: 443–60.
  1990 *Civilized Women: Gender and Prestige in Southeastern Liberia*. Ithaca, N.Y.: Cornell University Press.
  1992 "Civilized Servants: Child Fosterage and Training for Status Among the Glebo of Liberia." In *African Encounters with Domesticity*, ed. Karen T. Hansen, 98–115. New Brunswick, N.J.: Rutgers University Press.
  1995 "Warriors or Soldiers? Masculinity and Ritual Transvestism in the Liberian Civil War." In *Feminism, Nationalism, and Militarism*, ed. Constance R. Sutton. Arlington, Va.: American Anthropological Association.
  1996 "Carrying the Queen: Identity and Nationalism in a Liberian Queen Rally." In *Beauty Queens on the Global Stage: Gender, Contests, and Power*, ed. Colleen. B. Cohen, Beverly Stoeltje, and Richard Wilk, 147–60. London: Routledge.
  2000 "Gender and Aging: Are Women "Warriors" Among the Glebo of Liberia?" *Liberian Studies Journal* 25: 25–41.
Moran, Mary H. and M. Anne Pitcher
  2004 "The 'Basket Case' and the 'Poster Child': Explaining the End of Civil Conflicts in Liberia and Mozambique." *Third World Quarterly* 25: 501–19.
Mudimbe, V. Y.
  1988 *The Invention of Africa: Gnosis, Philosophy and the Order of Knowledge*. Bloomington: Indiana University Press.
  1994 *The Idea of Africa*. Bloomington: Indiana University Press.
Murphy, William P.
  1980 "Secret Knowledge as Property and Power in Kpelle Society: Elders Versus Youth." *Africa* 50: 193–207.
  1981 "The Rhetorical Management of Dangerous Knowledge in Kpelle Brokerage." *American Ethnologist* 8: 667–85.
  1988 "Mande Politics of Written History." Paper presented at the Annual Meeting of the African Studies Association, Chicago.
  2003 "Military Patrimonialism and Child Soldier Clientalism in the Liberian and Sierra Leonian Civil Wars." *African Studies Review* 46: 61–87.
Murphy, William and Caroline Bledsoe
  1987 "Kinship and Territory in the History of a Kpelle Chiefdom (Liberia)." In *The African Frontier*, ed. Igor Kopytoff. Bloomington: Indiana University Press.
Nordstrom, Carolyn
  1997 *A Different Kind of War Story*. Philadelphia: University of Pennsylvania Press.
Nordstrom, Carolyn and Antonius C. G. M. Robben, eds.
  1995 *Fieldwork Under Fire: Contemporary Studies of Violence and Survival*. Berkeley: University of California Press.
Okonjo, Kamene
  1976 "The Dual Sex Political System in Operation: Igbo Women and Community Politics in Midwestern Nigeria." In *Women in Africa: Studies in Social and Economic Change*, ed. Nancy Hafkin and Edna G. Bay. Stanford, Calif.: Stanford University Press.
Osaghae, Eghosa E.
  1996 *Ethnicity, Class, and the Struggle for State Power in Liberia*. Dakar, Senegal: Council for the Development of Social Science Research in Africa.

Owusu, Maxwell
  1992   "Democracy and Africa: A View from the Village." *Journal of Modern African Studies* 30: 369–96.
  1997   "Domesticating Democracy: Culture, Civil Society, and Constitutionalism in Africa." *Comparative Studies in Society and History* 39: 120–52.
Paley, J.
  2001   *Marketing Democracy: Power and Social Movements in Post Dictatorship Chile.* Berkeley: University of California Press.
  2002   "Toward An Anthropology of Democracy." *Annual Review of Anthropology.* 31: 469–96.
Parker, Andrew, Mary Russo, Doris Sommer, and Patricia Yaeger, eds.
  1992   *Nationalisms and Sexualities.* New York: Routledge.
Payne, John
  1845   "The Journal of the Rev. John Payne." *Spirit of Missions* 10: 113–45, 241–303, 330–65, 395.
Piot, Charles
  1999   *Remotely Global: Village Modernity in West Africa.* Chicago: University of Chicago Press.
Ranger, Terence
  1983   "The Invention of Tradition in Colonial Africa." In *The Invention of Tradition,* ed. Eric Hobsbawm and Terence Ranger, 211–62. Cambridge: Cambridge University Press.
Reno, William
  1993   "Foreign Firms and the Financing of Charles Taylor's NPFL." *Liberian Studies Journal* 18: 175–87.
  1995a   *Corruption and State Politics in Sierra Leone.* Cambridge: Cambridge University Press.
  1995b   "Reinvention of an African Patrimonial State: Charles Taylor's Liberia." *Third World Quarterly* 16: 109–20.
  1998   *Warlord Politics and African States.* Boulder, Colo.: Lynne Rienner Publishers.
Richards, Paul
  1996a   *Fighting for the Rainforest: War, Youth, and Resources in Sierra Leone.* Oxford: James Currey and Heinemann.
  1996b   "Chimpanzees, Diamonds, and War: The Discourses of Global Environmental Change and Local Violence on the Liberia-Sierra Leone Border." In *The Future of Anthropological Knowledge,* ed. L. H. Moore. London: Routledge.
Riesman, Paul
  1992   *First Find Your Child a Good Mother: The Construction of Self in Two African Communities.* New Brunswick, N.J.: Rutgers University Press.
Rodney, Walter
  1967   "A Reconsideration of the Mane Invasions of Sierra Leone." *Journal of African History* 8: 219–46.
  1970   *A History of the Upper Guinea Coast.* New York: Monthly Review Press.
Rosen, David
  1983   "The Peasant Context of Feminist Revolt in West Africa." *Anthropological Quarterly* 56: 35–43.
Sawyer, Amos
  1987a   *Effective Immediately: Dictatorship in Liberia 1980–86: A Personal Perspective.*

Liberia Working Group Paper 5. Bremen, Germany: Liberia Working Group.

1987b "The Making of the 1984 Liberian Constitution: Major Issues and Dynamic Forces." *Liberian Studies Journal* 14: 1–15.

1992 *The Emergence of Autocracy in Liberia: Tragedy and Challenge.* San Francisco: Institute for Contemporary Studies.

Schaffer, Frederic C.

1998 *Democracy in Translation: Understanding Politics in an Unfamiliar Culture.* Ithaca, N.Y.: Cornell University Press.

Schröder, Günter and Dieter Seibel

1974 *Ethnographic Survey of Southeastern Liberia: The Liberian Kran and the Sapo.* Liberian Studies Monograph Series 3. Newark, Del.: Liberian Studies Association.

Schumpeter, Joseph A.

1942 *Capitalism, Socialism, and Democracy.* London: Allen and Unwin. Reprint 1976.

Schuster, Ilsa M. Glazer

1979 *New Women of Lusaka.* Palo Alto, Calif.: Mayfield.

Seyon, Patrick L. N.

2000 "Liberia's Search for Resolution to the Governance Puzzle." *Liberian Studies Journal* 25 (2): 3–25.

Shaw, Rosalind

1997 "The Production of Witchcraft/Witchcraft as Production: Memory, Modernity, and Slave Trade in Sierra Leone." *American Ethnologist* 24: 856–76.

2002 *Memories of the Slave Trade: Ritual and the Historical Imagination in Sierra Leone.* Chicago: University of Chicago Press.

Shick, Tom W.

1980 *Behold the Promised Land: A History of Afro-American Settler Society in Nineteenth-Century Liberia.* Baltimore: Johns Hopkins University Press.

Simons, Anna

1999 "War: Back to the Future." *Annual Review of Anthropology* 28: 73–108.

Simonse, Simon and Eisei Kurimoto

1998 *Conflict, Age, and Power in North East Africa: Age Systems in Transition.* Oxford: James Curry/Ohio University Press.

Smith, Daniel Jordan

2001a "'The Arrow of God': Pentecostalism, Inequality, and the Supernatural in South-Eastern Nigeria." *Africa* 71: 587–613.

2001b "Ritual Killing, 419, and Fast Wealth: Inequality and the Popular Imagination in Southeastern Nigeria." *American Ethnologist* 28: 803–26.

Snyder, Katherine A.

2001 "Being of 'One Heart': Power and Politics Among the Iraqw of Tanzania." *Africa* 71: 128–48.

Staudenraus, P. J.

1961 *The African Colonization Movement, 1816–1865.* New York: Columbia University Press.

Taussig, Michael

1980 *The Devil and Commodity Fetishism in South America.* Chapel Hill: University of North Carolina Press.

1987 *Shamanism, Colonialism, and the Wild Man: A Study in Terror and Healing.* Chicago: University of Chicago Press.

Taylor, Christopher
  1999   *Sacrifice as Terror: The Rwandan Genocide of 1994.* Oxford: Berg.
Tonkin, Elizabeth
  1979   "Sasstown's Transformation: The Jlao Kru, 1888–1918." *Liberian Studies Journal* 8: 1–34.
  1980   "Jealousy Names, Civilized Names: Anthroponomy of the Jlao Kru of Liberia." *Man* n.s. 15: 653–64.
  1981   "Model and Ideology: Dimensions of Being Civilized in Liberia." In *The Structure of Folk Models,* ed. Ladislav Holy and Milan Stuchlik, 305–30. London: Academic Press.
  1988   "Historical Discourse: The Achievement of Sieh Jeto." *History in Africa* 15: 467–91.
  1992   *Narrating Our Pasts: The Social Construction of Oral History.* Cambridge: Cambridge University Press.
Trouillot, Michel-Rolph
  1995   *Silencing the Past: Power and the Production of History.* Boston: Beacon Press.
Utas, Mats
  2003   "Sweet Battlefields: Youth and the Liberian Civil War." Ph.D. dissertation, Uppsala University.
Van Allen, Judith
  1972   "Sitting on a Man: Colonialism and the Lost Political Institutions of Igbo Women." *Canadian Journal of African Studies* 6: 165–81.
  1976   "Aba Riots or Igbo Women's War? Ideology, Stratification, and the Invisibility of African Women." In *Women in Africa: Studies in Social and Economic Change,* ed. Nancy Hafkin and Edna G. Bay. Stanford, Calif.: Stanford University Press.
Walker, Philip
  2001   "A Bioarchaeological Perspective on the History of Violence." *Annual Review of Anthropology* 30: 573–96.
Wallace, Samuel Yede
  1955   *Historical Lights of Gedebo or Glebo (Yesterday and Today Glebo).* Harper City, Liberia: Published by the author.
  1980   "The Complete History of Yesterday and Today Grebo." Unpublished manuscript.
  1983   "The Autobiography of Samuel Yede Wallace." Unpublished manuscript.
Warren, Kay B.
  1993   *The Violence Within: Cultural and Political Opposition in Divided Societies.* Boulder, Colo.: Westview Press.
Weber, Max
  1947   *The Theory of Social and Economic Organization.* Ed. Talcott Parsons. New York: Oxford University Press.
  1978   *Economy and Society: An Outline of Interpretive Sociology.* Vols. 1 and 2, ed. Guenther Roth and Claus Wittich. Berkeley: University of California Press.
West, H. G. and S. Kloeck-Jenson
  1999   "Betwixt and Between: Traditional Authority and Democratic Decentralization in Post War Mozambique." *African Affairs* 98: 455–84.
White, Luise
  2000   *Speaking with Vampires: Rumor and History in Colonial Africa.* Berkeley: University of California Press.

Widner, Jennifer
  1995   "States and Statelessness in Late Twentieth Century Africa." *Daedalus* 124: 129–53.
Willams, Raymond
  1973   *The Country and the City.* New York: Oxford University Press.
Wilson, John Leighton
  1856   *Western Africa: Its History, Condition, and Prospects.* New York: Harper.
Wilson, Monica
  1951   *Good Company: A Study of Nyakusa Age Villages.* London: Oxford University Press.
Wonkeryor, Edward L., Ella Forbes, James S. Guseh, and George Kaly Kieh, Jr.
  2000   *American Democracy in Africa in the Twenty-First Century?* Cherry Hill, N.J.: Africana Homestead Legacy Publishers.

Index

Acknowledgments

I am deeply grateful to many individuals and institutions for supporting this research over the years. First and foremost, my husband, Jordan Kerber, without whose loving support and computer expertise I would certainly be lost. My children, Pearl and John, who always give me so many reasons *not* to disappear into my study and write, also give me the inspiration to work toward a more peaceful, truly democratic world for their sakes. My students at Colgate University keep me constantly aware of the necessity to write in a style that is accessible to undergraduates without "dumbing down" the argument. Many of these ideas have been introduced in my classes, and numerous Colgate students over the years have helped me as research assistants.

I am overwhelmingly grateful for the vibrant community of Liberians and Liberianists who have listened to and argued with me for so long; I quite literally decided on Liberia for fieldwork because of the existence of the Liberian Studies Association, its wonderful small journal, and the sense that this group of people formed a true intellectual community. To Warren d'Azevedo, Svend Holsoe, Jane Martin, Jo Sullivan, D. Elwood Dunn, Soniia David, Amos Sawyer, Ruth and Verlon Stone, Al-Hassan Conteh, Gordon Thomasson, Ezekial Pagebo, Joyce Mends-Cole, Elizabeth Tonkin, Richard Nisbett, and others I am probably forgetting, thank you for teaching me so much about Liberia and about the joys of scholarly interaction. I am also grateful to the dedicated volunteers at Friends of Liberia, especially to Jim Gray and his email news network. Discussion with members of the new generation of anthropologists working in Liberia, including Mats Utas and Danny Hoffman, has sharpened my thinking and given me hope for the future.

The original fieldwork in Liberia in the 1980s was supported by grants from the National Science Foundation and Mount Holyoke College. Travel to interview Liberians in the United States and support for student assistance was made available by Colgate University through the Faculty Research Council. I have relied on the support of many good friends and colleagues in the Colgate community for so much over the years, from scholarly collaboration to reciprocal child care, but in particular: Anne Pitcher and Martin Murray for support, coauthorship, and the "backyard Africa seminar"; Carol Ann Lorenz and Chris Vecsey for always reliable Africa/Native America comparisons; and Kira Stevens and Philippe Uninsky for unending companionship and intellectual stimulation (and great food) deserve mention. Warren Wheeler and Ray Nardelli of Colgate University provided photographic and technical support. In the broader community of anthropologists, Kay Warren and Louise Lamphere have always been my inspiration and my guides.

Some of what appears here has been published elsewhere. The map of Liberia appears courtesy of the United Nations Cartographic Section. *Liberian Studies Journal* granted permission to reprint material from my article "Gender and Aging: Are Women 'Warriors' Among the Glebo of Liberia," 25, 2 (2000): 25–41 in Chapter 6. Taylor and Francis Group granted permission to reprint from my articles "Uneasy Images: Contested Representations of Gender, Modernity, and Nationalism in Pre-War Liberia," in *Gender Ironies of Nationalism: Sexing the Nation,* ed. Tamar Mayer (London: Routledge, 2000), 113–36 in Chapter 3 and "Carrying the Queen: Identity and Nationalism in a Liberian Queen Rally," in *Beauty Queens on the Global Stage: Gender, Contests, and Power,* ed. Colleen Ballerino Cohen, Richard Wilk, and Beverly Stoeltje (New York: Routledge, 1996), 147–60. Permission to publish the cartoons from the *Daily Observer* was granted by the publisher, Mr. Kenneth Best.

Finally, this book has benefited enormously from a close reading by an anonymous reviewer for the University of Pennsylvania Press and from helpful comments on the Introduction and Chapter 1 by Stephen Ellis; I am most grateful to both readers and have tried to incorporate their suggestions as much as possible. At the University of Pennsylvania Press, I thank Peter Agree for his patience, his encouragment, his faith that I would indeed finish, and most importantly his friendship for many years.